Beyond DRAGONS

an architectural romance

*A not entirely practical guide to creating an eccentric and
expressive home, to say nothing of tangential tales
of outside and in…*

Jo Jordan

Backbiting Beast Publications

First published in Great Britain by Jo Jordan/Backbiting Beast Publications.

ISBN: 9781999736200

Printed and bound in Great Britain by Clays Ltd, St Ives plc.

A catalogue record of this book is available from the British Library.

Typeset in Arsenal 11/13.2pt and Khand 26pt.

Typesetting, layout and cover design by Claire Spinks.
Design and layout of colour plate sections by Nigel Purdy.

To Michael Thacker who loved this farm

Thank you to *Team Polski*, especially Krzysz and Ewa, without whom it would all have been so much more difficult.

Jo Jordan

Contents

PART III

Contents

The building of a new house...is a demonstration of individualism and self-confidence and deserves to be given appropriate architectural form

The National Trust Book of the English House, 1985 Clive Aslet and Alan Powers published by the National Trust

...there must be room for innovation or even downright eccentricity...

Patterns for Suffolk Building published by the Suffolk Building Preservation Trust, 1993

Design your house to lift your heart

anon

We are always being asked about the origins of Belle Grove. As it's a somewhat complicated story, I thought, why not write it down?

As with the house, this book mixes the practical and the curious. It's not intended as a self-build manual. I lack the competence to drill down (no pun intended) into technical detail, so constructional ingredients are explained from the lay person's point of view, corrected as necessary by my husband and partner-in-crime Nick. I haven't allowed him too much in the way of engineering-speak though, my aim being to try to explain the process, how certain things were achieved or why decisions were made, in a way accessible to the general reader.

And that's without the shopping...

Foreword

Part 1

In the Beginning

It all goes back to the Sunday afternoon that Nick and I had spent clearing out a bedroom cupboard stuffed with tottering towers of old journals and magazines. Instinctive hoarders, even we are occasionally overtaken by a desire to dejunk, so most of these were destined for the tip. However, clustered between tatty copies of *World of Interiors* and *Farmer's Weekly*, lurked a few issues of the short-lived *Perspectives on Architecture,* doubtless sourced at a car-boot sale. Idly, Nick reached for one, murmuring without conviction, 'Maybe this will provide some inspiration'.

Just as these words fell from his mouth, the magazine flopped open at a torn, double-page spread featuring a swathe of unorthodox structures. Tucked top left, a small sketch arrested attention, all curved sweeping roofs, eyelid windows, cupola-topped tower and soaring chimney, topped by a nebulous impression of, well, what seemed to be some sort of animal. Yet the fact that the

building featured windows and a front door, albeit fit for a dwarf, suggested a dwelling and, sure enough, a surviving snippet of text suggested that it had been a proposal for a house in St Petersburg. No more information was to be found; more 'artist's vision' than blueprint, it seemed that the idea had never come to fruition. How frustrating not to be able to flip over to discover how the artist visualised the side and rear elevations. As it was, there were no clues.

That bedroom cupboard was just three miles from the austere farmhouse in which Nick had grown up and where, following the death of his father, his elderly mother lived alone. We'd been putting off the inevitable move there, finding it hard to face living in the spartan space occupied by Nick's parents for half a century. Built more to impress than for comfort, the farmhouse's nineteenth-century façade looked quite handsome from a distance, in a small-child's-

drawing-of-a-house sort of way with red brick façade, square windows, central door and slate roof pierced by the 'ears' of two chimneys. Cosy it was not.

A farmer of stubborn bent, Nick's father, Tom, had declined to countenance improvements, be they replacing ill-fitting metal windows, installing heating or modernising the antediluvian kitchen. The cellar would fill with water if left unpumped for more than a day, so it was left to itself, stagnant water infusing the house with a musty miasma. (The floor joists eventually rotted away, leaving just one strip of relative solidity on the far wall by the meter. To reach it, the hapless electricity meter-reader had been obliged to jump over the watery vault and scribble down the reading with one hand, while desperately clinging on with the other. His luck ran out when that last strip of floor gave way. After that, Tom laid a plank, which the meter-reader seemed happy to walk.)

With the flooded cellar pushing a tidemark of damp up the internal walls and with ominous cracks in the external walls, the house hardly lent itself to a quick fix. Moreover, each of the quartet of rooms on the ground floor was small, the usual knocking-through solution hindered by the position of two large chimneystacks. Nor would the hipped roof permit a straightforward side extension, yet to extend at the back would require building on the slightly uphill north side. Not ideal.

A complete rebuild seemed the best option.

'How would you feel if the old house was demolished and we built a replacement?' Nick had tentatively asked his mother.

'I'd be delighted,' she'd insisted, without an ounce of sentimentality for 'that cold old place'.

With that blessing, we felt free to plan razing it to the ground.

To be replaced with what, however?

Here was an opportunity to construct something fresh and original. Not a faux-Georgian mansion or mock-Tudor villa, and certainly not a neo-Palladian mansion. Although admiring of many modernist constructs, we knew we'd find it hard to live with concrete and steel (we don't have minimalist habits or tidy ones). In as much as we'd thought about it, we favoured an open structure, reminiscent of a traditional barn with soaring timbered ceilings and expanses of glass.

However, the organic lines of the drawing plucked from *Perspectives* had evidently stimulated Nick's imagination. Waving the page at me, he asked, 'What would you say to a house like this?'

Presumably expecting a response along the lines of, 'Are you quite *mad?*'

A troika of obstacles stymie aspiring self-builders: lack of suitable plot; lack of finance; lack of building experience. How fortunate were we to bypass these tiresome difficulties. Firstly, the site of the farmhouse would be our plot, south-facing at that, and connected to electricity and water, albeit with no mains drainage. Secondly, we calculated (optimistically) that a DIY new build could be financed by dint of raising a loan on our existing house, pending its eventual sale, meaning that we wouldn't need to conform to a lender's likely conservative expectations of a new structure. Thirdly, as shall be seen, Nick had already acquired some off-beat construction experience.

It seemed perverse to waste such a lucky fusion of advantages on the hackneyed and derivative.

The first editor of *Perspectives*, architectural historian Dan Cruickshank, had declared the journal's ethos as one 'committed to the evolution of a new architecture which combines contemporary technology with the inspirational ideas offered by traditional buildings'.

I liked that.

He asserted that new buildings should connect with their environs. 'The reconciliation of the old and the new, united with a concern for relating new buildings to their settings, will restore delight to our view of the world.'

I liked that too.

Yet, although important to build in a way sympathetic to the environment, the end result doesn't have to be solemn. What's wrong with imbuing a new build with *jeu d'esprit*, a playful spirit?

So, Nick's question had to be treated seriously. Perhaps I surprised him with my reply.

'Why not?'

Rooted in Suffolk

My mother had been born in Ipswich, the county town of Suffolk. Marriage carried her far away and kindred connections became tenuous. Many years on, a distant cousin sent me details of the maternal family tree traced back to the sixteenth century (he'd worked on this long before the internet popularised genealogical research). I'd had no idea of the degree to which mother's paternal and maternal bloodline – and therefore mine – was embedded in the county. Having always assumed that I'd issued from sturdy peasant stock, it turned out that my forebears had been well-to-do farmers and industrialists. Suffolk had been in the van of revolution in agricultural practices, and one ancestor proved to have been the machine manufacturer Robert Boby, to whom there's even a building dedicated at the Museum of Rural Life in Stowmarket. His wealth trickled down his descendants and family legend has it that their extravagances included racing yachts moored at Felixstowe and Ipswich, solid silver tableware, fancy residences, posh schools and umpteen servants.

Another Boby scion, as it happens also a Robert, lived at Columbine Hall near Stowupland, where he farmed 540 acres. By extraordinary coincidence, I learned of this a mere two days before Nick and I were due to visit that very place. The 600-year-old, timber-framed building, with its jettied upper storey rising directly from the moat, had somehow called to me from an 'Invitation to View' pamphlet [1] so we'd booked a house tour with the owners. Once there, we'd learnt that the hall had been in the hands of a son of Sir James Tyrrell, the alleged murderer of the Princes in the Tower, and later, Sir Robert Carey, a favourite of Elizabeth I. It was Carey who, on the death of the Queen in 1603, had ridden hotfoot to Edinburgh to inform the King of Scotland that he had become James I of England. Anyway, in 1730 the hall came into the hands of

---

1 A scheme enabling owners of historically interesting houses to open to the public www.invitationtoview.co.uk

a rich merchant, and for the next century and a half, the property was let to farming tenants of whom Robert Boby was the most prominent.

Both Boby lines eventually converged with that of my grandfather Scott. It seems that this was the point at which the family wealth began to dissipate, the Scott gambling habit reputedly propelling the family from Stanstead Hall, a substantial moated farmhouse near Lavenham, to a cramped terrace house in Phoenix Road, Ipswich.

Although blown by the wind to Suffolk, I had a sense of coming full circle...

They say that unless your family has been rooted in Suffolk for about 300 years, you are deemed a newcomer. Paradoxically, in the light of my antecedents that makes Nick more of a newcomer than me. He had begun his own metamorphosis into 'southfolk' man after Tom and his wife, Frances, acquired a holding in the village of Westhall in the 1960s. This was the not so aptly named Belle Grove Farm, a beguiling designation for what was a plain East Anglian holding. (Put that name into a search engine and it will return results of eighteenth-century plantations in Virginia and Louisiana, a far more romantic reality.)

At that time, farms constituting anything less than prime land managed to avoid assimilation into larger units, so Belle Grove's inconveniently small fields and heavy soil brought it within reach of a down payment and a mortgage. In the early days, Tom maintained the virtuous circle of the traditional mixed farm, with grass pasture providing summer feed and sugar beet tops supplementing the hay in winter for the hundred head of cattle whose manure fertilised the land. He improved the lumpen clay through drainage, but while in those days a family could extract a reasonable, if not exciting livelihood from a limited acreage, this eroded with the economic exigencies of small-scale farming. As expected of a farmer's lad, Nick had laboured on the farm and, even now, wintry conditions turn his mind to the cold snaps in which the pipes would freeze and leave the farm without water, on one occasion for fourteen weeks. People can get by without water on tap but cows can't, so the fire service would come to the rescue with the loan of a firehose. Every morning before school (in the dark), the young Nick would connect the hose to a hydrant 100 yards away and after school (in the dark), roll it up before the hose itself would freeze solid. That surely explains his work ethos.

It was clear that the land could not sustain both father and adult son so there came a point when Nick had to choose: to stay and work full-time with little prospect of sufficient independent income or to break away from what may be viewed as the bondage of day-to-day farming to carve out a different life. Being Nick, he managed both. Sort of.

In those days, the ploughing season often extended through to Christmas, so the first part of his strategy was to acquire a brand new Track Marshall (crawler tractor) and invest in an innovative Dowdeswell plough.[2] In theory, this would give him a definite edge in offering a ploughing service to farmers whose conventional wheeled tractors struggled to cope with sticky clay. He and his ploughing partner (who, luckily, given the capriciousness of the brand new tractor, was a skilled mechanic), worked round the clock, Nick doing the night shift even though daylight hours were often spent rushing around after spare parts.

In the early 1970s, inspired by tales of those he met at various rock festivals to which he'd hitchhiked (including the early Glastonbury and Isle of Wight Festivals, a far cry from today's behemoths), he'd hit the 'hippie trail' overland to India and the Far East. Having acquired a taste for travel, he cast around for what next. 'Next' turned out to be a 20-week overland journey to South Africa, and after surviving in the back of a truck through North, West and Central Africa along with 18 other like-minded individuals, the second part of his break for independence kicked in. Calculating that he could organise a similar trip and be the one collecting the fares, he bought a truck, added seats and advertised for a complement of paying passengers across Africa, top to bottom. Of whom I was one.

Reader, I married him but retained my maiden name (for the record, Nick's surname is Fisher) and spent much of the next 30 years – first as Hobo Trans Africa Expeditions, then as Truck Africa – taking and organising overland camping expeditions, including an annual five-month, one-way Trans Africa from the UK to South Africa via the Sahara, West Africa, the Congo and East Africa. But that's a whole other story.[3]

To be exact, the trips set off from Belle Grove Farm, the vehicles prepared in a jerry-built workshop attached to the side of the outbuildings where all the equipment would be piled – tools, spare parts, sand mats, shovels, jerrycans,

2 Nick wants me to explain that this is a five-furrow, reversible plough invented by Roger Dowdeswell, who, having successfully designed a new linkage system, moved on to design this specifically for crawlers as one did not exist on the market at the time.

3 As recounted in African *Approaches: Roads to a Far-Off Place* pub. 2012, ISBN 978178003627.

tarpaulins, tents, metal boxes, cooking equipment, dry provisions and everything that might possibly be needed to make a five-month camping trip for 20+ people self-sufficient.

We fell into a routine: to avoid the worst of the heat of the Sahara and the rains in Central Africa, long-haul departures were scheduled for the New Year. As these were one-way journeys, the vehicles would be sold in East Africa and we'd fly home ready for the summer harvest. Much later, the company expanded to include year-round, short-haul, fly-in safaris. This required a London office, along with drivers and couriers, which allowed us to continue an increasingly multi-faceted life, including acquiring form with building projects...

The Learning Process

Come the late 1970s, we'd planned to participate in the Peking to Paris Race. This was intended as a re-creation of the famous 1907 Peking-Paris Rally and we even paid a substantial deposit to guarantee our place. The ambitious scheme failed – ultimately the organisers failed to conquer the bureaucracy of the Soviet Union (as it then was) through which it would have had to route. [4] Although our deposit was returned, it looked as if we'd sacrificed a year when we could have run a trip through Africa.

Instead, we bought a house.

I lived in London during the week and at weekends found myself hurtling up the A12 to Suffolk in my draughty (rust holes in the floor) Morris Minor, the very car that we'd have taken on the Peking-Paris run. The journey becoming tedious, I eventually made the quantum leap to country living. For £5,500 Nick and I purchased a late Victorian, four-storey townhouse in the market town of Halesworth, three miles from the farm. The nineteenth-century writer, Sydney Smith, famously bemoaned being 'twelve miles from a lemon'. Halesworth wasn't quite that challenging, but a request to the greengrocer for a green pepper or avocado pear did result in a distinctly glazed expression. For quite a while afterwards I found I needed to pop down to London for an 'urban fix'. Yet Suffolk gradually drew me in.

The house had been occupied (read trashed) by tenants from the American base at RAF Bentwaters and needed a lot of love. The 'expert' mortgage valuer disliked what he insisted on calling 'the Lighthouse' and stressed that 'there's no point spending much on this, it will never be worth more than £12,000 whatever you do'. We ignored him, taking walls down, sacrificing a fourth bedroom to make a bathroom and building a kitchen extension – although we do hold up

4 Several re-enactments have occurred since the dissolution of the USSR, notably the Motor Challenge in 1990 – too late for us.

our hands to the woodchip wallpaper. Apologies to our successors! Difficult to credit now, but back then, all things Victoriana were in vogue and we had fun tracking down suitable fireplace surrounds, light fittings, paintings and knick-knackery. Alongside the weekly livestock market opposite the house (now long gone), two 'deadstock' sales ran simultaneously, that 'inside' selling half-decent furniture and antiques, the 'outside' offering lower-grade, household items.

Thus, the Lighthouse gradually became equipped with mirrors, chests of drawers, tables and chairs from 'inside' and ladders, buckets, brooms and miscellanea from 'outside' from whence also came a pair of new double mattresses that had been caught in a flood leaving them with an off-putting tidal mark. These we acquired for the grand sum of 50p (kept for 30 years, they were the most comfortable ever, even more so than the mattress long before retrieved from a skip in Bayswater). If the auctioneer couldn't attract a bid on a lot, he'd throw it in with the next and on one famous occasion, I ended up with 14 lots for 50p, including many boxes of obscure paraphernalia, which were stored at the farm.

Long forgotten, the boxes re-emerged when the farm sheds were cleared. Having financially matured with age, the contents, mainly collectable bottles, stoneware vessels and leather harnesses, yielded an unexpected windfall. As will be seen, *never throw anything away* became our mantra.

Our son Jaimie was born in this period, much petted by the coming-and-going Africa crew and whichever wingman happened to be helping Nick with his ploughing schedule that season.

Peter, for example, did duty on all fronts despite being profoundly deaf. His lip-reading was excellent but could cause problems in the dark, whether trying to follow quick-fire repartee around a campfire or conducting disembodied conversations. At the time, I had succumbed to the then craze for freezing industrial quantities of seasonal produce and pig carcasses, so required Nick and Peter to shift a bulky chest freezer into the basement. Nick manhandled one end down the narrow light-less stairwell while Peter steered from the top but, the freezer becoming wedged, Nick was trapped at the bottom. With no verbal communication possible, the resourceful Peter focused a torch beam on Nick's lips, which could just be seen poking between the edge of the freezer and the wall (an occasion when a Mick Jagger mouth would have been handy). He could then read instructions of the 'left hand down' or 'back up' variety so, after several hours, the wretched freezer was manoeuvred into place and Nick released from his prison.

'That's never going to get out of there,' we prophesied.

Then there was Simon: he'd been travelling alone when we'd picked him up in Zaire [5] and he had come back to work with Nick. Between ploughing seasons, he made a trip to South America, on his return producing two enormous tins

---

5 Now the Democratic Republic of Congo.

of talcum powder from his backpack. Now, Simon enjoyed a recreational spliff of an evening and these turned out to be packed with 'weed'. He never did appreciate his good fortune: the first thing an alert Customs Officer would have thought was 'why would this guy have two tins of talc in his grubby rucksack? He doesn't look as if he's washed for weeks as it is.' Simon was royally vexed when his brother came to stay and smoked the lot. For ourselves, we preferred the sociability of wine.

With all this activity, the Lighthouse was becoming cramped, and with only roadside parking, inconvenient. Looking around for an alternative we noticed a 'For Sale by Auction' sign on a handsome house at the far side of town. Enticingly, the particulars referred to outbuildings, suggesting lots of storage space. And parking. Although the Grade II listed property had started life as a plain farmhouse, an aspirational Regency façade had been added along the way and over the years it had seen life as doctor's surgery, veterinary surgery and nursery school. On inspection, it was clear that nothing had been touched for at least half a century.

'We can do all the work,' we told ourselves, naively calculating on a five-year plan. 'Not that we stand a chance of getting it anyway.'

To our surprise – almost consternation – it was knocked down to us for a relative snip (£32,000 since you ask), only one other couple having half-heartedly bid. Not having sold the Lighthouse, we had pre-agreed a bridging loan with the bank (as one could in those days) but, in the event, were able to sell smoothly.

Q. What is the best way of broadcasting the fact that your house is up for sale?

A. Mention it to the person most likely to spread the information – your hairdresser!

I did.

It sold.

In fact, it sold to that very hairdresser, and for considerably more than the valuer's limit.

'Tell you what, we'll throw in the chest freezer,' we added, munificently.

'Wow, that's great, thanks.'

The house has changed hands several times since. I have a pang of conscience on going by in case the freezer, doubtless defunct by now, is still incarcerated. Even better, there were no expenses associated with that move: no legal costs (as a solicitor I could attend to that side of things), no estate agency commission and no removal charges. We simply heaped our less-than-impressive furniture onto a low loader towed behind a tractor, in full public view through the main (and only) street of the town.

The fact that the new house, Wissett Place, was in such a poor state had doubtless accounted for the dearth of buyers. We became accustomed to living in one room at a time, surrounded by the grimy chaos created by pulling down ceilings, renewing the roof, counteracting settlement in the extensive cellar, plumbing, heating, electrics and plastering. The chimney flues also needed attention and Nick maintains that rebuilding them brick by brick from the inside, all the time gagging on clouds of up-borne dust, is the worst job he's ever undertaken, in a long line of horrible jobs.

There was some excitement though; in the process of rejigging internal spaces, he knocked through a false wall at the end of a long corridor used as a storage cupboard, only to find a long-drop toilet exiting onto a strikingly healthy cluster of rose bushes. Although not cited on the Listing, this *garde robe* must have been original to the house and would have been highly unusual for the time.

The previous life of the house having been as an infant's school, it seemed that every second person was familiar with it. *'Oh, you live in Mrs Evan's place!'* In the very early days, we opened the door to a lady from New Zealand who was visiting her sister. Her family had lived there during World War II and she remembered the garden in its 'Dig for Victory' mode, when there was just an outside privy. She was astonished to see the *garde robe*, though she did recognise the pre-war lino still on the landing. Then there were the Pedgrifts, a family of local medical practitioners who occupied Wissett Place for much of the nineteenth century. Out of the blue, a twentieth-century descendant knocked on the door, having identified the house only through a portrait of a prominent ancestor standing before his estates in an 'all I survey is mine' posture (a device typical of its day), with the surprisingly recognisable house in the distance. The descendant was delighted to see the final piece of evidence, the family name, on a painted wooden sign found in the cellar.

Over the next twenty years the sprawling house, with its six bedrooms and outbuildings, accommodated the mainly Antipodean Trans-Africa crew. They ebbed and flowed through the sprawling attic and an outhouse which was occasionally raided by local police who, not having much else to do, got it into their heads (wrongly!) that it was occupied by a drug dealer. Eventually, it was colonised by an Australian called Wal and forever after known as Wal's Room.

Black Wednesday

With all the deep restoration work going on only as and when we could, that five-year plan looked increasingly unrealistic. Indeed, it was only when we worked on it before its sale twenty-eight years later, that Wissett Place reached its apogee. The experience Nick gained through the restoration process, as well as his innate hands-on ability, gave him the confidence to undertake sporadic building projects alongside farming and travel commitments. Encouraged by the economic boom of the mid to late 1980s, his first significant commercial scheme had been an extensive site off Halesworth's Chediston Street, consisting of two stark Victorian brick warehouses, a pair of pretty Georgian cottages and an adjacent Grade II listed seventeenth-century house, all of which had lain empty since World War II and, at the rear, an acre of low-lying land bordering a stream. Once a labyrinth of small terrace cottages and narrow alleys peppered with taverns and taprooms, the nineteenth-century incarnation of Chediston Street, 'Cherry Bow', had enjoyed a naughty reputation, the nearest thing Halesworth had to a red-light district. Ghosts are still said to haunt the area including a heavy-footed spectral presence connected to the murder of PC Ebenezer Tye, his murderer being the last person to be publicly hanged in Suffolk [6], an episode that sealed the street's reputation as lawless.

May I stress that the neighbourhood had become perfectly respectable by our time, so the plan was to create seven residential buildings comprising three street-front dwelling houses, and four carved out of the warehouses.

On account of being within the curtilage of the important seventeenth-century house, all the buildings were caught by its Grade II listing. This stymied any easy upgrade into the late twentieth century, but we were permitted to substitute traditional lime render and pargetting [7] for the Victorian brickwork under which a timber frame had lain hidden. This, Phase 1, achieved a healthy

6 In 1862

7 Decorative plasterwork particularly associated with Essex and Suffolk.

profit. Phase 2 moved onto the pair of Georgian cottages, producing a modest profit. Nick's thoughtful concept for the warehouse conversions eventually found favour with the planners, but it was in this Phase 3 that we took a spill: over eighteen months of work, the economic boom moved into bust and we found ourselves caught in the downdraught of a major recession. By the time the units were ready, Black Wednesday [8] had come and gone, the country's GDP recorded its sharpest drop in ten years, inflation was in double figures and bank interest rates peaked at 15 per cent, putting bank borrowing in excess of 19 per cent. There were no buyers. The bank having taken it as security, Wissett Place was on the line.

Despite the completed project achieving critical acclaim and award-wining status, we emerged with scorched financial fingers. While it would be easy to regret ever having touched the scheme, I believe that no experience is ever wasted and the project proved a showcase for Nick's virtuosity, on the strength of which he became a member of the prestigious Federation of Master Builders.

His strong visual sense transformed him into designer as well as practician, realising many innovative ideas without recourse to architects. His ethos has always been to find solutions and as he had no fear of tackling the tricky or unusual, it wasn't long before he found himself in demand, converting ancient barns, chapels, cowsheds and stables into homes. These consolidated his reputation for lateral thinking and his diplomatic dealings with conservation officers and planners kept them on side. In this he was greatly supported on the technical side by structural engineer John Rawlings. In an earlier life John had worked on the construction of power stations and was adept at resolving the sort of structural problems that defeat the average architect. Many a time he

8 16 September 1992 when the British government was forced to withdraw the pound sterling from the European Exchange Rate Mechanism.

and Nick managed to devise simple and inexpensive solutions to construction problems that had vexed owners and their expensively hired advisors alike. John was given to committing complex equations and calculations direct from brain to foolscap in old-fashioned longhand, something that, as will be seen, came to pose problems.

My physical input into Wissett Place had been limited to a paintbrush, but Nick and I discovered that we made a good team when it came to problem-solving and assessing aesthetic outcomes. We juggled all this between farming, raising a family, running the overlanding business, regular sorties to Africa and my own work as a locum solicitor.

Gothic Tendencies

Having no background in art or architectural study, somehow, I had never consciously registered the built world. Certainly, I had not fully appreciated the way that English architecture seems to fall into three overarching forms: the Gothic, the neoclassical and the modernist (within which, of course, are many sub-movements such as Baroque, Rococo and various Revivals). Gothic is compellingly expressed in the spectacular churches and cathedrals of the Middle Ages, a style that famously provoked Giorgio Vasari to describe it as '...monstrosities vomited up in torrents by barbarians throughout the centuries of ignorance'. [9] Vasari instead championed the classical aesthetic, resurrecting interest in the architectural language of the Greeks and Romans, epitomised by columns, pediments, rounded arches and domes. He effectively underwrote today's view of the Renaissance and by the eighteenth century, pilgrimages to study ancient buildings and ruins had become *de rigeur,* classical orders forming the language of all structures that aspired to importance.

It was Horace Walpole, with his romanticised notion of the Middle Ages, who gave birth to the Georgian Gothic Revival, but much as it amuses and delights, his house at Strawberry Hill is but an impractical pseudo-medieval piece of theatre. [10] And although the eccentrically brilliant Sir John Soane later subverted neoclassicism with Gothic elements, classicism continued to dominate British architecture. By the mid-nineteenth century, their appetite for the exotic fuelled by Empire, the Victorians had fallen for the Middle-Eastern flavour of Venetian Gothic. With steeply pitched roofs and spires, narrow pointed windows, exposed wood and heavy patterns, it was the very antithesis of classical form, nevertheless becoming 'the' style for high-status institutions designed by Gothic Revivalists, Augustus Pugin and Gilbert Scott amongst others. Perhaps

---

9 Italian painter, architect, writer and historian, famous for the book, *Lives of the Most Excellent Painters, Sculptors and Architects.*

10 Strawberry Hill in Twickenham, many of whose decorations are made of papier mâché.

reflecting the self-confidence of Victorian society, these represented a stronger interpretation of the medieval than that of the more tentative Georgians. By the early twentieth century, this disregard for stylistic purity had come to be viewed as a period of grotesque bad taste, summed up by P. G. Wodehouse in *Summer Moonshine*: '*Whatever may be said in favour of the Victorians, it is pretty generally admitted that few of them were to be trusted within reach of a trowel and a pile of bricks.*' Certainly, the ornate Gothic look was at odds with the Arts and Crafts movement, which, in reaction to nineteenth-century industrialisation, looked to honest use of materials worked by craftsmen.

The tide turned when the likes of Sir John Betjeman managed to see charm, wit and fun in Victorian architecture. Put simply, perhaps the British just aren't too concerned with architectural purity. Witness the quintessential English architect Edwin Lutyens, who didn't hesitate to mix traditional elements. The much-respected Pevsner also nudged mid-twentieth-century society into taking neo-Gothic seriously, in the process restoring the reputation of William Burges, an architect so in thrall to the decorative that he rebuilt Cardiff Castle as a sumptuous Gothic fantasy, leading to the tour de force that is Castell Coch. Seen by neoclassicists and modernists alike as 'mad architecture', Castell Coch is certainly at the extravagant end of Gothic Revival, its medieval mien and interior of sumptuous jewel colours and glittering golds making it thoroughly camp in the sense of theatrical and over the top. Mad architecture maybe, fun assuredly. Neither Nick nor I had had previous cause to analyse our respective visual responses but now recognised and embraced an undeniable leaning toward flamboyant Gothic romanticism, tempered by a parallel admiration for the honesty of the Arts and Crafts movement. In other words, we diagnosed a Gothic tendency, architecturally speaking.

No wonder we fell for that sketch.

'Hmm, Interesting'

As the years went by, the farm's modest acreage had limited its commercial viability and its future was uncertain. Tom soldiered on but died just at the time that Nick and I concluded we'd had enough of nearly three decades of the overland safari business. I had been very much involved with the Africa business to the last, despite combining it with full-time work commitments. Now I saw 'retirement' as an opportunity to escape the ever more tediously regulated routines of legal practice. But we had spent so much time in our own little bubble overseas that, as I'm wont to explain, 'we forgot to get a pension'.

We needed a plan. Something to propel us into the next phase of life.

We'd already dipped our toes into the waters of domestic tourism in the shape of a tumbledown stable adjoining Wal's Room. Having eventually wrestled Wissett Place free of the tentacles of the bank, we'd felt able to invest in it a bit more so, seeing the stable as a potential 'granny annexe' to attract a notional future buyer, we 'did it up'. Only later did we think to cover costs by letting it out as a holiday home. We'd harboured no great ambitions. Who would want to holiday near a busy road in an obscure town? So, despite the less than tranquil location, we'd been taken aback by the resulting 90 per cent occupancy and sensed an opportunity to replicate this on a grander scale at the farm. The redundant outbuildings could be converted into holiday lets, in the hope that these would provide a stream of income. Our tourism trajectory would thus continue from the ridiculous (rough-and-ready camping) to the sublime (five-star luxury). Furthermore, we reasoned that nothing the Great British public could throw at us could compare to coping with overlanders grumbling in the belly of the jungle.

Government subsidies were available to those small farmers who thought to diversify into holiday lets or bed and breakfast accommodation, but in truth, the hideously bureaucratic procedures were more a deterrent than incentive. Better to self-finance; something we would hope to achieve through the sale of Wissett

Place. Still, that original £32,000 investment needed to translate into a healthy sale price if we were to cover the conversions *and* a new house.

So it was that at the time we stumbled on that particular issue of *Perspectives*, we were already in discussions with the local planning authority concerning the lets. Winding up a session with the approachable but world-weary CPO (chief planning officer), Nick none too confidently flourished a photocopy of the sketch we'd carelessly dubbed 'Russian House', online research having suggested that it was probably attributable to the twentieth-century Russian architect, Ivan Kniazev.

'What do you think?' he asked, emphasising that while the challenge would be to make it function as a living machine, our vision definitely encompassed the curved frontages, the looming chimney, the cambered roofs, tower and turret.

'Hmm, interesting...'

The CPO wasn't given to hyperbole, but we were emboldened by the fact that he hadn't crunched the paper up and thrown it into a corner with a hollow laugh. But he was a practical man.

'Trouble is,' he observed, 'a planning application for something as potentially controversial as this would have to be considered by the full committee. I'm not even sure if my officers could get their heads round it, let alone the lay members.'

Used to assessing conventional plans, they could all have difficulty in interpreting the necessarily complex elevations.

'Sometimes ideas need help to translate them in a way that can be readily understood,' he went on. 'What you really need here is to show the design in three dimensions. Have you thought about an architectural model?'

Despite this excellent advice, we came away with the impression that he considered the idea a passing whim. An eccentricity.

It is said that something in the British psyche eschews the norm and embraces oddity. This is referred to as 'eccentricity'. Yet does cherishing and expressing individuality equate to 'eccentric'? For example, Britain is full of less than practical, indeed positively fanciful, edifices but these don't necessarily imply eccentricity, just the desire and wherewithal to be playful. Several exist more or less on our doorstep: the Temple of Dido at Gt. Saxham Hall, the gatehouse of Erwarton Hall, near Ipswich made from zany vertical brick tubes, and, in what may be England's oldest 'folly', Lord de Freston's six-storey tower by the shores of the River Orwell. Again, there's the strange Gothic building in the grounds of the long-gone Rendlesham Hall, consisting of a chimney supported by madly disproportionate flying buttresses. Yet, nobody damns as eccentric the ingenious and playful Balancing Barn at nearby Thorington, built by the architectural consortium MRDV. This is cantilevered over a mound so that half of it hangs in mid-air. Modern professional design evidently bestows credibility and insulates structures from accusations of 'eccentricity'.

So, allegedly eccentric follies have long played a role in romantically embellishing the landscape and became quite a cult during the Georgian Gothic Revival. These often took the form of 'ruins'. We had already contributed to romantic nonsenses by concocting our own ruin on that acre of ground at Chediston Street, a sham artfully made to look as if it had been there for centuries. That had come about not through eccentricity but by accident, a reclamation yard owner having airily waved toward the corner where Nick had spotted a few weathered flagstones.

'It's all yours.'

Neither had realised that the ditch, hidden by brambles, was bursting with stone slabs, columns and an incomplete window arch. The good-natured owner waved away a re-negotiation of the very reasonable price.

'I just want it cleared.'

'There must be a ton here. Maybe enough to make a 'ruin'?' Nick had mused, going on to construct a 'surviving corner' of an ancient building so apparently authentic that even visitors who had played on the site when young were prone to react with 'wow, I didn't know this was here – how old is it?'

Yes, this suggests a romantic imagination. But does it make him (or me) eccentric? One dictionary definition of the word is 'unconventional and slightly strange views and behaviour'. Admittedly ours *was* an unconventional course, but we don't think that we were strange in pursuing it and are encouraged by the sense that people, over time, do become attached to manifestations of caprice and that which Kevin McCloud dubs 'architectural porridge'.

Architect-free Zone

The philosophy of 'natural building' is enshrined in *Shelter*[11], a compendium of unconventional buildings aimed at back-to-the-land enthusiasts in North America. In this, Lloyd Kahn promotes natural building as a way to lessen environmental impact without sacrificing comfort. We're all for that, but it was his inspirational *Builders of the Pacific Coast* (published much later) that helped develop our instinctive preferences. In this, he shows how a swathe of carpenters on North America's West Coast used local cedar and Pacific driftwood to create astonishingly innovative and exciting buildings in a 'vortex of creative carpentry energy', no doubt helped by the fact that they had few, if any, building regulations to contend with.

In the search of the 'efficient, ecological and artistic', Kahn poses important questions to aspiring self-builders:

- Is the build practical?
- Are the materials sustainable?
- Will it be pleasing to live in?
- Does it fit into the landscape?
- Is there joy, wit and harmony to the design and construction?

In truth, we weren't sure how practical the build would be but otherwise felt that our project fitted these criteria. Another hallmark of the Pacific builders was that they dispensed with architects. We had to consider whether to do likewise.

As an artist works with line and colour, a sculptor works with form and mass. An architect has to combine both, but their work must also have functional purpose, so the best outcomes combine aesthetic vision with technical expertise. At one end of the scale is the so-called 'polite' where functional gives way to

11 Published 1973

style, with little regard for the practices and materials of a particular locality. At the other end is the vernacular, often described as 'architecture without architects', designed and constructed by local builders using to-hand materials and well-tried forms. In reality, cross-fertilisation ensures that the vernacular occasionally draws on sophisticated design and vice versa.

Our experience had been firmly at the vernacular end of the spectrum. Fairly or not, Nick tends to be sceptical of the value of conventional architects in the smaller domestic arena. He hadn't always enjoyed happy relationships with those he'd encountered, mistrusting their tendency to impose their own vision at any cost and, only too often, overlooking inexpensive and practical solutions in favour of over-engineering. In short, he has a lot of sympathy with the builder in Kahn's book who remarks, 'If a client hires an architect, I'm out the door'.

Having said that, we appreciate the refinement which professional design can bring, as well as the way in which good architecture can shape the landscape. Frank Lloyd Wright pioneered the notion of 'organic architecture' in the twentieth century by embracing the vernacular approach and positing that new buildings should harmonise with the environment. [12] His riposte to Le Corbusier's famous modernist aphorism 'the house is a machine for living' was a curt 'yes, just like the human heart is a suction pump'. Of a later generation, Bart Prince stretches the organic concept through exaggerated curvilinear forms and Arthur Dyson explains that his 'approach to design faces head on the reality that every part of human experience arises within a perpetual cascade of natural energies whose powers and workings are the very shape of our existence'. Eh? I *think* he means that architectural design must possess a vital spark of originality. But, however much Nick and I were seduced by photographs of Prince's and Dyson's sinuous buildings, the fact is that architecture at that level is only possible by way of serious financial patronage. Flying in the face of standard build wisdom tends to be expensive and, even at our level, we were conscious of Frank Gehry's observation that whereas a flat wall costs $1 and a curved wall $2, a double curve costs $10.

Interesting too that 'mad' (and rich) Ludwig II of Bavaria, he of those romantic castles clinging to crags [13], had turned to theatrical set designers rather than architects to put his fantasies into effect.

We felt that we'd have to rely on our own sense of theatre.

---

12 Exemplified by his design for Fallingwater, a house in Pennsylvania built partly over a waterfall, 1935.

13 In particular, the fairytale Schloss Neuschwanstein, a nineteenth-century Romanesque Revival castle in south-west Bavaria.

Thinking Spangly

The intention of post-1947 planning policy was to preserve the sanctity of the countryside by disallowing new private development in isolated rural areas. [14] This left little room for the creation of one-offs of the sort that had historically spurred architectural innovation. In 1974, the Victoria & Albert Museum had famously hosted an exhibition entitled 'The Destruction of the Country House' in which over 600 country houses were identified as having been demolished in the preceding century. This stark fact drove a new attitude to preservation, in turn leading to consideration of the merits of new building in that tradition. Consequently, in 1997 the Environment Secretary, John Gummer, introduced a policy that allowed new homes to be built in isolated rural positions, provided that they were 'of the highest quality, outstanding in terms of its architecture and landscape design, and would significantly enhance its immediate setting and wider surroundings'. The so-called 'Gummer's Law'.

This exception did not commend itself to the then Opposition who saw it as a perk for the privileged few. Nevertheless, the policy managed to survive later attempts to drop it, despite an Early Day Motion that 'this House believes that if the countryside is to be preserved by not building ordinary houses, it is even more important that it should not be polluted with big houses from the arrogant, vulgar and rich'. The revised Policy PPG7 emphasised that new buildings would only be allowed if 'truly outstanding and groundbreaking'. Attention inevitably focused on the country house or mansion possibilities and it was assumed that any such proposal would be architect-led, viz. this fairly typical comment posted on an internet forum: 'something truly "outstanding and groundbreaking" can only be produced by an outrageous architect in conjunction with a client with huge balls and very deep pockets'.

Or, as a *Guardian* article had it:

---

14 The Town and Country Planning Act of 1947.

...think pink, or purple, or starfish-shaped: the time has come for anyone with dreams of building a truly radical country house. Forget classical columns and a nice gravelled drive: something spangly and blobby like the Selfridges building in Birmingham, something jaunty like Will Alsop's Peckham Library... is more likely to win planning permission.

It went on:

The news was greeted with relief by architects, who may earn most of their livings from office blocks and attic conversions, but whose dream client has an untrammelled imagination, rolling acres, infinitely deep pockets and a sympathetic planning authority.

It wasn't clear at this point whether, as a replacement, but not like-for-like house, our proposal would necessarily fall within the PPG7 ordinance, but its prescriptions were likely to be taken into account.[15]

We weren't thinking spangly. We didn't have an architect, not even an outrageous one. Nor 'infinitely deep pockets'.

We did seem to have found a sympathetic ear at the planning authority, however, though it was still likely that 'huge balls' would be needed.

Even so, it was crucial that our building be perceived less as theatre than as a serious organic response to the landscape. Although Georgian symmetry works well in any environment, we felt that here the contours of the land required an unsymmetrical sort of symmetry, a balanced asymmetry if you like. Then there was the nature of the building in the sense of its personal purpose. Once, the word 'home' was used to mean more than mere bricks and mortar, evoking a sense of personal identity, a place of retreat from the world reflecting the occupant's history and dreams. So, a sympathetic architect will question clients closely in order to draw out their requirements for a home – including some they didn't know they had – and will be alert to subtext and nuance. Instead, Nick and I embarked on our own analysis of the dynamics of our life, how we envisaged physical space would be used. How we'd like to live. That is, matters to be considered as if we *were* briefing an architect.

Comfort and minimising household running costs were a given. To this we added a deeply personal mission statement:

- kitchen with Aga, wine fridge, slouching area (very important), walk-in pantry
- separate utility for laundry and the boring bits

---

15 The policy in respect of building homes in open countryside has evolved through to Paragraph 55 of National Planning Policy Framework (NPPF) 2012, which has a slightly different emphasis.

- massive table for family feasts and entertaining inebriated friends
- open fire for roasting chestnuts and marshmallows – and warming backsides after chilly walks
- master bedroom plus walk-in wardrobe to hide chaos
- several bedrooms overall for waifs and strays
- sybaritic master bathroom, emphatically not the hotel type of the current vogue.
- sumptuous linen cupboard so I could play domestic goddess (a role that has so far eluded me)
- two separate offices/work spaces/studies – this in an effort to separate the business from the personal, both of which seem to amass paperwork
- lots of windows with French doors in there somewhere
- internal double doors
- oodles of storage for things we won't be able to bring ourselves to get rid of and will probably go on acquiring despite best intentions
- miles of bookshelves – ditto

Critically, we'd aim to use materials and components from Nick's stockpile of 'useful one day' items.

These loose requirements were all very well, but if we *did* commission a model, we realised we'd need to come up with a much *more* detailed specification than as if going through this process with an architect.

The irony.

Mission Impossible

There is an idea that medieval England was covered in woodland but, in reality, much had disappeared by 1066. The remaining woods were hugely economically important, trees husbanded to produce bark for tanning, sap for pitch and tar, ash for soap and glass, and charcoal for gunpowder. Treated like a crop, trees were grown to the required size and felled for a specific job, not sawn up to await a buyer, as is the case today.

For us, the most practical and cost-effective way to proceed was to exploit timber (not to mention that a mistake made in wood is relatively easy to rectify) and, with no access to Kahn's cedar forests or driftwood, our choice fell on that stalwart of medieval timber-framing, oak.

Oak may be expensive but it is easily worked, versatile, durable, strong and, let's not forget, beautiful, qualities that make it the professionals' wood of choice to this day. The sheer density of an oak beam allows it to last longer in a fire than, say, steel girders, which will deform and lose strength under heat. In fact, the 'charring rate' of oak forms part of the calculations required for building regulations. Once completely dried out, the heartwood becomes so hard that nothing, not even the dreaded deathwatch beetle, can bore into it unless already degraded by damp conditions. Unseasoned oak does shrink but gathers character and strength with age, qualities to be seen in that pinnacle of timber-framed houses, the medieval hall house. To add to this paean, oak answers the call for sustainability on account of its low-embodied energy, that is, the energy required to extract, manufacture, treat and transport it.

Timber-framing has been a consistent form across the centuries, often taken to elaborate heights. One only has to look at the *stave* churches of Norway and wooden churches of Russia, all built without hammer and nails. English medieval carpenters were highly skilled in the geometry of green oak framing, knowing how to make proportions comfortable to the eye but, generally speaking, in this country timber-framing has stayed within a conventional tradition and confined to the domestic sphere. Across the Channel meanwhile, it has developed into a slick industry of off-site manufacture, often incorporating banks of glazing, the completed structure brought to site on the back of a lorry ready to 'plug into' mains services. (Of the firms specialising in such pre-fabrication, the HUF Haus is perhaps the best known.)

British builders *had* developed an alternative approach. This recognised the advantages of timber over traditional masonry, less from an aesthetic point of view than the speed at which the frame could be erected. Simple frames could also be enclosed entirely with manufactured structural insulated panels (SIPs) which reduced dependency on bracing, in turn meaning that much larger distances could be spanned. Consequently, there was a period in which construction became less complex while insulation significantly improved. Unfortunately, a *World in Action* television film, now acknowledged as misleading, suggested that timber-framed homes were a fire risk and prone to so-called 'intestinal condensation'. Modern timber-framing died virtually overnight.

That particular debacle may not have been of their making, but British builders do have a reputation for slow innovation, possibly because Britain has a greater history of speculative building than the individual-build traditions of mainland Europe. It's easier for the industry to stick to what it knows will sell – there hasn't been the public demand for cutting-edge modernity, although Channel 4's groundbreaking *Grand Designs* offers encouragement. However, an alternative model *has* emerged with the aid of modern industrial tools as a more individualistic affair than the Continental model. Thus, green oak framing has become an attractive option. This has solid timber post and beams erected on site, strategic members held together with traditional mortise and tenon joints fastened with wooden pegs (albeit complex structures will incorporate steel joinery for structural purposes) and infilled with studwork. Insulation, services and plastering follow.

This technique has given rise to numerous British oak-framing firms whose services include providing structural calculations to satisfy Building Control and making the frames in purpose-built workshops. The carpenter marks (scribes) each individual piece of timber into position above a life-size drawing on the floor, then transfers the particular shape of a piece of timber to its mate, creating a unique bond. The joints are cut by hand and pre-drilled for a final fix on site using handmade oak pegs, each piece of timber marked by the carpenter to indicate its precise location.

Armed with this knowledge, we felt confident that specialist firms such as Border Oak, Oakwrights and Heritage Oak Frames, to name but three (of many), should be able to process our design and assemble the timber structure. That'll leave us to do the easy bits, we thought. The 'easy bits' being the foundations, services, roof...!

However, we were aware that our ideas needed more detailed formulation. *Much* more. The starting point had to be that indeterminate sketch. With nothing but that single elevation to hint at the artist's overarching vision, we put the by now dog-eared drawing under a magnifying glass and attempted to interpret it from a constructional perspective. Subjected to this sort of scrutiny, it quickly became clear that a literal transcription would result in a very constricted living space; those rounded walls and sweeping rooflines significantly restricting the interior and the eye-catching roof hanging so low that, in reality, it would mean crawling on hands and knees through the hobbit-sized front door. Overcoming these issues meant shifting the roof upwards and the entrance sideways. Nick also slipped in one of his favourite architectural devices: a jettied porch.

I admit that I had concerns that this rectangular-ish addition would jar with the overall curved trope, but at least the new entranceway would provide access without the near decapitation that would surely occur by slavish adoption of the original. *Inspired by, not copying* became our mantra.

When a well-known oak-framing company promoted a tour of a completed house of conventional layout in Kent, we jumped at the chance to inspect their product and brandish the modified drawings.

'There shouldn't be a problem,' gulped a bemused 'suit'. 'I'll pass it on to one of our experts.'

Three months passed before said expert registered just how complex the scribing process would have to be. To be fair, traditional joints aren't generally compatible with the sort of curvatures and shallow pitches that we had in mind and for the firm's staff to devise a template for each and every joint would be impracticable and uneconomic.

So, the expert pronounced it 'mission impossible'.

In Kahn's book, one of the Pacific builders had shown his ideas for a sculptural building to a local builder who'd responded with the unequivocal 'you'd better get a hammer, boy, because nobody is going to build that stuff for you'.

Nick had to get a hammer.

Not a traditionalist for the sake of it, his approach would combine the use of green oak with modern methods of cutting and fixing, without a scribe or wooden peg in sight.

Serendipity

With the rejection of the project by the timber-framing firm, it looked as if we'd need that model, not only for planning purposes, but as a practical aid to the build process – being built to scale, the model would, for example, facilitate calibrating timber to exact requirements and be cut accordingly.

One thing was evident: a Blue Peter version made from pipe cleaners, toilet rolls and egg boxes wasn't going to cut it. How to track down a professional model-maker? Bury St Edmunds? Cambridge? Even London?

Serendipity. First that sketch floated across our consciousness, sparking our imaginations. Then Yellow Pages led us to to Nigel Purdy's workshop, just a few minutes' walk from Wissett Place. Nigel had been working in the architectural model-making field for years, gaining experience on The Bull Ring redevelopment in the centre of Birmingham, Heron City in Barcelona and Castle Mall in Norwich. [16] By the time we stumbled on him, he'd branched out on his own, working with local architects on domestic houses and retirement complexes, as well as projects for public bodies. There are many models of castles, museums, parks and gardens to his credit, even a leisure complex in Nigeria.

His website echoes the chief planning officer's advice: 'The benefits of modelling are the ability of the viewer to recognise and understand the concept, arrangement or function based on its visual appearance'. In other words, a model is a powerful means of communication, more so than descriptive text and drawings alone.

We found the slight figure and intelligently domed forehead of Nigel half-hidden behind mounds of chisels, clamps, glues, hacksaws, rulers and wood shavings. Blessed with a calm disposition, Nigel demonstrated no disquiet.

'What we'll do first is make a small wood prototype to test structural viability' he said. 'But I do need fixed positions for the chimneystack and the tower, as it is these that will drive the external contours and internal layout.'

16 www.nigelpurdy.co.uk

After Nick and I calculated these rather key aspects, Nigel's dexterous fingers created a framework, scaled at 1:100, from slivers of balsa wood. The process permitted experimenting with differing silhouettes so, to pre-empt objections, we toyed with modifying potentially controversial elements. Low tower, no tower or high tower? Pointy witch's-hat-style turret or curved cupola? Narrow or wide chimney? To the extent that we began to lose sight of the proposition that if you have a good idea, carry it out with complete conviction.

Courage mes amis. It took the CPO to steer us back. 'Best not dilute it. In many ways, the more unorthodox it is, the better its chances.'

This early process was an exploration of a hypothesis, a test of the building's ability to conform to statutory regulation mindful that a timber frame must carry different sorts of loading – dead loads (the weight of the structure itself, especially roof tiles), live loads (gravity) and variable wind loads (anticipating its aerodynamic behaviour). The final maquette failed to throw up any unresolvable issues and became a blueprint in three dimensions, so Nigel started working on a fully scaled-up 1:20 model. In effect, he would act as architectural draughtsman in 3D, interpreting our ideas and turning them into a workable scheme.

Saturday mornings typically saw Nigel gingerly laying the work-in-progress into the back of his red Fiat Punto Mia, driving up the road and conveying it to our kitchen table, around which the three of us would circle, probing every crook, angle and projection and analysing practical issues. These regular engagements highlighted potentially difficult detail and, while striving to preserve the spirit of the building, decisions also had to be taken on grounds of functionality. For example, although windows are key to build aesthetics, we wanted to take advantage of solar gain. Consequently, much of the glazing was shifted to face south and west, the idea being that the solid floor would act as a heat

sink, catching warmth from the winter sun while deep overhanging eaves would prevent overheating in direct summer glare.

After a couple of months orbiting our kitchen table, the model became too unwieldy to manhandle in and out of Nigel's Fiat. Instead, we convened in Nigel's workshop to review progress and discuss resolutions, a process that was to continue every Saturday for a further three months.

A pivotal aspect of Gummer's Law is that a proposed building must be 'sensitive to the defining characteristics of the local area, including local or regional building traditions and materials' (a policy that has much in common with Kahn's 'natural building'). Thus, it was important that the model demonstrate constituent components, in this case the red brick, the peg tiles, the timbering, as well as the straw bales, to be used in the entire north wall and tower. Admittedly, straw is not a customary building voice, but it has deep credibility as a sustainable material, especially when sourced locally. In this case, the 'food miles' were minimal, all the way from the back field. If challenged on the break from traditional form, we intended to argue that even if arranged somewhat unconventionally, the main elements draw on the Suffolk vernacular: red bricks recycled from the old house, traditional oak, lime-rendered straw walls, all topped with reclaimed tiles.

Well, not quite all. The old house had been roofed with grey slates, but the peg tiles for which the slate had been swapped weren't suitable for the shallow pitch of the eastern roof. A more ductile surface was called for. Fashionable aluminium, zinc or copper sheeting perhaps? A seductively practical, if expensive, notion, but although our philosophy would occasionally be compromised for pragmatic reasons, a metal roof could be hard to justify on the grounds of sustainability.

The idea of 'green roofs' passed our consciousness. Apart from its ability to enhance any setting, a plant roof encourages wildlife (especially in urban situations) and has splendid insulation qualities. We also realised that its conservationist credentials were a point we could shamelessly flag in the planning process. A firm based just thirty miles away could supply sedum vegetation blankets grown in the region and which could be delivered to site in Swiss-roll-like rolls, ready for installation. [17]

17 www.bauder.co.uk

So it was that we were to be found training binoculars on the nearby Adnams Brewery distribution centre, a building with the biggest sedum roof cover in Britain.

Samaki House

Funnily enough, it had been the experience of self-building a house in Africa that provided the confidence to tackle what might be considered an insane project.

In the 1990s, we had bought a plot of land in Tanzania, just below the equator. Why would anyone do that? Well, the refocusing of our Trans-Africa expeditions onto short-haul safaris (meaning anything from three to twelve weeks, as well as the regular twice-yearly 20-weeker) had implications not only for taking on more crew but for the maintenance of the company's expanding fleet of vehicles. So, we sited a workshop in the town of Arusha, itself a natural traffic hub sitting on the north-south highway connecting Kenya to South Africa and the east-west line between Mount Kilimanjaro and the Serengeti National Park. Nick found himself increasingly on call and, feeling conscious of over-imposing on hospitable Sikh friends, had sought a patch of land on which to construct an affordable and accessible base, possibly resembling a tent more than 'proper' house. Eventually, a plot presented itself, although, being rather precipitously perched in the foothills of Mount Meru, the second highest mountain in Africa after Kilimanjaro, it rather overturned the prerequisite of accessibility. Its elevation could also bring cold winds, so the tent concept was the next to evaporate.

The first battle had been getting the materials to site. The second was in timescale, as we were only able to progress the self-build in short stints. It's always good to have an aim though and ours was to be ensconced by Millennium Eve, come what may.

From the safe perspective of the twenty-first century, it's hard to see why the coming of the Millennium should have generated such excitement yet also such a sense of menace. New Year's Eve thousandfold, the event begged to be celebrated with a bang, but the so-called Millennium Bug, or Y2K problem, caused profound panic on account of a perceived problem created by the practice of abbreviating a four-digit year to two digits. [18] Global meltdown had been anticipated or, at the very least, aircraft falling out of the sky the moment clocks rolled over into 2000. Spoofs like this were going the rounds:

Message from: Rome
January 18, 1 B.C.

Dear Cassius,

> *Are you still working on the Y zero K problem? This change from BC to AD is giving us a lot of headaches and we don't have much time left.*
> *Honestly, you would think that someone would have thought of it earlier and not left it to us to sort out at the last minute.*
> *I spoke to Caesar the other evening. He was livid that Julius hadn't done something about it when he was sorting out the calendar. He could see why Brutus was turning nasty. We called in the consulting astrologers but they simply said that continuing downwards using minus BC wouldn't work. As usual, the consultants charged a fortune for doing nothing useful!*
>
> *As for myself, I can't see the sand in an hourglass flowing upwards.*
> *We have just heard that there are three wise guys in the East working on the problem but unfortunately, they won't arrive until it's all over. Some say the world will cease to exist at the moment of transition.*
> *Anyway, we are continuing to work on this blasted problem and I will send you a parchment if anything further develops. I end this message short because I'm suffering from a terrible case of enscriber's syndrome – it's ever since you sent us the new, high-speed, rewriteable tablets.*

> *Best regards*
> *Plutonius*

We'll never really know whether the relative absence of computer failures was the result of government-sponsored preparation or whether the problem had been overstated, but Nick and I had been very glad to be removed from all the brouhaha, even if it meant saluting the advent of the twenty-first century from a flimsy verandah overlooking the town and precariously attached to nothing but a framework of poles.

18 The Y2K problem was the name given to the issue caused by hardware and software which uses only the last two digits of the year rather than all four. Essential computer systems could be vulnerable when they ticked over from '99' to '00', making some of them interpret the year as 1900.

We hadn't needed planning permission nor had the benefit of a model. The design evolved, quite literally, on the back of a few envelopes, but the experience of using whatever materials were to hand, watching cost, communicating across language barriers and daily problem-solving, came to stand us in good stead.

Eventually, the build evolved into a one-and-a-half-storey house of timber and rock just about clinging onto the side of the hill and Samaki House has featured in several publications including the *Guardian* supplement and *Grand Designs* magazine.

Genius Loci

With no motorway or even a frequent train service, it is the very inaccessibility of north-east Suffolk that has protected it from being absorbed into commuter land and makes it so appealing.

'Twas ever thus. According to the *Suffolk Chronicle & Mercury*, 'hidden down a rural byway, Westhall is somewhat difficult to find... after leaving the small town of Halesworth the traveller can easily mistake the way.'
That was in 1928.

Westhall is still a bit of a backwater, if a little easier to find. Belle Grove Farm itself perches on Lower Common at the fringe of the village and is reached by way of Stone Street, a nine-mile stretch of Roman road between Halesworth and Bungay, known locally as the Bungay Straight. Part way along, take a turn east and follow a single-track lane. Once bounded by oaks felled in the great storm of October 1987, [19] the byroad is edged with burgeoning replacements that will one day screen the coppice-punctuated fields favoured by racing hares and swooping barn owls.

Running parallel to Stone Street is a small road extending to the left and right of the minor crossroads known as Dead Man's Corner. This marks the western boundary of the parish of Westhall. Straight ahead, the fields disappear behind flanks of arching trees funnelling through to a brick-built bridge straddling the road and which carries the railway line linking Ipswich and Lowestoft. Through the bridge is a section of road called The Danger – no one seems to know why except that it's prone to flooding (crossings were fords rather than bridges until well after World War II). However, if you find yourself at The Danger you've gone too far because Belle Grove Farm is off to the left, just before the bridge. Halfway between the unmanned railway stations of Halesworth and Brampton,

---

19 The once-in-a-lifetime storm, with winds of hurricane force, caused extensive damage, cost lives and devastated woodlands, especially in the eastern counties. The denial of any impending gale by the BBC's weather forecaster, Michael Fish, has become a cultural meme, though he claims he was misquoted.

the site is bounded by the wooded embankment of the rail line to the east, a row of mature alder and ash to the south and a high hedge to the west. Cultivated fields slope down from the north.

As mentioned, Gummer's Law also required that a house should provide a 'significant enhancement of its immediate setting'. We felt keenly that our proposal acknowledged the *genius loci*, the spirit of the place, by slotting snugly into the topography and treescape.

Much of Suffolk lies on chalk, responsible for the sweeping tracts of downland that form its only significant hills. Although the land hereabouts is generally level, it is by no means the featureless flat of popular imagination, its essence captured by Simon Barnes's engaging description:

> '*Suffolk is fascinatingly but subtly curved. Think of Keira Knightley but without the pout. If you want flat – the sort of county where you can stand up and instantly be a landmark – go to Norfolk, Lincolnshire or Cambridgeshire. Suffolk is hardly ungenerous in the amount of sky it puts on view but it really does go up and down.*'[20]

Belle Grove lies in an expressive dip between the higher grounds of Westhall and Holton; that there are now five wind turbines at Holton, 300 feet high, attest its elevation. Although modern Westhall lies in the midst of fields of wheat and barley, oilseed rape and sugar beet, the intransigent clay of the area had long sustained a mix of arable, livestock and fruit-growing. Livestock had once been

more commonplace, but nowadays, the odd few head of cattle seem almost an afterthought. Heavy though it is, this land is easier to farm than the light heathlands flanking the unpredictable coastline, itself a jigsaw of estuaries,

20 Simon Barnes, award-winning writer and journalist quoted from an article extolling Suffolk in *The Times*.

saltmarsh, crumbling cliffs and shifting bars of shingle and dashing waves. The soft underlying rock is prone to coastal erosion, the lessening shore devoured by Crabbe's 'greedy waters'. [21] Once one of the largest ports in the realm, nearby Dunwich has dwindled to a tiny coastal village (still with a great pub, it has to be said) a succession of thirteenth- and fourteenth-century storms propelling its destruction, significantly the *Grote Mandrenke*, the Great Drowning of Men. [22] Sea surges created by Atlantic storms coinciding with high spring tides continued to bite, and the last of eight churches fell off the cliff edge in 1919. Human bones from churchyards swept into the sea are occasionally found on the beach and, according to local legend, church bells can be heard ringing from beneath the waves on stormy nights. At the time of writing, a single tombstone remains.

Alluvium is dumped on the coastline just as inconveniently. The River Blyth between Southwold and Halesworth had become navigable in the eighteenth century after local businessmen funded a series of locks which allowed transportation of heavy goods in shallow-draught wherries. The 'Blyth Navigation' became a major factor in local prosperity, but the silting up of the harbour, combined with the coming of the Halesworth–Southwold Railway, a narrow-gauge line connecting the two towns in the late nineteenth century, knelled death for the river, which sank back into insignificance. The railway died too.

Villages with proximity to the coast were notorious for smuggling associations. The river, diminished as it was, continued to offer a route inland for illicit cargoes. *Jamaica Inn* [23] had nothing on it. The White Hart in nearby Blythburgh

---

21 Eighteenth-century poet George Crabbe in *The Village Book 1*, published 1783.

22 This affected the Low Countries and other northern European coastlines in 1362, causing thousands of deaths.

23 Daphne du Maurier's famous work of fiction set on Bodmin Moor, Cornwall.

was a particularly handy place from which to signal to small boats ferrying kegs of brandy. Contraband is said to have been stored above the fireplace at the Queen's Head, Blyford and bootlegged liquor hidden between pews and altar in the church, moved there from the pub along a secret tunnel. Westhall's St Andrew's Church held a similar secret, with kegs allegedly hidden in the valley between two roof ridges. At its peak, and as Rudyard Kipling suggests, smuggling was a lucrative enterprise that required the tacit support of the community:

> If you wake at midnight and hear a horse's feet,
> Don't go drawing back the blind, or looking in the street;
> Them that asks no questions, isn't told no lie,
> Watch the wall, my darling, while the gentlemen go by.

It's feasible that the folklore of rural Suffolk was deliberately exaggerated to encourage ordinary people to stay at home after dark, leaving bootleggers free to pursue their activities unremarked. A spot on a regular smugglers' route only four miles away is said to be haunted by Black Toby, a Negro drummer boy hanged for rape and murder. A spooky story about disembodied silver shoes dancing across Cox's Arch, a bridge in upper Westhall, is thought to have been put about by smugglers hoping to unnerve folk from venturing too far under the arch where booty was stowed.

Such tactics probably weren't needed to broadcast the legend of Black Shuck. The huge black dog...

> ...prowls along dark lanes and lonesome field footpaths...
> you may know him at once, should you see him, by his fiery eye;
> he has but one, and that, like there is in the middle of his head
> like Cyclops. [24]

In August 1577, this legendary devil dog is said to have burst in through the doors of Blythburgh's Holy Trinity Church accompanied by a clap of thunder, killing a man and a boy in the congregation and causing the church steeple to collapse. Leaving as balefully as he came, he scorched the 'devil's fingerprints' on the north door, still to be seen, and descended on the church in nearby Bungay, where two more people were killed.

It's thought that Sir Arthur Conan Doyle came up with the idea for *The Hound of the Baskervilles* after hearing tales of Black Shuck.

---

24 W. A. Dutt, in *Highways & Byways in East Anglia* 1901.

The Green Shed

Lowestoft, Great Yarmouth and Norwich may have been the primary East Anglian targets, but in the early days of World War II a German Dornier had emerged from the clouds to bomb Halesworth's railway yard. It scored a direct hit, killing three people. Apparently, Lord Haw-Haw, broadcasting from Germany that night, stated that a successful raid had been carried out on major marshalling yards in Suffolk, but German intelligence had evidently credited the station with far greater significance than it warranted. Other than that, until the adjoining airfield became operational, Halesworth wasn't particularly in the firing line, although a local lad did witness a Heinkel spraying the school with machine-gun bullets and the town 'circled with fire bombs', while a young girl saw a fighter swoop over Chediston Street, leaving bullet marks in the side of the house next door. [25]

At eight miles inland, RAF Halesworth (also known as Station 365) was the closest to the North Sea of all eastern counties airfields, having come into being for the use of USAAF fighter and bomber groups following America's late-1941 entry into the war. During daylight, it wasn't unusual to witness dog-fights, surviving aircrew drifting down on parachutes. At night, searchlights criss-crossed the sky, also lit by tracers and flak. 'The skies were never still. Every time you looked up, the war intruded into your thoughts,' recalls an American gunner. [26]

Shot-up aircraft trying to land in bad weather and bombers taking-off at maximum load were particularly vulnerable, mid-air collisions by no means unknown. One Sunday evensong, a crippled aircraft exploded by Halesworth's church, causing the entire east window to glow orange. Living proximate to the airfield, which included much of Westhall, was potentially hazardous, although it was mainly the aircrew who suffered. Scarcely a half-mile from Belle Grove

25 SW and LG interviewed in 1998 by Marjorie Shiers as part of an oral history project.

26 US gunner John Rainey in the booklet *Our Tour in Europe – 1944. Shroyer's Crew.*

Farm, the B24 Liberator 'Fay Day' crashed on clipping a tree behind Westhall's mill, killing eight of the crew. The Flying Fortress 'I'll Be Seeing You' disintegrated directly in front of a Westhall farmhouse with a death toll of seven. Another Liberator crashed on the edge of the parish and so it went on. As Allied sorties from RAF Halesworth stepped up, there were many retaliatory attacks and a German bomber, presumably targeting the airfield or adjacent railway bridge, managed to blow up Belle Grove's outbuildings instead.

These outbuildings had long outgrown their original function of accommodating the paraphernalia of Victorian farming. Claiming war reparations involved positive sierras of red tape and one stipulation, presumably to avoid 'improvements' at taxpayers' expense, was that damaged buildings were to be rebuilt only as they had originally stood. Thus, by the 1950s, the farm benefited from sturdily built, brand new sheds suitable only for horses and carts. (*Plus ça change.* You may be forgiven for thinking that not much changes with bureaucratic processes.) Modern materials, if not modern design, *had* been permitted so sharp-edged modern bricks bound together with cement took the place of mellow stocks held by lime mortar, while asbestos sheeting replaced ageless Suffolk pantiles. Robust and solid, yes; beautiful, no.

Over time, the buildings became stuffed to the rafters with aged farm equipment and the myriad parts and tools required for our African ventures: worn tyres, pieces of engines, jerrycans, shovels, tools and old tents squeezed in on all sides. Not to mention a 1948 Armstrong Siddeley Hurricane drop-head coupé, acquired from a friend in Nairobi whose late mother had had it sitting unused in a Brighton garage for more than twenty years. Nick had been talked into towing the Armstrong from Sussex to Suffolk and, as I suspected would be the case, his dreams of swanking around Europe being put on hold while it gently rusted in one of the outhouses along with the, by now, superannuated Morris Minor that had been destined for the Peking-Paris Rally. Body rust covered by black *Dulux* and rusty chrome with the same Caterpillar Yellow used on Nick's farm machines, I'd sold the number plate for a great deal more than the car's value.

On the face of it, the outbuildings appeared unpromising holiday-let material. Yet they did have potential to generate a revenue stream, more so than traditional cultivation of the farm's modest acreage. Local authority policy encouraged genuine farm diversification so we felt reasonably confident of achieving planning permission provided we observed the constraints. Applications to convert agricultural buildings to domestic use were not treated sympathetically if they included inappropriate fenestration, infelicitous rooflines or dormer windows. These restrictions meant that our buildings could never be fashionably 'flooded' with the light of agentspeak.

Planning permission duly given, the outbuildings had to be completely cleared before work could begin and, anticipating the need for an alternative dumping ground, Nick had already sought and received formal consent to erect a monumental 'shed' in another corner of the farm. This would house all the tools, equipment and junk as well as the Morris and the Armstrong. He'd spotted a promotion for an almost indecently low-priced shed frame in a farming magazine so duly rang the advertised number without success.

'I'll give it one last try,' he muttered.

'*Bore da.*'

'Pardon?'

'*Ydym yn ei werthu siediau ie.* Oh, sorry you're English! Yes, we sell sheds.'

'Whereabouts are you?'

'Wales.'

The outcome, after a surreal conversation conducted in respective Welsh and Suffolk accents, was: 'That's fine, *fy unig enaid* (my darling). We can do that and deliver it too'.

It was so well priced that Nick, thinking it had to be some sort of scam, cautiously asked, 'How do I pay?'

'Oh, that's OK my lovely. *Fy unig enaid*, just hand the driver a cheque.'

How refreshing to do things 'old school'! The shed frame arrived in good order and once erected, Nick and a friend clad its sides and roof with green corrugated sheeting. While at it, Nick placed two redundant 40-foot shipping containers alongside, extending the roof over them so as to end up with a 80 x 40 foot shed and workrooms. Inevitably, if unimaginatively, it became the 'Green Shed'.

Then everything went on hold.

Nick felt he couldn't turn down an exciting commission to refurbish an Arts and Crafts house in North London. As it turned out, the job was more a rebuild than refurbish and took the best part of a year, but this blip in the timeline not only paid financial dividends, it delivered a future workforce. Following the same procedure by which we'd recruited drivers and mechanics for the Trans-Africa operations, we advertised in *TNT* magazine, a London weekly give-away. Once upon a time, the majority of applicants would have been Australasian; this time the ad provoked a flood of applications from the many Poles, Romanians and Czechs seeking economic betterment, following the expansion of the European Union.

After scores of telephone interviews, two or three of the more promising candidates were persuaded to venture into the depths of Suffolk where, in exchange for the train fare and holing up in a scruffy caravan, they were 'road-tested' over the course of a week. At least they took the trouble to find out where they were, geographically speaking; more than a few of our Australasian workers vaguely thought we were somewhere 'up north', even when they'd been working there for weeks. The first to arrive was Krzysztof, a rangy, whip-thin Pole who spoke so little English that his phone call had been fronted by a 'fixer', the marginally more communicative Andrzej, also known as The Professor. Krzysz turned up with the Professor in tow, who was also on the lookout for work. Nick was doubtful. Somehow, the Professor didn't have the look of a horny-handed son of the soil.

The first test was to dig a narrow trench for the foundations of a high brick wall. Nothing unusual in that except that this wall would have no apparent purpose, being located just a few feet to the east of the workshop. We knew the workshop was to be demolished but they didn't. The other thing Krzysz and the Professor didn't know was that a huge pond was to be excavated on the far side of the trench, out of which an ostensibly 'ancient' brick wall was to rise, suggestive of a one-time moat. Whatever private thoughts he might have had, Krzysz never flinched from the task. Indeed, it became apparent that, rather than being a drawback, a major advantage of workers who don't speak the lingo was that they had no words for 'what the hell is this?', 'you can't do that' or 'what a crazy idea'. He simply knelt in the sludge and got on with it.

Out of the blue, a call. A heavily accented voice announced that his company was making a documentary about Polish workers. 'It's to explore how they're coping with life in the UK. I understand you have Poles working for you.'

'Who is it to be made for?'

'Oh, it's just for Polish television,' he said airily.

It turned out that the canny Professor had done a deal with a Polish production company, allowing them to follow him in his hunt for work.

'Would you be willing for us to film on the farm and interview you as the Professor's employer?' the voice wanted to know. 'You needn't worry, it's low budget so a minimal crew.'

We had nothing to hide, but it's always a bit nerve-wracking going on camera. The fact that the film was to be exclusive to Polish television, however, meant that it wouldn't be seen by anyone we knew, so hey ho.

'Alright then.'

'I work in office in *Polska*,' the Professor explained on asking to be driven to the railway station as soon as the camera crew had done its work. 'I too old for this.'

We harboured deep suspicions that it had all been a put-up job to give the cameras something to film out of London.

But the Professor *had* brought us to Krzysz, the first to be offered a regular job. He promptly joined Nick in London where he not only introduced compatriots who'd registered under the UK's Worker Registration Scheme – labourers, carpenters, plasterers, plumbers – but eventually shipped over his willowy and deceptively fragile-looking wife, Ewa (pronounced Ava). Nick had been dubious about this injection of domesticity; in our experience in Africa, husband-and-wife work teams could become political and problematical. But it transpired that Ewa possessed an amazing virtuosity, turning her hand to dry-walling and plastering, painting and decorating. Crucially, she wielded a benign feminine influence in the household and made valuable suggestions: to save rent, almost all the workers (peaking at 12) camped out in the house, keeping ahead of the game plan by moving their mattresses from room to room. Many were prone to overdosing on cheap vodka, so levering them out of bed in the morning could be a challenge.

As a result of Ewa's intervention, they agreed that Nick could be trusted to pay a weekly advance on wages, a sum just enough to live on (and a little bit for *wódka*) with the balance to be paid in one lump at the end of the job, safeguarding their earnings rather than frittering them away. (Every so often they'd entrust their savings to the driver of a bus shuttling between Victoria Coach Station and Warsaw who, in exchange for a modest commission, could be relied upon to deliver envelopes stuffed with cash to the right recipients.)

Despite Ewa's efforts, it wasn't that unusual to find the workforce sadly diminished on a Monday morning, many languishing in bed with vodka hangovers. The other commodity on which cash was dissipated was *papierosy*, cigarettes. In recent years, the UK has been largely weaned off smoking, but it's unexceptional in Poland, so a thick fug hung inside the building until smoking was banished to the street.

With the London job concluded, Krzysz and Ewa returned with Nick to Suffolk, together with the handful who didn't baulk at the idea of country life. Effectively team leader, Krzysz picked Wieslow as his fetcher-carrier and fall guy. Piotyr (Piet) may have been a vodkaholic, but was he was still an excellent bricklayer, his *niewolnik* (brick slave) being the young Michel. Marek's seniority meant he became *de facto* head carpenter and deployed whenever anything needed 'brain power', whereas Damian, not known as The Incredible Hulk for nothing, was simply there to offer 'Big Power'.

One and all, they shacked up in a pair of decrepit but weather-worthy static caravans connected to electricity, water and drainage. As in London, they embraced living on site as it meant longer hours in which to earn the money to send back home.

The team had almost no regard for the concept of Health and Safety and rather than *wódka* consumption, a resistance to safety helmets proved a persistent vexation. At least hard hats weren't critical to the early stages, including the demolition of the Nissen huts that had stood for half a century, so that was a battle postponed. With the emptying of outbuildings, an extraordinary amount of 'stuff' (others may call it junk) had to be shunted into the Green Shed, an operation that could have spun to eight weeks but took two. The price for such speed was an enormous muddle. After all, Nick could only direct operations from one end at a time; while he supervised what came out, he couldn't possibly be on the spot to direct what went in where.

Cleared, the outbuildings were exposed as the hovels they were, the walls strong enough for a siege but crushingly ugly. How could we hope to transform such unpromising material into tranquil retreats, welcoming boltholes, havens of comfort? We'd simply have to draw on the experience of our old holiday-let, which, in order to distract guests from the proximity of the road, had flaunted rich wall colours, antique furniture (read second-hand) and highly eclectic furnishings. But we'd have a long way to go before reaching that point.

Time to refocus on the house...

Part 2

A Doll's House

A message from Nigel.

'It's ready.'

The model was a work of art in its own right. At 39" long, 30" wide and 28" high, it was constructed in seven interlocking sections that, when dismantled and upended, revealed a stunning matrix of timbers. Nigel's attention to detail encompassed individual roofing tiles cut in MDF, the chimney with contrasting brick motif and a front wall of herringbone brick infill, not to mention lead flashing, gutters, window mullions and green roof. Rooms, staircases and even a hinged coffin hatch were detailed inside. After much discussion, we'd agreed that a trap door linking the landing and top floor would be useful for objects too large to be manoeuvred around the upper circle of stairs. I hasten to add that we had furniture in mind rather than coffins, the term harking back to the days when it was commonplace for those who died at home to be removed in their casket.

Colour-coded detail differentiated structural elements such as the blockwork, insulation and straw bales. Nigel had even included a pair of owl boxes in the turret. The one missing detail was the whatchamacallit or thingamajig topping the chimney.

Judy Boyt is an internationally acclaimed artist, specialising in figurative sculptures. In 1998, her bronze rearing horse, the heroic twice-life-size *Rebellion,* had been the very first sculpture by a female artist to be exhibited on a plinth in Trafalgar Square.[27] As an old friend, Judy had kindly offered to come up with a prototype of 'whatever'. In the meantime, the model's chimney had

27 Judy Boyt MA FRBS SEA – www.judyboyt.com

to be topped with *something*. Did that indeterminate shape on the sketch resemble an elongated cat slithering downward or a great-crested newt crawling skyward? We just couldn't agree.

Even Nigel lost patience. 'Oh, for heaven's sake!'

Deftly twisting a piece of copper into a head, body and tail, he jammed it on top of the chimneystack. What we *did* all suddenly agree on was that this gave the unfortunate impression of a rat doing something improper to the chimney.

We had lived with the idea of the house for so long, we could no longer see it objectively. So the question was, what would others make of it?

Cue Karen and Ignatius *aka* Ikki, our near neighbours. They had lived in many exotic corners of the globe before retirement to their pretty timbered house. At the time of Tom's purchase back in the 60s, it had been a pair of run-down farm labourers' cottages on Belle Grove Farm but, going through a pious phase of condemning anywhere lacking indoor plumbing, officialdom had insisted on their modernisation. Tom, who had other calls on his resources, received the inevitable letter. 'I have no alternative but to report the matter to my Public Health and General Purposes Committee with a view to the council carrying out the work in default and recovering the costs from you.' In other words, do as we ask or we'll pull it down and send you a bill for £200. [28] (Over thirty cottages in Westhall were demolished in this era and this procedure was repeated throughout the land, surely contributing to the dearth of inexpensive rural housing today, although you'll never hear the planners admit it.)

Not being able to afford either option, an indignant Tom managed to find a buyer who would undertake all work necessary to remove the death notice. The rescued building passed through various owners before Karen and Ikki who, luckily for us, had the typically relaxed temperaments of former ex-pats. Unbuttoned they may have been, but Nick was concerned about their reaction as, while the English (and in Ikki's case, Dutch) purport to liking idiosyncrasy, they might not necessarily want it next door. Consequently, we had shelved a discussion until there was something tangible to display.

'Do pop down for a gin and tonic. We've got something to show you...'

The G&Ts did their work. Karen and Ikki inspected the model with characteristic equanimity and, considering the noise and site disruption that could be expected, became wonderfully supportive. I expect they saw that after

---

28 This was 1960. In 2017 values, £5,000 by inflation or £12,000 calculated by income value.

initial chaos would come improved order. After all, the current environs were hardly attractive, jammed as they were with bits of lorries, engines and rusting farm implements.

However, it is always wise to anticipate objections. Before formalising the planning application itself, we laid the groundwork by presenting the model to the parish council and canvassing individual district councillors. We were also aware that the views of the local conservation officer and the Suffolk Preservation Trust would be sought by the planners. It was all very well to seek consent for a new build, but permission had to be granted to demolish the old house, not a given by any means. With this in mind, we invited these interested parties to view the model in the front parlour of the farmhouse with the artful idea that this would emphasise its shortcomings, what with the cracks in the outside walls and water stains washing up its inside walls. The exquisite detailing of the model did prove quite a distraction even to hardened professionals, but we had the feeling that while they were sympathetic, even excited, they doubted the project's viability.

Thus, I compiled the formal application citing Eric Sandon, who, in *Suffolk Houses: a Study of Domestic Architecture* observes:

> *Twentieth-century houses in Suffolk show two major design trends – the first is a continuation (of the traditional), the second a radical re-interpretation of traditional norms...*

I liked to think we were doing both and wrote:

> *Although domestic design frequently takes inspiration from the past, there is a danger of pastiche. At one end of the alternative spectrum is the modernist model, which often employs unforgiving and environmentally unfriendly materials. Here the applicant has set out to explore ways of employing traditional materials whilst thinking beyond the rectilinear, literally 'thinking beyond the box'.*

Years later, a visitor pointed out that 'Eastern Lodge' near Plymouth bears a stylistic similarity and is described in its Grade II listing as 'picturesque vernacular revival style'. Fine language that could have been deployed had I but known.

The submission was also careful to emphasise suitability to site, reading:

> *The natural features of the landscape mean that the proposed dwelling will nestle comfortably into a sheltered spot, set 70 metres back from the highway. It will take advantage of the levelled site, on which the existing house is situated, the roofs of old farm buildings visible at the rear. Ground relief is provided in several ways – the land rises gently from the road to the level and, at a more significant gradient, to the north (behind). There is a gradual gradient down to*

the confluence of two ditches in the south-east corner. Grass-covered mounds formed by pond excavations form a boundary to the garden area on the eastern flank. The railway embankment to the south-east and east is some six metres higher than the surrounding land (at its highest point), the embankment heavily wooded and adding a further dimension to the site. This also benefits from the scale and sense of maturity provided by a number of large trees particularly on the eastern and western fringes. These factors together create a sense of enclosure and will allow the dwelling to fit comfortably in its surroundings.

The unorthodox absence of elevation plans and reliance on a model had also to be explained:

Due to the unconventional form of the proposed building, the physical and practical possibilities necessitated consideration of certain issues at a very early stage. Thus, the structural, functional and aesthetic implications of this design were carefully worked through with the aid of two architectural models. The first was a maquette, made to highlight and resolve fundamental structural issues and to explore the application of timber and other materials; the second carried this through in far more detail. The finished product is presented to you in support of this application. It should be noted that this does not show secondary timber members or any steel support that may be required to conform to building regulations, as any such requirements will be incorporated within the structure and not on view.

Crucially adding:

The twist of metal on the chimney is intended merely to give an approximation of the final piece.

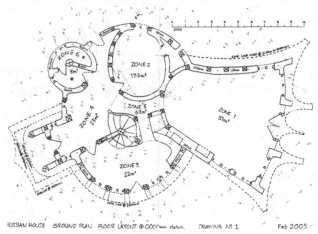

RUSSIAN HOUSE   GROUND PLAN   FLOOR LAYOUT @ 0000mm datum.   DRAWING Nº 1   Feb 2005

John Rawlings filed the application documents on our behalf. In doing so, he used the code 'Russian House', which is why it will forever be known by that moniker in the council's annals, although not by anyone else! Floor diagrams and views of four elevations (straightforward south, east, north and west) were extrapolated from Nigel's computerised calculations, but in lieu of more comprehensive elevation plans (which would normally detail every face and aspect), a 360° revolution of the model was saved on disc.

Designing the project thus far had cost considerably less than if we'd retained an architect, but we were only too aware that it was a huge gamble.

'Still,' I convinced myself, 'we'll end up with a fabulous doll's house if nothing else.'

The summons arrived. 'Will you be able to get back from London for the hearing?' I asked Nick. Minor planning applications are decided by senior planning officers with 'delegated authority', but larger or potentially controversial proposals (such as this) are referred to the Planning Committee. So, this summons was to attend the Rural Area Development Control Committee, held monthly on a Wednesday evening and which gave members of the public a voice.

Nick couldn't make it, but Nigel stepped in to provide moral support and to help lug the unwieldy model (it needed manhandling at each end) into the intimidating room at Beccles Public Hall and plug in the lead for the interior lights. It was to be kept under cover until I gave him the nod. There was no certainty as to the recommendation of the planning officers, nor that of the organisations whose opinions had been canvassed as part of the process.

One or two of the councillors were in favour I knew, but ultimately the decision would be in the hands of their colleagues on the committee. Things didn't look too promising when, listed just before us, an application for a 'radically different' eco-house, submitted on behalf of a marketing director of Marks & Spencer was refused outright. Our turn. My heart sank further on hearing the opening words of the Suffolk Preservation Society's report: 'The proposal seems, on the face of it, outrageous'.

Given that opening salvo, I was startled to hear that the Society's statement summarised in our favour. The CPO also put himself on record as 'strongly recommending approval', commenting 'there has to be room in the planning process for individually designed homes of quality'. This only left the fifteen-strong committee. Time to play our ace. An imperceptible nod to Nigel saw him surreptitiously switching on the model's lights, and whipping off the cover with a flourish worthy of the big reveal of a TV-makeover show. I raced through my allotted three-minute address, all that is permitted to applicants or their agents. No member of the public stood up to object and much to the indignation of the architect who had just seen the application on behalf of his big-cheese client unceremoniously dumped, our application received unanimous approval.

'If I'd put a policemen's helmet on my house, maybe it would have got through too,' he was heard to mutter.

Were we the first house to be given approval without a set of conventional plans? Possibly not, but there can't be many others. The only detailed record is on that disc and I do sometimes wonder if even that still lurks in the council's archives.

'Fantasy home is given approval,' shrieked the East Anglian Daily Times, adding, 'two "radically" designed homes proposed for north Suffolk met differing fortunes at a planning meeting last night. While a Russian-style "fantasy" home at Westhall, complete with a tower and a bell-like turret won over Waveney Councillors, a modern eco-house planned for Southwold was turned down.'

And the Eastern Daily Press commented:

> Sweeping curves and round rooms are key to a "Russian House" to replace an old farmhouse. The environmentally friendly home has a four-storey turret, a giant brick chimney and a sedum-covered roof. The existing farmhouse will be demolished although many of its components will be reclaimed. WDC's rural area development committee backed the plan after seeing a model of the house, which will be visible from the nearby railway. Committee members were "bowled over by the design" and members of the public said it had "almost a Disney feel to it". The committee added that while the building "might reasonably be called a fantasy house and would certainly cause a stir", it had been designed boldly.

I'm not keen on allusions to Disney or Harry Potter. Nor references to fairy tales. By all means call us outré, oddball, outlandish, idiosyncratic, peculiar or just plain batty – I'll even allow eccentric if you must – just avoid the term 'Fantasy House'!

A Splendid Lark

The planning consent was granted. With a caveat. The details *must* correspond to the model. This necessarily included the 'creature' straddling the chimney, even though I'd stressed that the built version wouldn't simply be an enlarged copy. If Judy were to come up with a design quite unlike Nigel's twist of metal, we would probably procure dispensation, however she was completely bound up with a prestigious public sculpture and we were reluctant to divert her attention to anything as trifling as our 'thing', much as it would be thrilling for a renowned sculptor to be involved.

Yet in a way she had already created a precedent for the unexpected at roof level. After its stint in Trafalgar Square, Judy's *Rebellion* had been craned up to the top of the 100-foot East India Building in Spitalfields where, from below, the wildly rearing horse looks deceptively precarious.

In an entirely different context, sculptor John Buckley had proposed a similar idea for a house in Oxford.

'How about a horse on the roof?' he'd suggested, partly in jest, to his friend the broadcaster Bill Heine, owner of an unassuming terrace house in Oxford. His was the roof in question, its slate tiles viewed by both men as a blank canvas begging for drama. Driven by the need to create edge and transgression rather than the comfortable or gimmicky, they jettisoned the horse idea and evolved the idea of a shark diving through the roof tiles. To abridge the gripping story, [29] on the 41st anniversary of the dropping of the atomic bomb on Nagasaki, a fibreglass shark was 'dropped' by crane, its tail pointing skyward as if it had made a giant leap from the Southern Ocean head first into the attic. In effect, it's a piece of pacifist conceptual art, intended to convey 'a sense of impotence and anger and desperation', a political as well as artistic statement referencing 'CND, nuclear power, Chernobyl and Nagasaki'.

---

29   As told in Bill Heine's enjoyable book *The Hunting of the Shark: The Story Behind the Tale that Crash Landed on an Unsuspecting Oxford Suburban Street*, OxfordFolio, 2011.

The political message was sidelined by the uproar, the shark's sudden appearance on the roof prompting bewilderment, puzzlement and outraged calls for police action. (The police sensibly took the view that it was hardly a criminal act for a shark to be put on a roof.) Years of controversy followed. Should the shark have had planning permission? Did it constitute a work of art and, if it did, was planning permission even needed? Opinion was sharply divided between the 'it's brilliant' and the 'they should be locked up' brigades.

'It's as much to do with attitude as age,' Heine observed. 'Some people are up for an adventure, others want their cup of cocoa and an early night.'

The influential *Times* columnist Bernard Levin weighed in, describing the advent of the shark as a 'splendid lark'.

Arguing that public sculpture doesn't need planning permission and undeterred by the refusal of retrospective planning permission by the city council, Heine appealed to the Secretary of State for the Environment, who in 1992, six years into the debate, published his decision:

> *The case should be decided on its planning merits... the basic facts are there for almost all to see. Into this archetypal urban setting crashes (almost literally) the shark. The contrast is deliberate... and, in this sense, the work is quite specific to its setting... An incongruous object can become accepted as a landmark after a time, becoming well known, even well loved in the process. Something of this sort seems to have happened, for many people, to the so-called 'Oxford shark'. The Council is understandably concerned about precedent here. The first concern is simple: proliferation with sharks (and heaven knows what else) crashing through roofs all over the city. This fear is exaggerated. In the five years since the shark was erected, no other examples have occurred... But any system of control must make some small place for the dynamic, the unexpected, the downright quirky. I therefore recommend that the Headington shark be allowed to remain.*

Of course, we did have planning permission for a 'creature', which, although not politically transgressive in the way that rendered the Headington shark so compelling, would certainly be flouting the norm. And while we didn't think for one minute that ours would provoke an outbreak of mythological creatures on roofs, we were happy to make an atypical contribution to architectural mix.

A splendid lark indeed.

'Flonking the Dwile'

So how would it be living in Westhall? The tiny community goes back a long way, having a history of pre-Norman settlement even though it's not mentioned in the Domesday Book. In 1870, the *Imperial Gazetteer of England and Wales* recorded a population of 468 but against national trends, the population was down to 390 by 2005. In the 1950s a national newspaper crowned it 'The Sleepiest Village in England'. Not, I suspect, a compliment. However, as studies have shown [30], community isn't about geographical boundaries but social interaction and networking and, in that, Westhall shows a strong spirit, having twice been awarded the title 'Suffolk Village of the Year'. Yet despite medieval farmhouses and a number of Suffolk's 700 medieval moated sites, it is unlikely to be pronounced the prettiest. This is because it's *real*, not a place of fanciful quaintness.

Earlier inhabitants worked on the land as seasonal labourers, sometimes spending part of the working year in the fishing industry (perhaps explaining the many pubs called 'The Plough & Sail' hereabouts). Their cottages may have been picturesque but were also small, inconvenient and draughty; in contrast, nowadays many commute to jobs and live in twentieth-century brick houses. And whereas children of the working poor (which at one time was most of the village) once attended the village National School [31], local children are nowadays bused to schools in nearby market towns.

The shape and nature of the surrounding land has changed profoundly too although fragments of ancient hedgerows do survive as living evidence of medieval field patterns. In *Suffolk Scene*, written before World War II, Julian Tennyson lovingly describes the hedgerows as '...fascinating, extravagant and

---

30 A 2011 BSc dissertation conducted through the case study of Westhall, which also drew on Jonathan Finch's 2007 *Death of the Village Fete: a Community Study of Westhall, Suffolk*.

31 The National Society for Promoting Religious Education brought education to the children of the poor and provided the first near-universal system of elementary education in England.

dramatic... anything that can find a place in them runs amok in a dizzy tangle'. Subsequent government improvement schemes led to the pulling out of most of those very hedges to create fields suitable for the increasingly monstrous agricultural machines that turned farming into an industrial process. (It's fair to mention that schemes now exist to encourage farmers to go into reverse and maintain habitats.) Tyneholme Estate, on the western edge of the parish, is an example of the changes wrought by modernity: once it had produced strawberries, apples and blackcurrants for the owner's Newcastle jam factory (hence the name). Over time, it absorbed many small-scale farms and nowadays is an arable-only spread of 3,000 acres in the hands of overseas owners.

Once upon a time, the village had a thriving market, a mill, a blacksmith's forge, its very own police station and two public houses, The Racehorse and The Greyhound. Both betting names you'll notice. Only The Racehorse survives. The market has long since vanished, the mill demolished decades ago. Of three shops, only the general store/post office remains through the assiduous attention over 60 years of proprietor Tony.

In every community, there are people with particularly fascinating personal hinterlands. Tony was born and bred in the locale and as a boy had served in the Home Guard in World War II. Night duty in Westhall consisted of one of a team of three cycling to the nearest public phone box (two miles distant) with the specific remit to await an invasion alert and, in that event, to pedal speedily back to rouse the others waiting in the village hall!

By 1944 and aged 18, he had been sucked into the wider world via military service. Army training in Glasgow was enough of a culture shock to a lad from Westhall, let alone being posted to India. He recalls crossing the Ghat mountains, 'The Indian soldiers guarding the bridges between Bomaby and Deolali threw stones at us because of Gandhi. Deolali had a large mental hospital so we used to say someone was 'doolally'.' From there he went to Malaya, the journey through the peninsula toward Singapore taking several months as Japanese soldiers were still very active despite the war having ended. As a location giveaway, a fire was out of the question and at one point Tony and his comrades became isolated from the regiment. 'We had no choice but to drink water out of the river. It killed a lot of our lads, but I stayed healthy because I was brought up on village pond water.' (Mains water only reached Westhall in the 1950s, before which households made do with ponds and wells.)

After the dropping of the atom bombs on Japan in August 1945 (as registered so forcefully by Bill Heine), Tony had been despatched to Nagasaki as part of the occupying forces, finding that 'you could see the outline of bodies on the pavements where they had been incinerated'. He admits to picking up small household items as souvenirs and keeping them in his backpack, subsequently lost in the calamitous 1946 Nankai earthquake. You may think the loss just as well for Westhall's radiation count but, as he observes, 'at the time, we didn't know about radioactivity'.

His duties included guarding the National Diet in Tokyo (the Japanese Parliament), where Japanese soldiers, humiliated by defeat, would come to commit hara kiri. 'We weren't permitted to intervene, you just watched the trickles of blood getting nearer and nearer.'

The annual pantomime (on hold at the time of writing) was for many years scripted, acted and directed entirely by villagers, many of whom, including the local copper and the rector, had no diffidence about public displays of buffoonery guaranteed to induce gut-aching laughter in the audience not to mention the corpsing players.

Social glue of another sort was once provided by the 'noble art' of dwile flonking. Otherwise known as morris dancing with mops, its annual championships were hosted by The Racehorse to rules set out in *Ye Olde Booke of Suffolk Harvest Rituels*, discovered (supposedly) in a local attic. In essence, it's about lobbing a beer-soaked rag at members of an opposing team. [32] For years, teams competed for a pewter chamber pot, the gazunder trophy so called because it 'goes under' the bed, in an event that took on international status after The Racehorse applied for a licence extension for the dinner dance of the Waveney Valley Dwile Flonking Association.

'Exactly what does dwile flonking entail?' the Magistrate was said to have enquired.

---

32 One team holds hands and dances around in a circle while trying to avoid being hit by a beer-soaked mop (the 'dwile') thrown by a member of the opposing team (the 'flonker'). If the dwile misses completely, the team forms a line and the flonker has to drink the contents of a chamber pot filled with ale, but before the wet dwile has passed from hand to hand along the line, chanting to the ancient ceremonial mantra of 'pot pot pot'. The team with the highest number of points wins after deducting one point for every player still sober.

Both the licensee's representative and the police inspector on duty had to admit they didn't exactly know. Fortunately, a woman sitting in the public gallery was able to enlighten the court and the licence was duly granted. The ensuing publicity saw the Flonkers on prime-time television, following which letters requesting the official rules flooded in from Australia and New Zealand, Hong Kong and America. A television series about bizarre sports featured a contest[33] and a local paper reported the flonking championships at The Racehorse (by then, the sport's 'international headquarters'), in the same breath as 'tennis greats battling it out at the French Open and the European football championships'. It went on, 'No one could remember the score, although team members recalled feeling "pretty fragile" the following morning...'

So, is dwile flonking a long-established country tradition or just an excuse to have a skinful of beer? I favour the theory that it originated with Michael Bentine's 1960s irony-laden skit in 'It's a Square World', in which pith-helmeted explorers stumble across a group of natives playing a very similar sport in the darkest reaches of the English countryside.

Drinking games, free alcohol prizes and binge-drinking promotions have since been banned by law and, sadly for free spirits everywhere, dwile flonking has faded away. Dare we hope temporarily? The championship trophy has vanished from sight and it's not an unreasonable hope that it's been secreted under a bed in readiness for a revival.

It might be observed that never was the soubriquet 'Silly Suffolk' more apt, but then again, this is said to derive from the German *selig*, which means blessed or happy. Yes, happy Suffolk.

---

33 Presented by Paddy McGuinness and Rory McGrath and viewable on YouTube: https://www.youtube.com/watch?v=J0kxQ-osmKQ

On Notice

The customary template for self-building is:

- acquire a building plot
- organise the finance
- appoint an architect and approve the design
- arrange the mandatory energy-performance evaluation
- obtain detailed planning permission
- obtain advance building regulation approval
- find a good builder
- appoint a project manager and quantity surveyor.

Our circumstances allowed us to deviate from this paradigm; we already had the site, finance was sorted, assuming Wissett Place was sold, we'd source our own materials and Nick would act as quantity surveyor and project manager.

Planning consent had been granted, but there was also the not-so-little matter of building regulation approval. In contrast to the non-existent building codes of those unorthodox Pacific timber builders, we faced strict UK regulations which require detailed information relevant to carrying out the work, from the depth of the foundations to the height of the chimney. Provided that our notions complied with current building standards, approval would be granted, but we knew that long delays could occur if additional information was required or plans needed amending. As no work is supposed to commence until final approval, building can be held up for weeks if not months.

Luckily for us, there was an alternative. That was, to proceed by way of Building Notice, a system that permits work to get under way quickly. A formal application and fee has to be submitted to the local authority, accompanied by a block plan after which, under Notice procedure, our build would be subject to site inspection at key stages: excavation and covering of foundations, installation of damp-proof course, laying and testing of drains, floor and roof structure, insulation and electrical safety. Significantly, detailed technical drawings would be required to 'prove' a solution to any complex structural issue. Only when the building inspector was fully satisfied would a Certificate of Occupation be issued. This do-it-as-you-go-along approach was useful for the likes of us who often didn't know what we were doing until we did it but, to all intents and purposes, we would be gambling that the work *would* be regulation-compliant.

In the meantime, Nick was consolidating his working relationship with *Team Polski*. As a much smaller squad than that in London, he would be working with them in a more direct way. They had little English. He had less Polish. (They gave little away in expression, so we had no way of gauging whether their response to the model had been wonder or horror.) The language barrier limited Nick's explanations of the overall programme, so he spent much of each day whirling between them, relying on hands-on demonstration.

Gradually, they developed a new version of pidgin. It helped that some words are similar in both languages. Polish produces a clipped-sounding *banan* (the emphasis on the first 'a') so at least the word banana is recognisable, providing a handy linguistic shortcut meaning 'not straight'. A 'little bit banana' came to mean anything from a warped piece of wood to a poorly fitting door and, if unacceptably out of true, 'all is banana'. Usefully, *maksymalna* means 'maximum', so 'max' became an all-purpose word for 'no more than that'. For some reason, 'small' became 'small small', usually accompanied by manic gestures and a 'little bit more long' speaks for itself. Nick couldn't find a Polish phrase for 'that'll do' or 'that's near enough' so the sentiment was conveyed and understood by the words 'somehow like'. And everyone got it when Nick called on Damien to produce 'Big BIG Power'.

So, you could say that as well as building a house, we were also learning the art of linguistic bridge-building.

Shopping Adventure No. 1

Not so long before the London project, we had journeyed to Kuala Lumpur in Malaysia. Years before, while on secondment to the Royal Malaysian Air Force my elder brother, Keith, had married Rosey, a spirited Chinese-Malay and, invited to her niece's wedding, we had taken the opportunity to visit Bali. Many opulent hotels and spas cater for affluent visitors to Ubud (later made into a hot spot by the film *Eat, Pray, Love*) but ours was the modest but beautiful *Taman Harum*, whose magical gardens, with backdrop of emerald paddy fields, were crowded with basalt carvings, carved teak benches and limpid pools, heady frangipani perfuming the air.

Having anticipated a plethora of authentic artisan work, we were disappointed by slick galleries offering 'tourist' carvings of the polished variety and our wallet opened only for a pair of tall metal candlesticks in the shape of wingless dragons.

Until the last day.

'Stop the car. *Berhenti!*... Stop!'

Inyoman, the obliging hotel manager who had volunteered to double as our driver, screeched to a halt. Propped against the outside wall of a small backstreet shop were a few pairs of elaborately carved and painted doors and phantasmagorical figures based on Hindu mythology. The interior

of *Sukama*, stuffed with yet more doors and carved *Garudas* (mythological creatures with the head of a bird hatched from cosmic eggs) was truly a cave of fabulousness. We particularly liked those baroque doors.

'What could we do with them?' I remember saying.

'They could be used in the lets I suppose,' replied Nick thoughtfully. As the idea took hold, he continued, 'How about if each unit were to be styled differently?'

I instantly got it. The business needed a unique selling point, a personality that would make it stand out in a fiercely competitive market. I was (and still am) uncomfortable with the expression 'theming', so preferred to think of it as imbuing each property with a flavour, a thread, a leitmotif.

Intending to put them in a shared container, we closed an amazingly reasonable deal for a dozen traditional doors, complete with frames, and several traditional figurative carvings. However, *Sukama* wasn't the sort of shop that was familiar with the export process and we were running out of time.

At this critical juncture, Inyoman casually interjected, 'My friend is a shipping agent. He organised a consignment for some Americans a few months ago'.

'Call him!'

On discovering that, at USD $600 it was only $100 more to send a whole 20ft freight container to Felixstowe than to share one, the decision was easy.

'Let's go for it.'

Easy to say, not so easy to do. It was 1pm. We were due to check in by 4.00pm for our flight back to Singapore. Three hours to find enough goods to fill a container and finish packing. Where had I read, 'The soul of Bali is unhurried?'

Inyoman confirmed that he could source some of the teak benches that we had admired at his hotel but more – *much* more – was needed. I recalled passing a roadside display of the huge volcanic stone pots, bowls, basins, urns and

jardinières with which Balinese love to fill beguiling gardens. Retracing our steps, our manifest 'now-or-never haste resulted in highly favourable terms for gigantic stone planters and granite troughs. For a modest commission, the resourceful Inyoman undertook to oversee the packing and loading. As well as the items from *Sukama*, we left Inyoman to cram the container with some teak garden benches and the troughs and planters, filling pockets of space with a hundred thatched Balinese lanterns as well as the lengths of *ikat* and silks, shell curtain tie-backs, bamboo soap dishes and woven palm-leaf boxes I'd picked up in the market. Once home, we aimed to sell surplus items (if any) to defray costs.

Off we flew to Singapore, secretly wondering if we'd ever seen any of it again.

My father had been stationed at RAF Changi from 1957–1960 so, having spent a few years there as a girl, this was something of a sentimental stopover for me. Before setting out, I'd found this card tucked inside an old photograph album:

INVITATION TO A BALL

OFFICERS' MESS, FAIRY POINT, CHANGI

ON THE OCCASION OF

THE EIGHTEENTH ANNIVERSARY OF
THE BATTLE OF BRITAIN

CARRIAGES AT 2.30AM

Seeing it afresh, two things stood out.

Firstly, the relative time proximity of the Battle of Britain and World War II, underlining that the Far-Eastern theatre of war had ended only 13 years before. Despite my having found a Japanese sword lying in the grass in its sheath and although our *amah*, Lo, jumped a mile when anyone crept up on her unawares, the fact that a war had been fought on the island had never sunk in at the time.

Secondly, carriages at 2.30am? I hadn't realised that their social life was that interesting...

Mind you, while Mum and Dad did engage in the service social rounds, they weren't particularly immersed in the partying/drinking scene. Rather, they were interested in their surroundings in a way that I now recognise was quite atypical of 1950s ex-pat culture. Dad's passion for photography gave him licence to circumvent that scene in favour of spending family time exploring local cultural traditions. Lo, accompanied us as we drove all over the Malay peninsula including the, as then, unfrequented east coast. [34] I suspect Mum and Dad *were* considered eccentric by their peers.

With the perspective of time, I recognise how their interest in 'the other' has rubbed off on me.

Even then, I had yearned to see beyond the line of paddle-leaved traveller's palms that protected the periphery of the celebrated Raffles Hotel. But the hotel was for rich 'civvies', not the likes of my prudent parents. By the time, fifty years later, that I did manage to see inside, the Long Bar, patronised by the likes of Ernest Hemingway and Somerset Maugham – and where the Singapore Sling cocktail had been invented – had long been relegated to the hotel's shopping arcade.

---

34 In view of the dirt roads and the Malayan Emergency – reaching its endgame at the time – some insurgents were still operating in the jungles of the East.

The parents' instinct had been spot on: our Singapore Slings came a close second to the most expensive drinks we had ever ordered (that honour going to gin & tonics at La Mamoumia in Marrakech). A visit to the hotel shop would have broken the bank too if I hadn't seized on the very cheapest item, a pack of 'Reproductions from the Golden Age of Travel' hotel stickers of the kind you see on vintage trunks and suitcases. Bought with the vague idea that they would come in handy 'one of these days', they had wonderfully evocative names like The Continental Palace, Saigon, The Grand Hotel de Pekin, The Hotel Majestic, Kuala Lumpur, Shepheards Hotel, Cairo, The Phya Thai Palace, Bangkok and more.

Back in Malaysia, Nick and I were still into buying mode so were delighted to note the labyrinthine antique shop dead opposite our Malaccan hotel, a restored Peranakan[35] merchant house on Jonker Street. This emporium yielded an authentic Chinese bed, ornate cabinets, side tables and a traditional roped armchair.

The cabinets were highly decorative, one featuring red-lacquered doors decorated with gold, another intricately carved and inlaid with porcelain plaques hand-painted with Chinese landscapes. This time they *were* crated up for a shared load to which I added intricate leather shadow puppets as used in *wayang kulits* and irresistible *songkets* and batiks. And, unbeknownst to a disapproving Nick, several cartons of the noxious black clove cigarettes – *kreteks* – for which I had developed a taste, their very name meaning the crackling sound of burning cloves.

Back home, reality kicked in. We were going to need far more than a few doors, carved gods and a Chinese bed to kit out five barns.

Our thoughts turned to Rajasthan...

---

35 A term used for the descendants of the early Chinese immigrants to British Malaya.

Shopping Adventure No. 2

During Nick's time on the London project, he'd been in the habit of attending a weekly north London auction room and proudly bearing home treasures about which I could be quite sniffy. These included an ornately framed painting measuring six foot by four, depicting a column of mounted soldiers. There was something about the background and uniforms that spoke to me of the Raj, perhaps a British regiment in nineteenth-century northern India.

As Nick pulled it out of the van I had asked, with notable lack of enthusiasm, 'Where on earth are we going to put *that*?' – little thinking that it would become the anchor of the décor in one of the barns...

Special Offer
16 nights in the forts and palaces of Rajasthan.

The tour had been advertised at a seductive price. Under the British, the Maharajas of the 565 'princely states' enjoyed unconscionable wealth and power. However, in 1971 they had been stripped of their privileges overnight and, faced with multi-million-dollar tax bills, most were forced either to sell up or convert their palaces into hotels. Hence, this tour which, even though it implied group travel, appealed to our interest in architecture and the exotic. Bearing in mind that we ourselves ran a tour operation, our idea of luxury was not to have to think about organisational matters. Even so, I was apprehensive as to who would be our travelling companions and spent most of the flight trying to identify the rather off-putting possibilities. So, when Austrian Airlines spewed us out at Delhi to be greeted by a marigold garland-bearing rep, the first thing to ask was, 'Where are the others?'

'There are no others. Only you.'

Ah. We had overlooked the fact that the reason the tour was startlingly cheap was that it was at the hottest time of year, June. That a SARS epidemic was raging hadn't helped. Which is how we came to spend 16 days in an air-conditioned saloon car driven by one Gopal, with time to take in more nooks and crannies of Rajasthan than we could otherwise have hoped to see.

People comment on India's mad driving and they're absolutely right – Africa had nothing on this (well, maybe Lagos). Gopal steered a course through preposterously overburdened lorries and motorbikes balancing absurd loads of pots and pans, and passing road gangs of women in bright yellow and red saris desultorily mending potholes.

A diet of truly magnificent Hindu and Jain temples culminated in the Karni Mata, the 'Rat Temple' near Bikaner, famous for its 20,000 freely roaming black rats, venerated for their association with Ganesh, the elephant-headed god.

In need of contrast, we persuaded Gopal to include collections of the deluxe motorcars once thought so desirable amongst the Indian ruling classes. The main thrust of the tour, however, was architecture: the gems of Agra and the Taj Mahal, Jaipur and the Palace of Winds, Udaipur and Chittorgarh. Finally, Jodhpur, a fifteenth-century city surrounded by ten kilometres of wall set with pointed iron spikes and where the battlements of the Mehrangarh Fort tower over a panorama of blue-washed houses. Heading into the city, we passed a high block wall running parallel to the highway for half a mile or so. Scores of enormous old wooden doors could be seen leaning up against it and the tops of yet more poked above the wall from the far side.

'Hold on. Gopal, what is that place?'

Gopal jammed on the brakes and in the casual Indian way, headed across two lanes of oncoming traffic to investigate further.

'People come all world.'

'What you mean?' His argot was catching.

'Young people build new, throw old house – bring here. All world.' (Jodhpur is the only Indian city with its own customs bonding system – it means that a shipping container can be filled and sealed on the spot, thereby avoiding the need for inspection in Bombay.)

'Let's take a look.'

There followed a lightning tour of the 53-acre reclamation site including the carved stone department, the metal department and the fake antique department (furniture made and left in the sun to age) along with architectural impedimenta. The doors turned out to be the huge gates and double doorways salvaged from *havelis*, traditional fortified merchant houses, whose massive outer doors were often inlaid with iron or brasswork. Windows looking inwards to a courtyard, rather than outward, provided further security. Alas, family *havelis* are considered by many to be out of date so are being demolished and replaced by modern houses. So, there are plenty of originals on the market, but Westerners are also catered for by a plethora of fakes, sorry, *reproductions*.

The cost of shipping a 40-foot container from Jodhpur to Felixstowe, via Bombay, was USD $1200.

We filed this information in our brains under, 'Remember this, you never know when it may be useful'.

Three years later, we remembered. With no direct flights to Jodhpur and internal flights not slotting into our limited timescale of a week, we opted for the overnight sleeper from Delhi. Although impressed by the facility to book Indian train tickets from England, I remained sceptical, so, on landing, we immediately made for the Old Delhi Railway Station. Even at 7am the air was torrid, and after much sweaty floundering, it transpired that the office where we were to exchange our internet confirmation for 'real' tickets was up a long, long flight of stairs.

Hallelujah! At the top we found the only space in the entire complex that enjoyed air conditioning. Expecting a bureaucratic muddle, we were more than happy to settle there to while away the hours until the overnight train to Jodhpur, but not only did our names instantly flash up on a computer screen, in an endearing mistrust of their own technology, our names had also been handwritten into a 'shades of Empire' leather-bound ledger. Just when we could have done with a bit of inefficiency. So, a cool retreat was provided by the unwitting five-star Ashok Hotel (many years of crashing hotels in African capital cities, often the only source of a cold drink and somewhere to wash one's hair, had made us inclined to take a few liberties). Although 'first class', our eight-berth carriage compartment was shared with a friendly family eager to share its parathas and pickles, as well as businessmen whose opening gambit was the inescapable 'how much do you earn?' No one snored.

The burly Mahaveer greeted us. He was one of five Jain brothers who ran Maharani Art Emporium, the business behind that long wall, between them managing retail and wholesale furniture, textiles and manufacturing. We had just three days and four nights for this shopping adventure.

Once on site, a youth was designated our 'guide'. 'Just point me,' he said, motioning to his camera.

A tad confused, we eventually understood that his job was to digitally record anything and everything we found of conceivable interest. This proved addictive and soon we were pointing wildly at painted *almirahs* (large cabinets or wardrobes), bedside tables, enormous mirrors with carved frames, carved arches, doors and frames, pillars, boxes, brass-inlaid furniture, painted teak chests, carved panels, bookcases, garden benches with iron ends shaped as serpents, *kudia* (decorative pots) candle stands, paintings, iron lamps, lanterns and chandeliers. We were also much taken by a pair of life-size teak beasts misleadingly described as tigers – while their 'distressed' yellowy finish was reasonably authentic, the spots were definitely more leopard-like. At the end of each day, Mahaveer would load the images onto a disc, which included a pre-loaded form comprising columns of trade prices in USD, size, volume and running tally. Lucky that I'd taken my laptop – I hadn't expected such efficiency. We'd spend each evening making a shortlist, very much a speculative exercise, the outbuilding conversions not even having been started at this point. Sadly, practicality ruled out those 'tigers'...

The focus was the main site outside the city walls, but from time to time, we were ferried to the wholesale textile shop tucked down a narrow street in the old town. The chauffeur thought nothing of driving against the traffic and randomly parking in the centre of busy junctions, tooting aggressively at any hapless policeman who had the temerity to get in his way while directing traffic. I revelled in the tottering piles of silk bed throws, gold-threaded saris sold by weight, Kashmiri shawls and elaborate Gujarati wall hangings. Bale-ends of 'exclusive' and/or 'designer' embroidered silks woven specifically for the Western market were irresistibly good value, I suspect, sold illicitly, off-contract.

Every day at noon, we were summoned to share a delicious vegan luncheon at the family mansion of carved red sandstone where we learned that pretty well the only thing the family *didn't* deal in was granite and marble. Jaipur to the south is better known for stone, but we were running out of time so had to make do with one hour-long hit at a local supplier. A  ten-foot length of polished black granite was priced at £10 and an unpolished four-foot square of green granite, £5, that price reflecting its unpopular figuring, which was considered too 'random' – exactly why we liked it. Fortunately, the exchange rate was in our favour. Along with the furniture, doors, several tons of black and green granite, plus some white marble for good measure, we'd ordered a set of metal gates to be made up to a design drawn on a hastily torn sheet from a school exercise book, all of which managed to fill not one but *two* 40-foot containers.

For our final night, Mahaveer wangled an off-season deal for us at the Umaid Bhawan Palace. Designed by a renowned English architect for Maharajah Umaid Singh, this Art Deco showpiece surely reflected Kipling's sentiment that *'Providence created the maharajas to offer mankind a spectacle'*. It is worth recording that this 'spectacle' came about through the wish of the Maharajah to provide employment to his people during a period of terrible drought and famine in the late 1920s. In this he succeeded, as it took 3,000 workers over 14 years to complete the million square feet of flamboyant marble detailing. A third of its 347 rooms have since been turned into a stunning, if hugely expensive, hotel.

The disadvantage of our off-season stay was that we were alarmingly visible. Embarrassing to be greeted by a drummer and bugler and have servants bowing and scraping despite our distinctly non-five-star appearance, not to mention the personal butler.

As the hotel blurb said, 'In those long ago days of languid afternoons and indigo nights, the Maharajah and his guests were waited upon hand and foot by the palace butlers. The resourceful butler was a silent force, fulfilling his master's wishes before they were voiced, heeding his master's voice seemingly before it even passed his lips. Their direct descendants are here to look after your needs and can be summoned with a quick call...'

Our own needs were catered to by the splendidly attired Pavak. Whether he was a direct descendant of a palace retainer is doubtful, but he certainly looked the part in his crisp white shirt, high boots, khaki jodhpurs (of course) and matching khaki *pagari* or Rajasthani turban with its magnificently stylish 'tail' flowing from the back of his head to his buttocks.

'You wish tour of Palace?'

'Yes please!'

The hotel was virtually empty at that time of year, so Pavak guided us around its secret corners, necessarily avoiding the wing containing the former women's quarters, in which the current royal family lived. We were ushered over inlaid marble floors and past lavish furnishings through to the immense rotunda, colonnaded balconies and whispering gallery as well as the subterranean swimming pool. Every pillar – and there were many – consisted of sections of tightly interlocking sandstone, a result apparently achieved by placing dry ice between the blocks. On the ice melting, the sandstone settled into perfect alignment. The final flourish was to have been the installation of custom-designed furnishings and decorations shipped from England but, it then being 1942, a torpedo had sunk the ship carrying it all. Remarkably, everything had been replaced in time for a Christmas Eve party that very year. (One does wonder how this could have been achieved in wartime.) The original art deco flavour of many of the hotel bedrooms had all but disappeared under a wave of 'modernisation', but happily the original splendour of the suite occupied by such luminaries as Jackie Onassis Kennedy, Prince Charles and the Queen of Bhutan had been preserved intact. Our tour ended in the Trophy Bar where elephants had sacrificed their trunks and feet to make table lamps and stools. However lavish the surroundings, it's hard to enjoy a cocktail while balancing on an animal appendage.

'They [the butlers] will draw a soothing bath, recommend the perfect meal or help you choose an ideal treatment at the Spa,' the blurb continued. 'Throughout your stay, discreetly and unobtrusively, your butler will gladly guide you through the pleasures that lie within and without the palace walls, no task too insignificant, no demand too unreasonable.'

Doubtless we disappointed Pavak by our failure to 'request tasks' or 'make demands'. Although taken aback that we were to take the regular sleeper to

Delhi not the (highly expensive) Maharaja Express, he escorted us to the railway station. In full butler fig of jodhpurs and a *pagari* that swished as he shouldered our decidedly un-designery baggage, he nonchalantly disregarded the sneers and whistles of the regular porters, much as Eton schoolboys sporting uniforms of collars, striped trousers and tailcoats, must learn to ignore the derision of their non-Etonian peers.

With the best part of a day to kill in Delhi before the return flight, we flagged down a tuk-tuk.

'Take us to the tassel souk!' (There's usually a whole street of shops for whatever it is you want.) A wizened old man seemed very happy when we randomly halted the tuk-tuk outside his tiny shop, and hoovered up his stock of tassels. Long, short, dainty, chunky, beaded, beribboned and bejewelled, all for not much more than the price of a pair of curtain tassels in an upmarket UK store. One problem, this booty meant hopelessly exceeding our luggage allowance. In the end, we could be seen waddling shamelessly onto the plane, every pouch, pocket and purse overflowing with tassels.

Some weeks later a message filtered through. Maharani Arts has started to load the containers.

'There is a little more space. Would you like more sideboards?' Mahaveer asked.

'Not really. But wait, are those 'tigers' still available?'

Backbiting Beast

Furnishing interiors before there were any interiors to fill was admittedly a back-to-front exercise so it was definitely time to progress the holiday lets. But first we had to undertake some landscaping.

You may recall talk of a pond at the time of Krzysz's test task. We had recognised that the sometimes sullen landscape could benefit from visual interest and, in the absence of mountain, rock or forest, this meant water, a generous pond if not a lake. The idea was to dig it out early on to give it time to mature. However, at the time the excavation was scheduled, the outbuildings were also being cleared so the pond, which would obstruct the way to the Green Shed, needed to be bridged.

At the time, the contractor, Colin, had pointed out a difficulty: a pronounced fall in the land.

'I'm going to have to dig out two separate holes, one higher than the other,' he said. 'That way, any floodwater can flow from the top pond to the lower one and drain off into ditches.'

This called for a dam between the upper and lower ponds but rather than presenting a problem, it made the job of building the bridge much easier. So, Colin spent a week gouging out the earth, after which, Nick, true to form, cobbled the dam/bridge together from materials from 'round the back'. Placing a pair of colossal steel beams (he'd been offered these for free if he took them away, which of course he did) from bank to bank, concrete railway sleepers were then butted together at right angles across the steel and topped with four inches of concrete and shingle.

The spoil from the dig created a high bank to the side. Once planted with native hawthorn, blackthorn and willow, this should (eventually) shield the unlovely Green Shed from view.

In my mind's eye, I saw idyllic lily-strewn pools fringed by graceful willows and reeds. By the time Colin had finished wielding his digger, the stark landscape of puddled yellow clay was more reminiscent of the desolation depicted by war artist Paul Nash than Monet's visions of water lilies. In despair, I wondered how it would it ever be possible for this mess to become the bucolic scene of my vision?

The bridge was adequate for toing and froing but needed refinement. So telegraph poles were brought in to do duty on the outer edges and, for safety, Nick fixed reclaimed metal railing, which had already been through several incarnations in his hands. As the bridge would form the entrance to the courtyard used by some of the guests, I decided that a theatrical flourish was called for. A massive pair of *haveli* doors was duly erected on a frame at one end. In my head, I could already see the huge leaves of a *vitis coignetiae* romping over it. In a final flourish, Krzysz heaped an outsize Indian *kadai* (metal cooking pot) with chunks of firewood, mounted it on a tripod stand and located it at the top of the track. Our somewhat romantic plan was to set the wood ablaze every Friday afternoon, by way of welcoming guests into the domain.

The next major step was to create independent access to the barns. This meant laying a track across the boggy field that hugged the railway line. East Anglia is hugely significant in terms of archaeological 'gold', so I nursed secret hopes that the track excavation would yield ancient treasures...

A cache of 180 golden Iron Age torcs, unearthed near Snettisham and displayed at Norwich Castle, has been declared one of the most important treasure hoards ever discovered in Britain, while the Mildenhall find of sensationally beautiful Roman silver, dishes, bowls, goblets and spoons, is exhibited at the British

Museum. Then there is the late Roman silver plate and gold and silver jewellery from Thetford, not to mention the Hoxne hoard, an extraordinary accumulation of 14,000 late fourth-century gold and silver coins. And more recently, there was a further spectacular discovery of an exquisite gold, jewelled pendant dug from a muddy South Norfolk field.

Westhall has a 'hoard' too. Though not exactly 'treasure', the collection of objects unearthed in 1855 following construction of the railway line, has nevertheless been deemed significant. The exact find spot isn't clear, but it is known to be within the boundaries of Sallows Farm, our immediate neighbour. Pottery, Celtic metalwork of the highest quality and a Roman lamp dated to AD 50-75 (similar to those at Pompeii) suggest a Romano-British farmstead. Reconstructed fragments of a small badge portraying what has been described as a 'backward biting beast with two tails' (which has since become the village emblem) is now kept at the British Museum, as well as strap unions or terrets inlaid with expensive champlevé red enamel, which were used to guide the reins of chariot-pulling horses. Julius Caesar is said to have been amazed to find chariots in use in such a barbaric country as England, but in fact, they had long been used by the Celts and open almost any book on Celtic art and you'll find an illustration of the most glamorous of the Westhall Iron Age finds, the Great Terret.

How long had these lain undisturbed in the earth? Empress Faustina's head on a coin shows it must have been post AD 125, that is almost 100 years after the Romans conquered the area and 60 years after Boudicca's unsuccessful revolt. (Westhall is within the area that was home to her tribe, the Iceni.) There again, the coin may well have been a random addition to a heap of scrap bronze collected for smelting. We'll never know, but the assortment provokes a powerful sense of persons unknown leaving their mark, a tiny window onto their world.

The most famous Suffolk site of all is Sutton Hoo, located on an exposed bluff overlooking the River Deben where

*'a thousand winter winds
keen through
tattered leaf
spiny root
clogged down
glistening mud...'* [36]

In the summer of 1939, archaeologists uncovered evidence of a buried ship in one of the earthen

36 From 'The Dig' in *Wild Path: A Sutton Hoo Quartet* by Jan Farmery, published by Salters Lane Press 2013 (available from Amazon).

mounds that rise so abruptly out of the landscape. All things organic had long been consumed by the soil's acidity but waiting to be unearthed was a sword, a spectacular helmet[37], spears, chainmail and shield, personal jewellery and an intricately decorated purse lid. A gold buckle inlaid with red garnets was so perfectly preserved that, after 1700 years, its spring mechanism worked first time. These objects had been laid alongside eating and drinking vessels almost as if a journey were about to take place. And in a sense it was, because this was clearly the burial chamber of a very high-ranking personage, possibly even Raedwald, King of the Angles. The find sheds light on early Anglo-Saxon society, inviting comparisons to the legendary world of Beowulf.

Nick complains that in all the years of cultivation of the Forty Acre (otherwise known as the 'back field'), he has uncovered nothing more interesting than old horseshoes. Small objects tend to be hidden within soil turned by a plough, but a local metal detectorist *has* unearthed a single George III gold coin and a fascinating assortment of Elizabethan half-groats, Georgian pennies, buttons, buckles and musket balls – indicating that a footpath  that crosses the field had been a busy thoroughfare at some point. Alas, no precious objects emerged from our own 'dig'. Old tin cans aplenty and cannon shells, presumably jettisoned by wartime aircraft but not even any of the common aviation artefacts found at other crash sites, such as instruments, plexi-glass and flare cartridges. (I digress to mention that Nick had had better luck digging down the back of the proverbial sofa, a pristine George III silver crown rolling out of the springs of our second-hand settee.)

As a cheaper and more manageable alternative to wet concrete, Nick took what he called the 'rolling road' approach to the land sacrificed to the track, the forklift dumping four reinforced concrete railway sleepers at a time. Laid on a bed of sand and stone, the sleepers were butted together and topped with road planings, sand and gravel, soil and grass seed, then tipped along the track's spine in the hope that a grassy strip might suggest a decade's worth of wheels had already ground up and down.

'I'm off to the sale preview this afternoon,' Nick reminded me. 'That farmer who's emigrating to New Zealand, remember?'

Bidders tend to concentrate on agricultural equipment at farm sales, which leaves the door open for building material bargains. After scrutinising the usual

---

37 The helmet has become the symbol of the Sutton Hoo burial but had survived only as a mass of small pieces, reconstructed after years of painstaking work at the British Museum.

heaps of bricks and pantiles, Nick pottered around the periphery of the site and spotted a large, gnarly and very dead elm tree interred in a nettle-filled ditch. Given that there were several other dead trees lying nearby, it was reasonable to infer that they all succumbed to Dutch Elm disease in the 1970s. Elm produces poor heat, so no one had bothered to chop them for firewood but nor had the trees rotted (which is why elm is valued for coffins). Nick's inventive mind stirred. Perhaps the trunks could relieve the starkness of the ponds if dropped at random on their banks?

He found the farmer who was selling up.

'I'm interested in those tree trunks if you've no use for them. How about £30 for that one?' pointing first to the one in the ditch that caught his eye. 'Or £50 for them all. I'll come and drag them out with my tractor if that'll help. I know you're busy.'

The farmer was known for being a bit tight. His eyes lit up. Maybe the tree trunks had some value after all.

'No, no. They're going in the auction!' the farmer insisted. (Clearly not – it was 4pm and the auction was due to start the very next morning.) He duly hauled six tree trunks out of the undergrowth. These were divided into three Lots, a hurried addendum to the sale catalogue.

The day dawned, the last lot eventually reached.

'Who'll bid me...' the auctioneer wearily called.

No one was the answer.

It was with much satisfaction that Nick, the sole interested party, secured them at £5 for each of three Lots. The farmer wasn't best pleased and grumbled incessantly as Nick, gratified that he'd been saved the job of hauling them from the ditch, loaded them up.

With the aid of the forklift, the trunks were dropped on the banks of the upper pond in a manner we hoped was suggestive of trees falling where they'd grown. Yet Nick seemed reluctant to deploy that first magnificent leathery tree trunk, which now revealed a huge blackened twist to its trunk.

I recognised that uncommunicativeness. 'Bet he's up to something.'

We preferred to let the ponds fill naturally with rain so it would be months before they were anything other than giant holes in the ground. In the meantime, Marek spread yellow flag iris, courtesy of Karen's garden, on the banks together with rushes with the distinctive brown sausage pods that identify them as bulrushes. As anyone will know who has seen just how quickly these promulgate, this wasn't necessarily a bright idea...

They say that you can plant a cricket bat and it'll sprout, so instead of allowing them to be consigned to a bonfire, I retrieved discarded sticks from Karen and Ikki's recently pollarded willows and rammed them unceremoniously into the mud. They added little to the bleak scene.

To be honest, neither did the tree trunks.

French Connections

The roofs of the outbuildings required renewal, and while sourcing pine for rafters was straightforward enough, green oak was needed for the frame of the house. This took rather more research.

An old estate map of Westhall Hall and its environs reveals that swathes of woodland once bestrode the parish. This would have been oak, perhaps mixed with holly and yew. While English oaks had once been tall enough to supply post mills with the necessary 40-foot length, nowadays they are seldom so long, a problem often solved by connecting two pieces by way of special joints to form one continuous member. In our case, we'd need several lengths of 33 feet (minimum) for the house, something that had been causing problems. Phoning round for quotes, Nick would run through his lengthy cutting list, adding, 'And half a dozen 33-foot long beams.'

'I don't know about that mate.'

Silence. 'Well, we could find it, but it's likely to cost double.'

We considered sourcing from Poland, but probing deeper into the internet led us to an operation in the Dordogne, which, by chance, happened to be run by an Englishman. Specifying the extra-long timber, Nick expected the usual red flag.

He could sense Andrew's shrug down the phone. 'Fine,' Andrew said. 'Next?'

After an exchange of friendly emails of the 'let's talk over lunch!' variety, we flew EasyJet to Bergerac, hired a car and tracked Andrew – or *André* as he is known in this milieu – down to his yard. Chestnut was abundant, oak plentiful and Nick spent many happy hours (and I, truth to tell, bored ones) scrutinising towering stacks of timber, discussing sapwood, sound or dead knots, boxed heart and the pitfalls of end shake, frost crack, curly grain and bark pocket.

The unlikely story goes that Napoleon planted extensive forests to provide oak for his fleet and, as it had never been cancelled, planting continues to this day. It seems that as French oak is grown in single-species woodland rather than the mixed deciduous woods of England, competition between the trees as their canopies reach for sunlight results in the enormously long straight trunks we were looking for.

I perked up with the promised *déjeuner* and over many courses, Andrew enquired, 'Where do you actually live?'

'Suffolk.'

'Where in Suffolk?'

'The north-east, near the Norfolk border.'

'But *where*?' he insisted.

'Oh, you wouldn't know it.'

'Try me.'

'It's just a small place called Halesworth.'

'I know it well, I worked there for five years!'

Delivery was keenly priced too, courtesy of taking advantage of Norfolk-based lorries returning to the UK after delivering agricultural machinery to Spain.

Nick's cutting list was by no means definitive, so quite a lot of size 'guesstimation' was involved. The order settled at various lengths of six by six (inches) together with five of those extra-long (ten-metre) beams. (Yes, for long obscured reasons the French mix imperial and metric measurements when dealing with timber.) As an afterthought, Nick added a stack of inch-thick floorboards, their bargain price due to knots, cracks and size inconsistencies, making them difficult to use in practice. Nick figured they'd 'come in handy one day'.

Tentatively I enquired, 'What have you in mind for them, then?'

'Well, they've got to be worth having because they're so cheap, but actually I'm thinking they could cover that ugly 1950s brickwork.'

It's a gift to see a use for just about anything. Certainly, a timbered veneer would go a long way to soften the outbuildings' unprepossessing exteriors, adding texture and character. They'd be practical too, needing no staining so long as we'd be happy to allow the oak to silver with age, which we were.

January 2007. The lets needed to start producing income as soon as possible, so rather ambitiously, we aimed to open the following summer. Rather than using a commission-led agency, our small let at Wissett Place had been marketed through a property-owner's co-operative, Premier Cottages. We liked the way it allowed owner autonomy and hoped to take this path again. They are selective, however, and we would have to prove a VisitEngland 4-star or 5-star rating. The problem lay in a vicious circle of timing. The deadline for details and photographs for the next year's brochure was the end of June. In other words, we needed to be completely finished down to the last teaspoon, table lamp and butter dish as required by VisitEngland's rating scheme, before we could *be* star-rated. Yet, we couldn't participate in the next brochure *until* we were rated. We'd almost certainly miss a year, so there would be an inevitable lacuna in the first summer. Even so, we could expect a few guests from other sources and treat it as a test run.

We had a concern that the new access track would be taking arriving guests past our unlovely building site, as yet unshielded by vegetation, so we aimed to at least complete the house footings so as not to disturb them with noisy diggers and cement mixers. (Ironically, although I had seen this as a negative, the house-building process proved a great attraction, several guests frequently returning to check how we were getting on.)

So, just 18 months to:

- rehouse Nick's mum
- demolish the old farmhouse
- lay the foundations for its replacement
- rebuild the barns
- furnish them
- open for business.

What's that well-known Japanese proverb, *a journey of a thousand miles begins with a single step?*
We'd better start walking...

Team Polski

A friend telephoned in high excitement. He was watching television.

'You're on, you're on!'

'What do you mean we're on?'

'*Panorama.* It's all about Polish migrants. Couldn't believe it when I saw Nick's name pop up!'

'Oh noooo! That's only supposed to be shown in Poland!'

'Well, it's going out in front of several million UK viewers right now, mate.'

The programme began with a portentous voiceover:

> *Over the period of a year Panorama has filmed the reality of economic migration, following eleven east Europeans who came to the UK seeking work. For some the going seems easy. Weislow, a bus driver from Poland [not our Weislow], is recruited to drive for a British bus company. His boss says he can't find enough British drivers who want to work. He tells Panorama, Poles 'are used to work', while in Britain 'it's very easy not to work and still make a living'.*
>
> *But for some the going is pretty tough. Andrysz, "the Professor", came here from Poland last year and struggles to get a job. He even resorts to working for no pay at all, just for his accommodation. With no income he sleeps rough, even living for a time in a coal hole under the street.*
>
> *Panorama shows that many east European migrants who cannot find legal employment are easily absorbed into the black economy, and reveals how some are employed, illegally.*

[Interviews various people]

Then...

> *Voiceover:* There are lots of unconventional alternatives to the official paid job market for migrants. The Professor goes to work as a labourer on a farm. He gets accommodation but no pay. The farmer who employs him had put an advert in a magazine aimed at Australians travelling abroad.'
>
> *Cut to Nick:* We were looking for workers and local people seemed to be doing other things, so we put an advert in the TNT magazine in London and we had about 50 people reply. Out of those 50-odd people, there were only three Australasians and all the rest were east Europeans.
>
> *Voiceover:* The Professor said he could start the very next day.
> *Andrysz:* I didn't agree with any money, you know.
> *Voiceover (in horror):* You never asked how much?
> *Andrysz:* I never asked, no, no. Because it wasn't the point. The point was to get out from underground for a couple of days at least, to have fresh air.
> *Nick:* He's only on a week's trial at the moment, but he'll get his train fare and his accommodation and food and so on, and if we take him on, then he'll be above minimum wage as a labourer plus accommodation.

End

We sat in stunned silence until the phone started to ring with friends adding teasing commentary of their own.

As previously mentioned, the Professor hadn't made it past a few days and the existing *Team Polski* didn't seem to mind shacking up in the caravans if it meant they were on site and able to put in long hours. The bevy of farm cats, in the habit of importuning Nick's mother for food and milling around under her feet so dangerously that she would have to bat them away with her stick, saw an opportunity for even more belligerent begging and had become reliant on Polish scraps.

Having by now cleared the outbuildings, dug the ponds, made the track, rehoused Nick's mum and emptied the old house, Nick and I deemed it safe to allow its demolition to proceed in our absence, as we needed to look to affairs in Tanzania. Promoted to foreman, the not-yet-English-speaking but conscientious Krzysz had, by now, a good understanding of Nick's thinking and knew that, come what may, the ancient crooked apple tree near the house was to remain untouched and the materials from the flattened house were to be preserved for reuse.

Intellectually, we knew not to expect the house to be standing but emotionally, it was still a shock to return and find nothing but a void, the branches of the solitary apple tree lacking familiar bricks for its branches to caress. But the roof slates had been diligently stacked and the carefully cleaned red bricks stood in neat piles, all 30,000 of them. Bound with old lime mortar, there had been very little wastage on demolition and Krzysz had even sorted the regular old stocks from some that were plainly different at 9" long but 1⅓" deep, with creased faces and irregular arris (edges).

Nick examined the 'skinnies', as he called them.

'I think these must be Tudor.'

Many were soot-blackened, but despite the inference that they had come from the chimney, Krzysz waved his hands. '*Nie, nie. Ściana.*'

It appeared that they came not from the chimney but an inside wall.

Recycling has always been taken for granted in rural communities and Nick surmised that the skinnies had been part of a chimney of a much earlier house on the site and used to 'infill' the walls of the structure that superseded it, the one just demolished. Ironically, Karen and Ikki's timber-frame cottage survived because earlier farmers hadn't thought labourers' dwellings worth upgrading, yet someone had been happy to pull down what would have been a substantial timber-frame farmhouse to replace it with an inferior structure.

The first consignment of oak arrived via a haulier based in nearby Wymondham, a giant lorry carrying a combine harvester having been despatched to Spain with orders to collect our load on its way back up through France. Having gone all that way without problem, the lorry failed to make the final furlong, the hedge and ditch lining the single track from the highway to our gates robbing it of wiggle room as it tried to turn into our entrance. The timber had to be unloaded on the roadside and ferried to site by forklift and tractor-trailer. This manoeuvring took most of the day, causing the sort of country lane congestion that isn't exactly the best way to foster happy neighbourhood relations.

By this time, the barn roofs had been stripped and the gable ends built up with block and brick to accommodate the steeper pitches required for traditional clay pantiles. The arrival of this first load triggered work on the framing of the roofs across all the letting units, a complex operation as no two were of the same height. With an eye to the Upper Barn, Nick had been holding back a pair of curved oak beams acquired from a bankrupt reclamation yard many years previous. Split from one 'banana' beam, the two symmetrical blades would form an apex in the form of a semi-cruck frame.

Then insulation, a matter of packing it in as densely as possible. A supplier in Cardiff sold 'spoilt seconds' of foil-backed *Celotex* at significantly lower prices than those paid at a builders' merchant. The 'spoiling' proved to be little more than wrinkles in the foil or broken corners, so the sheets were perfect for cutting up and tucking between rafters. Nick zealously sealed each and every crack and gap with a combination of not-particularly-eco-friendly-but-very-effective expanding foam and aluminium foil tape. Tile battens, breather membrane (felt) and reclaimed pantiles followed.

The other significant job was the normally straightforward carving out of window and door apertures, but the tough post-war brick walls dictated the attentions of a diamond-tip chainsaw, after which Team *Polski* glazed the window apertures and doorways with temporary sheets of transparent plastic.

At last. Wind and watertight.

This meant serious work could begin inside. Starting with staircases and fireplaces.

Trying to encourage guests to feel that they had exclusive enjoyment of the site, we had already come up with an *external* configuration that minimised shared elements such as parking. It was then a matter of considering the *internal* layouts, the drawings produced for planning purposes having been ditched (interior layouts can be adjusted without permission provided building regulations are satisfied). Key to this was the siting of the staircases, driven by rules that govern headroom as well as the depth and height of each and every tread. Marek and Krzysz became stairmakers-in-chief, building four dog-leg staircases in situ from chunky, pitch-pine beams that had begun life as floor joists in a Great Yarmouth maltings. The fifth unit was fitted with the straight, no-nonsense staircase reclaimed from the old house.

We also had to think about fireplaces. Open fires and wood-burning stoves were, we knew, very popular with visitors.

'Come and have a look at this.'

At the back of Womack Building Supplies, Nick's favoured reclamation yard, sat a pile of stone. There were about 70 pieces, many weighing in at around 100 kilos.

'How much?'

'Bid me,' invited the ever-affable proprietor, Gene.

'£10 each?'

'They're yours.'

'I only wanted two or three.'

'Why don't you have the lot? My muscles ache through people getting me to sift through them for matching ones and then not having any because none do!'

Those people sought a perfection that didn't exist. Rather than reject imperfection we embraced it, and now Nick was able to fabricate four distinctive fireplaces (the fifth was made from the old bricks) with plenty left over. (That stone has come in amazingly handy over the years.)

The fireplaces added character but the rooms still threatened bare, bland and boring. This would not do; minimalism isn't our thing. We're not fond of twee either but recognised that guests love a timbered look, as well as a living fire. Thus, our minds turned to more of Nick's accumulated rejects, this time oak and old pine. The gnarled, the crooked, the contorted and the moth-eaten had been picked over many times, the remains languishing in distinctly unpromising heaps.

Rusticity is hard to fake. We've been in too many pubs where a couple of oak posts carelessly nailed in place are thought to constitute authenticity, but if anything could integrate them as 'original' studwork, it would be Nick's unerring eye.

Crucial Services

Water in, sewage out. We mustn't overlook the basics. Following the concept of 'natural building' to its logical conclusion would require natural waste treatments and water reuse, but in our business context, compromises had to be made. For example, we abandoned the idea of using *greywater* (recycled from washing machines and baths) for flushing toilets as that had complications in commercial situations, but collecting *rainwater* for flushing and for watering the garden was worth doing. Nick acquired a 40,000-litre tank and spent a day burying it for the purpose. But come the next day, the tank had popped right out of the ground. Clearly, the water table was higher than we had thought. The tank was reburied, much deeper this time, and weighed down by a layer of concrete sleepers and a starter dose of water.

With no mains sewer nearby, all properties hereabouts rely on septic tanks. In the old days, they would have been cesspits. We explored the feasibility of rush treatment plants, but the lie of the land made a suitable location difficult to pin down. In the end, we opted for a *Klargester* – a sewage-treatment plant which allegedly produces such a clean product that you can drink from its outfall. I didn't anticipate trying.

The capital cost of capturing on-site energy, whether through wind or photovoltaic systems, was beyond our means at this stage of the game. Our priority was to get the business off the ground as quickly and economically as possible, so, in the end, opted for a straightforward oil-fired system, despite the risk of hiking oil prices. Well, maybe not *that* straightforward; a separate building would house a highly complex and futuristic arrangement of three boilers (as failsafe), three cylinders and criss-crossing pipes. From here, solar-heated water (topped up by the boilers where necessary) would be pumped on a loop around the properties so that hot water was literally 'on tap', the solar also contributing to the underfloor heating.

Given Marek's self-professed plumbing experience back in Poland, Nick, not without trepidation, put him in charge of laying the underfloor heating pipes and first-fix plumbing. Jon Lewis, who had worked with Nick on several projects, was shipped in for the electrical first-fix. Rendering followed and as we were not after a modern, polished plaster surface, Ewa applied a layer of plaster bonding, which would provide a slightly irregular matt finish.

It must have been confusing for them. The London job had required immaculate attention to detail, precision and perfection; this time, Nick was asking the team to *deliberately* make things look a bit wonky, as if they'd been there forever.

Dragons – Part 1

We had taken time out to attend the Chelsea Flower Show. Not that we are particularly into horticulture – my idea of gardening is clutching a glass of wine while watching the weeds proliferate and thinking, 'I really must do something about that'. But Chelsea can offer across–the-board inspiration and sure enough, our Gothic tendencies had homed in on a finely carved stone griffin and its twin, a dragon.

'They'd look quite handsome topping-off the gateway,' I'd observed, with a resigned, '... if we ever get around to doing it.' Turning the bedraggled approach to Belle Grove into something elegant and welcoming was becoming something of a bête noire.

Befitting their quality, the carvings were not cheap, so we circled back and forth, humming and hawing. The clincher had been the waiver of the hefty

delivery charge, so in due course, they arrived in Suffolk to await installation. In the meantime, we had taken to driving around the countryside inspecting and photographing gateways for inspiration, to the extent that it was a wonder we were not arrested for 'casing joints'. In the end, Piet was put to flanking the entranceway with curved brick walls constructed of the reclaimed skinnies. From the London job's requirement of flawless brick courses laid by spirit level, he adapted admirably to laying by eye. Touches of moss, missing corners and imperfect lines created the impression

that the entrance walls had been in situ at least a hundred years with only the, as yet, unblemished stone of the dragon and griffin atop the piers signalling otherwise.

Driving past those creatures every day revived our wrestles with the issue of the 'creature'. Taking inspiration from the stone dragon, we wondered, could a dragon be the answer? Its shape would work well, long neck, dumpy body (to hide the flue), dramatic wings and long tail to wrap round the chimneystack.

There are so many depictions and descriptions of dragons that it is hard to remember that they are only make-believe. Even as late as the seventeenth century, the naturalist Edward Topsell published *Historie of Foure-footed Beastes and Serpents,* portraying dragons as if they were real creatures. The idea of fire-belching dragons engendered genuine fear. Some believed they had seen them and there were a great many who, if they had not seen them themselves, were sure others had.

The Anglo-Saxon Chronicle records the first Viking attack (in AD 793) at the monastery of Lindisfarne: '... dreadful fore-warnings over the land of the Northumbrians, terrifying the people most woefully: these were immense sheets of light rushing through the air and fiery dragons flying across the firmament.' That description doubtless owed much to the fact that the Viking longships displayed fiercely carved dragons on their prows.

According to Pliny the Elder, a dragon was seen and killed on Vatican Hill during the reign of Emperor Claudius. Freak weather and phenomena, such as ball lightning, were attributed to dragon activities and in 1222, dragons were 'seen' flying over London, an event followed by severe thunderstorms. A medieval chronicle [38] describes 'great earthquakes, lightning and thunder, with a huge dragon and a blazing star'.

---

38 From 1274, held in the Norwich Record Office.

I'm inclined to think that the sightings of dragons in the Middle Ages equates to the sighting of UFOs today.

It's hard to escape tales of St George and the Dragon. Of the many legends about the saint, the most widespread concerns that of the dragon. It seems that on a lake by a city in Libya (or possibly Lebanon – there are differing accounts) lived a ferocious flesh-eating dragon whose breath poisoned the countryside. Terrified citizens appeased it by a daily offering of sheep. The supply of sheep running low, they began to provide human beings, chosen by lot. One day, the lot fell upon the daughter of the king of the city. George happened to be passing by on horseback and struck the dragon with his spear, but the scales were so hard that the spear broke into a thousand pieces and George fell from his horse. Fortunately, he rolled under an enchanted orange tree and was able to wound and tame the dragon, leading it back to the city using the lady's girdle. He then threatened to release it unless the inhabitants became Christian. They agreed and George killed the dragon. Variations of this story were long known in Britain, but it became particularly popular during the Crusades with St George so highly regarded that he became England's patron saint. (I love the paradox: his feast

day, 23 April, has become synonymous with the very essence of 'Englishness', yet he had no connection to England whatsoever!)

Anyway, back to *our* dragon. If we were to pursue this idea, we'd have to consider what a dragon actually looks like. That said, the great advantage of a mythical creature is that while the dragon permeates art and iconography, no one can definitively say what 'lifelike' is. The name stems from the Latin *draco*, which in turn derives from the Greek *dérkomai* meaning to look fixedly. In other words, to stare – and staring is an essential characteristic of any self-respecting dragon. Other than that, the imagery varies, the earliest depictions being of giant worms and serpents with the later additions of legs and wings creating the more familiar trope.

Western narratives focus on cunning monsters guarding vast hordes of gold within deep caverns, threatening maidens and creating mayhem, all designed to test the courage of knights whose job spec was to protect the vulnerable. Greek mythology gives us Perseus, who, travelling on his winged sandals, noticed the captive Andromeda awaiting the attentions of the dragon monster that Poseidon had called from the depths and which, naturally, was destroyed by Perseus' sword. Or  the dragon that tried to keep the Golden Fleece from Jason. Or the gigantic Typhon, who caused such damage on Mount Olympus that the gods put him under Mount Etna where he still breathes fire.

Britain's even scarier variant – fire-breathing, scaly-bodied creatures with razor-edged talons, bat-like wings and spiky dorsal spines – derives from age-old Saxon and Celtic myth, and several British saints were noted for their dragon-slaying activities. St Sampson of Cornwall led a dragon from its cave to its death over sea cliffs, for example. Otherwise inexplicable events could be explained by dragon activity. In early 1400s Suffolk, a dragon 'vast in body with crested head, teeth like a saw, and tail extending to an enormous length' was spotted in the River Stour. An enormous fire-breathing monster had emerged from the river and, although attacked with bows and arrows, remained unhurt 'for the arrows bounced off his back as if it were iron or hard rock'. [39] The 'dragon' reappeared a couple of times before eventually plunging into a lake, never to be seen again, although an inscription in the nearby church suggests that the dragon was slain by a knight called Sir George of Layer de la Haye. This has led to speculation that this is the real source of the St George and Dragon legend. A more credible theory is that it was actually a crocodile brought back from the Crusades, which

39 The chronicles of the monk, John de Trokelowe, as mentioned in *Wormingford: An English Village* by Beaumont & Taylor.

had escaped into the River Stour. Whatever, the legend holds sway and today a huge striding dragon can be seen carved into the hillside. [40]

Dragons magical, predatory and benign turn up in literary sagas from Beowulf to Tolkien's Smaug in *The Hobbit*. The creative imaginings of Lewis Carroll, Kenneth Grahame, C. S. Lewis, E. Nesbit and, more recently, Ursula LeGuin, Terry Pratchett and J. K. Rowling are a staple of children's literature and adult fantasy. Instructive that such an ancient symbol should feature so prominently in manifestations of the modern, from screensavers, fantasy video games to *Game of Thrones*.

---

40 On the hillside facing St Stephen's Chapel, Wormingford.

Samaki House Revisited

By now you'll have noticed our tendency to take a 'back-of-a-fag-packet' approach and Samaki House had been no exception. Its appearance had to depend on available materials, the ability of those materials to be physically transported up the hill and, not least, the width of our wallet. All considerations that pointed

to one design solution: a timber frame. Not oak, of course, nor expensively imported termite-resistant cedar, but two lorry-loads of pine poles originally destined for a matchstick-making factory bankrupted hours before the poles were due for delivery, allowing the supplier to divert them to other buyers (us) at a
rock-bottom price. This wasn't necessarily the wisest move, given that termites relish snacks of easy-to-digest softwood. We did take steps to moderate their depredations, firstly with the used sump oil reputed to repel termites (it didn't) and then with chemical pellets of the sort that had been used to treat

 an extremely upmarket Game Lodge (which did work – we think).

The long verandah and roof of *bati* (corrugated tin) may have created a classically colonial look, but there were similarities to our Suffolk project. For example, the infilling of its frame with rock hewn from our own rock pit echoed the infill of straw in the oak frame, not to mention its 30-foot tower with its sensational views across the town of Arusha, 500 feet below. A fledgling compared to the one we were to build, but notice a certain pattern?

Local subsistence farmers working under Nick's direction provided hands-on labour. Marshalling them to their tasks reinforced Nick's already-useful ability to communicate across linguistic barriers in a technique that came to be deployed to good effect with *Team Polski*. His ad hoc methodology – if that's not a contradiction in terms – was dubbed by the workers as the 'daily plan', a version of which was to become familiar at Belle Grove.

Architecturally, Africa may bring to mind pretty thatched rondavels, but nowadays it's all concrete blocks and tin roofs. In its use of rough timber and raw rock, Samaki House was, and is, considered wacky by local standards. During construction, local rumour had it marked down as a safari lodge, never mind that it lacked mains electricity, running water and drainage.

Modest African interiors are typically enlivened by colourful oilcloths, bright enamel kitchenware and vividly printed cloth used as room-dividers. Sometimes paint is applied to walls in chevron patterns, geometric designs and mysterious runic shapes. We couldn't help but observe that many European ex-pats created domestic interiors that wholly mirrored Western style, rather than acknowledge the continent in which they lived. We tended to veer the other way and Samaki House became adrift with African ephemera: Tanzanian *tinga tinga* paintings, *kanga* curtains, hand-crafted tables and four-poster beds with *kitenge* throws[41], as well as tribal masks, decorative gourds and wooden carvings bought and

41 *Tinga Tinga* paintings are made using several layers of bicycle paint to create brilliant and highly saturated colours. The subject matter, usually animals, is depicted in a naïve, caricatured manner. The *Kanga* is a colourful piece of printed cotton, often with a border along all four sides and a central motif, worn throughout East Africa. *Kitenges* are similar to kangas but of a thicker cloth and have a patterned edge on only one side.

bartered across the continent. Yet our mélange was merely a Western construct, a mishmash that by no means reflected an authentic African domestic interior – whatever that is.

You'd assume that with our strong African connection, we'd have been thinking of incorporating African motifs in the barns rather than those of the East. If we *had* been thinking of creating an 'African look', we'd have drawn on the elegance of the colonial era – all steamer chairs, campaign furniture, rattan, woven mats, deep-sea trunks, artfully draped muslin, mosquito nets and zebra skins. Yet while all that works well in a hot climate, somehow it doesn't give off the warmth required for a chilly British milieu. In my view, it's nigh-on impossible to pull off a convincing yet cosily comfortable African-inspired interior in northern Europe, or assimilate even a soupçon of the continent's ambience.

Not Quite a Grand Design

As the cliché goes, 'if I'd had a pound for every time I'd heard the words "this should have been on Grand Designs…"'

At the end of each edition of Channel 4's long-running and hugely popular TV programme, self-builders are urged to submit details of projects that might be suitable for filming. Against my instincts, Nick persuaded me that exposure on national television could have a beneficial, knock-on effect on the new business. We duly downloaded the lengthy application form and submitted it, complete with photographs of the completed model.

'That looks interesting. Contact us again when you have planning consent,' responded a sceptical assistant.

In the fullness of time, I notified the production company, Talkback Thames, that planning consent *had* been granted.

'Oh sorry, I can't find anything about that, can you send the details again?'

I did. In fact, they had to be sent three times. After a certain amount of toing and froing, during which Talkback expressed active interest in following the build, all went quiet. In late autumn, I sent a reminder that we were hoping to commence construction in the New Year.

'We're in the process of negotiating airtime with Channel 4 for the next series,' they explained, 'but we'll be back in touch shortly.'

'Shortly' failed to materialise. Following the demolition of old house, I made final contact. 'We're starting to dig the footings next week.'

'That's fine. We don't need to film the groundworks unless there's something particular going on. We'll be back in touch by next Wednesday for sure.'

Needless to say, Wednesday came and went without word. Having a team of workers to keep busy, we couldn't hang around, so we focused on the foundations and forgot all about *Grand Designs*.

It's surprising the passionate debate that such an ostensibly dull subject triggers. The thing is, a foundation has to bear structural loads and allow proper drainage of ground water (to prevent soil weakening from frost heave). In this country, structures built more than 200 years ago have natural foundations built on bedrock or firm clay and most have remained completely sound. Indeed, Wissett Place had had no foundations and although the expansion and contraction of the clay soil, combined with 100-year-old wisteria, had caused localised issues, it had stood firm since 1810.

Ideally, we were searching for an environmentally friendly alternative to concrete, with all its high-energy manufacture ramifications. For a while we favoured 'rammed earth' foundations where old car or lorry tyres are placed in line, stacked one on the other, the gaps are then filled with rocks and plastered over. After all, there was no shortage of old tyres around the place. On the other hand, we had to recognise the potential for damp at the interface with the materials above – very significant, given our plan to build with straw bales. Self-draining foundations, such as the rubble trenches popularised by Frank Lloyd Wright, would probably work. These utilise loose stone or rubble in lieu of concrete but are not recommended for earthquake-prone areas. That's one thing we didn't have to worry about in Suffolk.

A rubble trench requires structural engineer approval, but what really killed the idea were the exceptional loadings (the tower and the chimneystack), along with the planning requirement to keep the footings as close as possible to the original footprint, meaning that the tower was to rise more or less over the old cellar. In light of this, the first diktat of Bob, the experienced and possibly horrified building inspector assigned to us, was that we should follow the well-tried concrete route.

Although concrete has become something of a dirty word in sustainable terms, it has been around for a long time. In the Monty Python film *Life of Brian*, the answers to the question posed by the People's Front of Judea, 'what have the Romans ever done for us?' has become comedic code for the practices they introduced (only sanitation, medicine, education, wine, public order, irrigation, roads, public health...) but the script could also have included concrete. The refined concrete they used is very similar to that of today. Architectural historians even refer to the 'concrete revolution' that allowed Roman builders and designers to aspire to complex and beautiful constructions including the Pantheon dome, even now the largest unsupported concrete dome in the world.

Resigned to the concrete route, we could at last proceed, and armed with his trusty tape measure and a ball of nylon string, Nick brought his practical geometry to bear. Creating a grid that he scaled-off with bamboo poles, while following the floor plan of the model, he drove in stakes to denote the curvatures of the footings. Actually, excavating these proved trickier. When you think about it, a digger simply has to pull its bucket in a straight line to make a slot. Here, we were asking the digger operator to manoeuvre around bends.

Generally speaking, a footing is twice as wide as the foundation wall it supports and as deep as the wall is thick. However, the footing for the tower

had to be excavated to at least one metre lower than the cellar's base – already eight feet down, although the final depth would depend ultimately on the level at which undisturbed soil was found. Following Nick's grid, the digger cut diagonally across the cellar, a process that revealed it had been lined with narrow 'skinnies', hitherto hidden under a coat of cement. Wieslow and Piet lowered themselves into the pit and continued the dig by hand. Luckily for them, at 6' 6" below the cellar floor level (that is, nearly 15 feet down), the ground proved to be undisturbed clay. Bob confirmed that this was as far as we needed to go and also that the part of the old cellar *outside* the new footings could be shuttered up to its ceiling height and filled in. With what? Well, a one-ton gravel sack had been the receptacle for empty vodka bottles and was now full to the brim. Instead of laboriously feeding them one by one into a bottle bank, the bottles were pitched *en masse* into the void. Diverting to contemplate what future archaeologists might make of it.

It took three days for the trenches to be gouged into the curves dictated by the model. Accustomed to rectangular footings, this looked seriously weird to me; a wavy model was one thing, a wavy house quite another. The layout looked smaller than in my head too, but I was familiar with the phenomenon whereby with no walls, rooms can seem small, but as walls go up, rooms appear bigger. You'd expect it to be the other way round.

Bob having signalled his approval of the excavations, the next stage was to fill the trenches, ideally before it rained. Needless to say, a series of steady showers set in, initiating one of those interminable spells that turn the ground into a morass. So several weeks passed before we dare order the ready-mix. Once, a concrete pour was all about the capacity of the site's concrete-mixer; now, we had to calculate an exact figure in cubic yards, no easy matter with our irregular trenches. Order too much and, apart from the unnecessary cost, the driver would have to find a place to dump the surplus; order too little and the driver must make another costly journey. Dreading the sort of last-minute concrete panic than can occur, we could only sigh with relief when our dawn-to-dusk 'pour' proved spot on and singularly undramatic.

The concrete had to be left 'to cure' before the floor could be laid, so Nick turned to the sole plates. In a traditional timber frame, these comprise sturdy oak beams, but it would be impossible to bend oak to the shape of these footings and, in any case, the straw would require protection from possible water penetration from below. Thus, the damp proof course was laid on block plinths.

The monumental chimney also required robust foundations. Although not positioned over a cellar, its footings had to be dug with critical precision as its position would dictate the location of the main fireplace and, on the other side of the chimney, the flue for the hoped-for Aga. It was frightening to think just how many issues would be affected by decisions taken in these very early stages. Soil pipes were another example – where they were laid affected the locations of bathrooms so we had to keep an *approximation* of the interior in our heads.

Eventually, the floor could be laid, comprising separate layers of compacted rubble followed by Malteser-like clay balls topped with insulation (more *Celotex*) and a final layer of concrete, then to await the underfloor heating pipes.

A coda. Jumping several months to June, Nick and I had headed off to the Norfolk Show with the idea of researching wood-burning stoves, when Nick's phone rang.

'Hello, this is Madeleine from Talkback Thames. I'm on the team dealing with *Grand Designs*. We've found some papers about your self-build and are extremely interested in including it in the next series. When are you starting?'

'Er, we commenced the build in February,' he replied, forbearingly adding, 'as we told you.'

'Where are you up to then?'

'The tower and the chimney are built.'

'I see... what a pity, that's just too advanced for us.'

In a way, it was the opposite of the Polish TV/*Panorama* scenario – there we found ourselves with unsought publicity; here, we had pursued it to no avail. That's the media for you.

Still, although Nick mourned the lost opportunity to promote the business by association, I confessed to enormous relief that we were not having to justify to a tooth-suckingly sceptical Kevin McCloud, in front of millions of viewers:

i) the lack of architect

ii) the lack of 'proper' plans and

iii) the use of unskilled workers, with whom we couldn't properly communicate.

Committed

Another Christmas came and went and January 2008 was upon us. There we were, bowling along the A12 toward London, when Nick's mobile phone chirped its annoying ringtone. Scrambling to retrieve it from his pocket, Nick passed it to me.

'Hello?'

'I read about Stable End Cottage in *The Times* a year or two ago and kept the cutting,' a crisp female voice pronounced, going on to enquire, 'Do you have availability for August? We need two bedrooms.'

We had to explain that Stable End, being part of Wissett Place, was off the market pending its sale. Only at the last moment did I have the wit to add, 'We do have new properties coming on stream – there's information online'. (Brian, a photographer friend,[42] had left his London lair to take a few shots for a 'coming soon' web page, although, it had been more a question of what needed to be left out of sight than included at that stage.)

42 www.bbphoto.co.uk

'Can you describe the new place?'

I did my best – difficult as we only had a vague idea ourselves at that point.

'Will it be as nice as Stable End?'

'Well, we're planning to make it even nicer!'

'By the way, we have three small dogs.'

Although we don't have dogs ourselves, we are mindful of Bunyan's aphorism that 'An Englishman would rather walk with a dog than with a fellow Christian', and long recognised that accepting pets was part of the ethos of hospitality that is 'thou shalt' rather than 'thou shalt not'. Although three dogs was going it a bit. Still, we couldn't afford to be picky at this stage.

'That should be all right.'

'But can you *guarantee* it will be ready for August?' the voice insisted.

I gulped and took the plunge, 'Yes'.

'Fine, we'll book for three weeks. Where do we send the deposit?'

Committed!

1

2

3

4

5

6

8

Back to the Barns

Now that the barns were pretty well *structurally* complete, it was a matter of organising second-fix electrics and plumbing, fitting kitchens, decorating and equipping everything ready for guests. Given the fact that we'd never actually stayed in a holiday let, our starting point had to be instinct. What would *we* want?

While the barns would have certain features in common, they wouldn't be cloned. Yes, all the kitchen floor cupboards would be fashioned from the chunky Rajasthani 'sideboards' made from cut down *haveli* doors, but each of these was of differing style. The units were to be topped with either black or green Indian granite, shaped to size by Piet, the surfaces then polished with a diamond polishing disc while, in some cases, deliberately leaving an irregular rough rim on the nose and the top face of the upstand.

We planned to give one of the units an Indonesian feel by fitting some of those striking Balinese doors. These days, the doors tend to be fitted with metal hinges but those from *Sukama* had retained the traditional construction: pivoting wooden post, traditional wooden hinges and a locking mechanism consisting of two rings fastened by a padlock. The doors were certainly decorative, but the need to step over the integral three-inch-high sill was inconvenient and potentially hazardous, not something which Bob could approve. So, Nick cut off the sills and re-hinged the doors. Conventional door furniture would have compromised their appearance though, so we stayed with the original design, the doors secured with a bar pushed between the two rings.

Elsewhere, it was a matter of utilising some of the old doors that Nick had accumulated. I say 'some', but over the years, he had collected a hundred or so panelled and ledge and brace doors, mostly other people's rejects. On the face of it, many were unusable, what with their short height, woodworm and gaping holes where locks had been removed. Not unnaturally, people prefer doors they can walk through without needing to duck, something we overcame by

deconstructing some of the worst offenders and transferring slices onto the tops or bottoms of better preserved versions, after which the whole thing was dipped in caustic soda, waxed and polished. Throwaways became things of beauty. Specific doors were then allocated to specific sites so that the frame could be made to fit the door rather than the other way around, the more typical method.

Our aforementioned electrician, Jon, hadn't allowed himself to become *too* exasperated by our first-fix electricity 'plans', which consisted of chalk scrawls where sockets and switches were to be located. For the second fix, we'd been researching alternatives to the ubiquitous white plastic switch and in the end, sourced Bakelite dolly switches from the period range of an Australian company, [43] which Nick later mounted on blocks of waxed oak. Unusually, these reproductions were an improvement on 1930s originals, which are seldom found in working two-way or three-way mode. We'd have liked to include wall and lighting circuit sockets which allow an assortment of table lamps to work off one wall switch but, with Australia using a different system, we were forced to return to British suppliers at three times the price. One can never have too many electrical sockets.

Turning to the private patios and gardens, these needed physical boundaries for which we found ourselves using a lot of the 'reject floorboard' oak from France, although the unrelieved effect was a bit stockade-like, a bit *High Noon*. So, we reached for visual relief in the form of rusted corrugated iron. All right, it's a material more commonly associated with farm sheds and refugee camps, but we liked its texture and colour, and, especially when partially encrusted with ivy, it befitted the agricultural genesis of this place.

Two of the barns had south-facing gardens and another faced south-east, but we were conscious that the remaining pair faced a sometimes unfriendly north. These would need protection from the sharp winds that can flail East Anglia. The farm was littered with discarded vehicle parts from the days of Trans-Africa preparations, including a pair of lorry bodies known as curtain-siders – that is, trailers with a floor, a roof, a solid side and an open side covered with canvas that can be pulled back for easy loading. At 24 feet long and eight feet deep,

---

43 www.palesinstyle.com.au

Nick figured these might work as buffers against the elements, doubling as south-facing sunrooms once French windows were substituted for the canvas.

The forklift lifted these into place on an east-west orientation leaving a ten-foot gap between them to act as a sort of vestibule leading into two separate walled gardens. Each came with a decent wooden floor, but Nick replaced the flat roofs with sloping pantiles, Velux windows and solar panels. The north side was covered with shiplap cladding and the south fitted with bifold doors. Somewhere along the way, he had acquired an assortment of oak panels and these were used to line the interiors. Panelled, plastered and painted, the 'curtain siders' were transformed into glorious suntraps, 'shabby-chic' repositories for a miscellany of squashy armchairs, barbecues and parasols.

I was also keen to endow the outside spaces with some maturity. The only trees to survive Nick's earlier transplanting efforts had been indestructible elders so, en route to Heathrow for a flight to Egypt (more of that anon), we just had time for a stopover at Paramount Plants in Crews Hill. In what was becoming a series of quick-fire shopping hits, we ordered mature bamboos, fig trees, acers, camellias, cordylines, olives and pomegranates, figuring these would convey an exotic contrast to the wider untamed grounds. Despite the relative substance of these new additions, the gardens retained an incomplete air. Something only time could cure.

At Home

The Professor (Andrysz) showed up unexpectedly.

'Can we talk?'

It appeared he was there to translate for Krzysz and Ewa, whose English had remained almost as non-existent as our Polish. We were worried. Were they going to quit? Convening under the spreading apple tree, we were stunned to learn that Krzysz and Ewa planned to bring their son aged eight and daughter aged four, who had been in the care of grandparents, to Suffolk. First, they needed to know, 'Will there be work for us in the hotel?'

In other words, what would happen once the construction was complete? Would there be further employment?

It was obvious to us that there would be months', even years' worth of work to finish the barn grounds *and* the house, let alone keeping the ship afloat. Ewa would surely make a good housekeeper thereafter. Even so, we were astonished that they would consider carving out a future in such a rural backwater.

'Are you sure you want to settle so far from a city and perhaps your Polish friends?'

It appeared that, as far as they were concerned, this was a beneficent place to raise a family and, we could only assume, an improvement on prospects back in Poland. The plan was that Krzysz's mother would come to look after the children, Michal and Patrycia, and accompany them to and from school while Krzysz and Ewa were at work.

'When do you want to fetch them?' I asked, assuming later in the year.

'Next week!'

'So soon? Are you sure?"

'Michal and Patrycia can start school in September if they come now.'

They had it all worked out. I don't think they envisaged anything going wrong. Such as the dire economic downturn that would shortly engulf the country.

Their decision begged the question, where would they live? At present, they were occupying one of the caravans 'round the back', but with only the most basic levels of comfort and privacy, it wasn't at all suitable for a young family. They needed a house, a home.

'Leave it with us,' was all we could say, as Krzysz and Ewa disappeared to Poland.

Not as easy as we made it sound. Suffolk landlords can be dubious about newcomers from Norfolk let alone Europe. Eventually, we found a small, unfurnished terraced cottage to rent within walking distance of the schools. They would need a car though. Wages may have been much higher in the UK than in Poland, but the cost of living – accommodation, utilities, council tax, food, driving and most material things – was very stiff by comparison, so they could expect challenges in making ends meet.

Flying into London would severely restrict their chances of bringing back any domestic paraphernalia, so the cottage was kitted out with furniture, kitchen equipment and bedding donated by well-disposed friends. As it happened, on the day they arrived, son Jaimie was due to drive up from London in a borrowed Transit van, so to avoid train fares it made sense for him to pick them up and convey them to Halesworth *en famille*. This may have saved money, but it meant that Ewa and Krzysz, their never-been-away-before children and their grandmother endured the ride north in total darkness, with no means of communicating with the cab. Their very own Black Hole of Calcutta.

True to stoic form, there was no word of complaint.

Shopping Adventure No. 3

We are all much more interconnected than we imagine. St George may be associated with England (even originating in Suffolk, if that tale from the Stour Valley is to be believed) but, as seen, the 'slayer of dragons' legend is much more likely to have been brought back from the Crusades. In fact, St George is venerated all over the Middle East by Christians and Muslims alike and medieval romances suggest that Ashkelon, the lance with which he slew the dragon, was named after a place in the territory which was to become modern-day Syria.

Syria had seemingly developed into one of the region's more tolerant cultures, with religions harmoniously coexisting alongside each other. Unfortunately, the Assad regime had achieved a bad-boy reputation through its relationship with Hezbollah, a terror group in neighbouring Lebanon, and its cynical playing-off of sects and factions while ignoring internal disaffection with the result that we all know today. So, I hope it's not insensitive to recall an interlude in Damascus that was '... a slice through history'.[44]

The visit was another off-piste occasion. Neither Nick, I, nor John, the Anglican priest who made up the third and last member of our party, whom we'd not met before, had been deterred by Syrian politics as seen through a distinctly Western prism. Still, conscious of the need to dress according to local mores, I packed all-enveloping black clothing. Our wariness was compounded by the troops of white-robed and sternly bearded men who also embarked on the Damascus-bound plane and stared disapprovingly whenever I or Nick ventured down the gangway.

'This is a bit heavy. Is it what Syria is going to be like?' I whispered.

The bearded ones were nowhere to be seen on arrival, it transpiring that they were a group of Pakistani fundamentalists taking the cheapest air route to Islamabad. The guide who met us at the airport had a beard too but was

---

44 'A journey to Damascus is an amazing hunt from beginning to end, a slice through layers of history in search of treasure.' *Travels with Myself* by Tahir Shah, www.tahirshah.com

chatty and welcoming. From the car, I spotted plenty of women in Western attire, their head coverings, if any, consisting of cheerful headscarves. Only a few were wrapped in a *niqab* or draped head to toe in a black *abaya*. 'Iranian tourists,' muttered our guide, curling his lip. By contrast, when it came to fashion, Syrian ladies didn't hold back on decorative detail, displaying a weakness for bows, lace and diamanté.

I ditched the black garments.

Damascus had long been a magnet on account of its strategic position, the beautiful vaulted caravanserai, Khan As'ad Pasha, hosting caravans from Arabia, Africa and across the Levant. At its heart is Souk Al-Hamidiyya, with its vaulted roof still admitting pencils of sunlight through the bullet holes made by machine-gun fire during the nationalist rebellion of 1925. Markets are a true evocation of place and this one overflowed with luridly dyed cakes, bales of damask, startling and unexpected displays of sexy underwear, egg-sized glass beads strung on ribbons and perfumeries breathing rose and jasmine. Alarming 'pharmacies' in the Seed Souk offered dried baby crocodiles, turtle shells, lizards, quills and horns amid miniature landslides of spices.

The old city is punctuated by monumental lumps of Roman masonry, Emperor Augustus' Temple to Jupiter standing to attention in the midst of the main bazaar while merchants and housewives, imams and pedlars pursued

their purposes under and around its massive arches. Resonating across the millennia, this casual juxtaposition of ancient and modern brought an atavistic quality to the scene, ancient yet vibrant. That a priest (dubbed Prester John) was a member of our party had been sheer coincidence. Like many nowadays, I consider myself a Christian by culture rather than belief, so I was nonplussed to feel quite so touched by the ancientness of the 'Street called Straight', referred to in the New Testament. Likewise, with Saladin's Tomb and *Bab Sharqi*, the Roman Gate of the Sun, which marks the crossing point from the Muslim into the Christian and Jewish Quarters.

Official print guides were provided for Christian destinations such as St Ananias Chapel (where Saul became Paul after his blinding Road to Damascus moment) and, given that friends had questioned the wisdom of visiting Syria at all, it was instructive that, waiting to enter the Umayyad Mosque [45] (heads

---

45 One of the largest and oldest mosques in the world, where the head of John the Baptist is said to rest.

respectfully covered), hardly any of the 2,000 worshippers streaming out of Friday prayers spared as much as a glance at supposed 'infidels'. Our Western self-consciousness was piqued only by the ubiquitous looming portraits of Bashar al-Assad, his father Hafez and the popular Hezbollah leader, Sheik Hassan Nasrallah.

While Syria isn't officially 'dry', the availability of alcohol tends to be confined to the Christian Quarter. Alas, this wasn't where our hotel was located. I learnt a few tricks from the surprisingly worldly Prester John, who had the knack of conjuring up bottles of wine and tumblers of Scotch out of thin air. (Nothing other-worldly about it – he simply bribed the staff!) Taxis were cheap, their drivers endowed with a seemingly infinite knowledge of what's what and who's who, their helpfulness reflecting *ikram al dayf*, the imperative to respect and welcome strangers. By this rule of hospitality, guests are to be provided with whatever food and drink is available to make them comfortable and happy.

Brother Keith and his wife Rosey had experienced the benign effect of *ikram al dayf* when driving overland from Dubai to England via Syria at the time of Operation Desert Storm (the First Gulf War) when sordid politics weren't allowed to sully the moment, albeit there had been a wobbly moment when Keith admitted to having had a military career.

Our own brief sojourn hadn't allowed for personal encounters of that sort, but we enjoyed the eateries that had sprung up in the Damascene houses of the Old Quarter. Crammed together in narrow alleyways, the crumbling and outwardly plain buildings provided privacy for their owners by simply omitting ground or first-floor windows by the public street; even the upper windows were covered by shutters designed to keep out curious eyes.

Every house was laid out around a courtyard floor made from a mixture of basalt and a rosy coloured stone called *mazzey* that keeps temperatures moderate. In the old days, there would be a gushing fountain also built of *mazzey*, a clever way of keeping the water cold and fruit refrigerated. In fact, the Old City had enjoyed a unique water system, with river water pumped into the highest fountain in a street, from where it would cascade over the edges and flow down through water pipes and into the fountains of neighbouring houses, down and down, a methodical and labour-saving system that had died out with modernisation.

After a long period of neglect and, possibly inspired by the success of *riads* in Morocco, there were clear signs of interest in restoring the quarters' historic buildings, some as boutique *pensions* or hotels. Some were being used as television and film locations, as we discovered on blundering into a courtyard being used to film a soap opera, and nearly featuring in the Syrian equivalent of *EastEnders*.

The shopping scene was oh-so seductive. At Abed al Razzack Alhosani 'all kinds of oriental embroiders deep-rooted Damiscene products' *(sic)* could be found and at Al Sharq Khalil al Dayeh, silk brocades, brass and copper inlays, ceramics and mosaics, swords and Bedouin silver.

While Prester John hunted for the perfect brocaded chasuble to which to treat his parishioners of a Sunday, Nick and I scoured side streets for items rather more readily transportable than Khalil's inlaid chests or rococo lamps,

tottering back under armfuls of embroidered tablecloths and cushion covers, ropes of outsize glass orbs, kilims, coffee beakers and a clutch of antique beaded light fittings from a charming octogenarian manning an obscure junk shop. Most of which were to find their way into the barns.

Of course, investment in the restoration of old Damascene houses has come to an abrupt halt. As we wonder whether this taxi driver or that waiter, the old boy or Khalil al Dayeh and others are even still alive, our 'finds' have taken on heightened significance. Back then, the main threat was to one's waistline; now, with ever spiralling violence, no faction has been without blood on its hands, but it is the regime that must answer to history.

As I write, Syria's tragedy has yet to reach its final act...

Verticals

Any building project requires a clear dialogue path between project manager, foreman and workers. Between Nick and *Team Polski* the dialogue was still of the banana variety, but they'd managed pretty well so far.

Time to test their communication skills while dealing with the house build. You may remember from the model that the dominant vertical elements comprised the tower and the chimneystack. We added another, not so tall perhaps but equally as idiosyncratic.

Tower

The house foundations had already been laid, of course, and convention dictated that the next step was to build the walls. Yet our first vertical element wasn't a wall at all but the tower, rising 40 feet to the top of its windows with the cupola adding another 16 feet or so. Admittedly, the tower *was* something of a design flourish, but it also had a practical function, housing a laundry room and cloakroom at its base and a staircase from the first to the second floor and up into the turret. While there'd be room enough to sip a G&T whilst admiring the view, there wouldn't, alas, be space for the coveted studio à la Vita Sackville-West. [46]

At 10 feet in diameter, the tower's skeleton required seven, dead-straight, 40-foot posts. Six for the circumference and one for the centre. Where to find such things?

'We could use telegraph poles, I suppose,' Nick deliberated. 'They're nice and straight and Andy down the road sells them.'

Bob didn't approve, pointing out that they'd be full of weeping tarry toxins. He was right, of course.

'OK, let's think laterally. What trees are telegraph poles actually made from?'

46 Poet and novelist, Vita Sackville-West, chose the small room at the very top of the Elizabethan tower in the grounds of Sissinghurst Castle as her writing room, her sanctuary.

Douglas fir, it seemed.

'Try Dunwich,' a friend suggested. 'There's thousands there.'

It appeared that the Forestry Commission was in the process of 'rewilding' Dunwich Forest, a radical shift from a conifer plantation to a mix of semi-natural habitats. The strategy was to regenerate the natural landscape, meaning that the southern part of the plantation was being progressively clear-felled. We spent a happy afternoon strolling through the woods, the words, 'into the forest I go, to lose my mind and find my soul' insistently pricking my mind. [47] Eventually emulating the medieval practice of felling for  specific purpose, we selected eight of the straightest and tallest Douglas firs (an extra one just in case), marking those for the chop with a satisfying large red X – another life goal fulfilled, on a par with instructing a taxi driver to 'follow that car'! Even at 80 feet or so, these were midgets compared to their American West Coast cousins, which can grow to over 275 feet (just think, that's more than 25 storeys high). Out of sentiment, I scooped up a bagful of the pendant cones that blanketed the ground, convincing myself that they'd fallen from 'our' chosen trees.

Logging is a hazardous occupation and Forestry Commission consent has to be obtained before a suitably certificated woodsman friend could undertake the felling. We couldn't resist chorusing bits from the Lumberjack Song on each cry of *Timm-berrrrr!*

> *I cut down trees, I eat my lunch,*
> *I go to the la-va-treeee...*

Before they could be fitted on the borrowed 40-foot trailer, the 60-80 foot trunks had to be shortened and shaved of their branches, so quite a lot of work was involved.

Nick had warned a puzzled *Team Polski* to expect another delivery of *drewno*. Not pre-cut planks or beams this time but *duże drzewo*, big trees. Soon they saw what he meant. The forklift heaved the tree trunks to the ground. 'That was

---

47 By John Muir, the Scottish-American naturalist and writer who devoted much time to the preservation of the wilderness.

easy enough,' the team doubtless thought but, as they were soon to discover, it's one thing to deliver the tree trunks to site, another to stand them up and keep them standing.

One approach would have been to concrete the trees *into* the ground, but to avoid foot rot, each pole had to be seated *on top* of the ground. In anticipation, steel brackets had been carefully arranged in a circle then concreted into the plinth so that the base of each post could be stood upright into the bracket and simply bolted in.

At least, that was the theory.

If felling trees is a potentially dangerous and awkward pastime, consider the hazards of the reverse: manoeuvring a sap-heavy, half-ton Douglas fir complete with bark, back into its natural vertical position. The first pole was duly chained to the tines of Nick's fickle *Sambron* telescopic forklift and lifted into the air, where it wavered alarmingly until manually teased into position under Nick's exhortations to 'make Big Power', scaffolding hurriedly erected all around to keep it upright and stop the bottom kicking out.

Uważaj! Watch Out! Words quickly added to our lexicon.

The danger lay in that the height and weight of each pole put it at risk of capsizing. If one fell down, it would pull the rest with it so each had to be hastily scaffolded. Each pole in the circle was to be three feet apart and it was only in the course of raising the second pole that we grasped the problem: the 8-10 foot of scaffolding surrounding the first pole effectively blocked access with the forklift. The scaffolding had to be dismantled and reorganised, the process repeated for pole numbers two, three, four, five six and seven (the circle and centre pole). Cue much cursing in *polski*.

Not helped by another little problem: although we'd selected (we thought) the very straightest of trees, they still had a touch of the 'banana' about them. By dint of scaffolding pipe, rope and much Big Power, they had to be rotated so that any curving tendency faced inward rather than out.

Two days later, the seven poles were in their final position, supported by scaffolding and bolted into those steel claws in the ground.

Nick cheerfully remarked, 'I think we've got the hang of it now'. No translation available.

As a mere onlooker to this drama, I relished the fact that these trees from the local forest created such a connection to the landscape. They would be part of the house forever, just as those skinny bricks from the demolished house carried over from its predecessor would also be absorbed into it. A satisfying continuum.

Chimney stack

Most chimneys are wholly integrated into the structure, but the stack here was to soar skyward on an outside wall, effectively freestanding. The idea was to face a reinforced concrete block core with brick, incorporating possible foothold' for the, as yet, unidentified 'creature'. It was by no means a simple job to lay the concrete blocks as the whole edifice slanted inward from a broad splayed base, but by now, Piet's brick slave Michel had been promoted and put in charge of all things block. He also had to install a clay flue liner as he went, to create a vertically stacked tube (later to be girdled with insulating vermiculite).

Piet worked behind him, facing the blocks with some of the 30,000 bricks reclaimed from the old house. For fun or for fakery, however you look at it, the sooty bricks recovered from the old house were used to line the inner surfaces of the large cavity left for the fireplace.

The triumphs of brickwork that are Elizabethan chimneystacks had inspired Lutyens to deploy chimneys boldly and dramatically. Unfortunately, our own stack, whilst dramatic, risked looking grimly monumental. We'd always planned to attenuate it with a pattern of contrasting bricks (as indeed Nigel had incorporated in the model) and researching this had been a fine excuse for more careering around the countryside. The most inspirational chimneystack was at Otley Hall near Ipswich, a stunning Tudor building described by Nikolaus Pevsner as 'one of the most interesting fifteenth-century and early sixteenth-century houses in Suffolk'. [48] The design we came up with wasn't anything like as elaborate as that at Otley, but then they probably had skilled craftsmen playing at it for months, whereas ours was afforded just a few days of Piet's attention.

We were all wary of irredeemable mistakes so decided that the pattern should initially be assembled *sans* mortar, after which Piet raised his eyebrows by way of enquiry. 'What do you reckon?' Yes, the grey bricks did provide a subtle contrast to the reclaimed reds and alleviated that monolithic quality.

'*Tak*. Do it!' I said.

The question then arose, what to use for grout? Ready-to-use mortar would look too sharp, too modern, the joints making too stark a contrast with the reclaimed brick. The Tarmac 'rep' and his box of mix-to-order samples duly summoned, I chose a muted reddy mix.

This was just one of the questions with which I was being inundated by Nick, the demand for decisions unremitting. One of the unexpected things about building

---

48 Best known for his 46-volume series of county-by-county guides, *The Buildings of England (1951–74)*, Pevsner is often referred to by just his surname.

from scratch is the sheer number of choices that have to be made, all of them with long-term implications.

Pre-empting a building-control query as to how he envisaged securing the 'creature', Nick had asked a puzzled Michel and Piet to incorporate footholds into the structure at what he guessed would be strategic spots. He also clambered over the scaffolding, 40 feet up, to fix three pipes into the top of the concrete core, intending that these could act as sockets for the framework that would one day secure, well what...? Possibly... a dragon...?

Even with the pattern relief, without surrounding walls and roof to give it context, I had to admit that the completed chimney bore a passing resemblance to a commemorative war memorial.

'More like a crematorium,' commented Ikki, while walking his dog.

Rationally, we knew that as long as the chimneystack followed the model, it would work. But doubt set in. Maybe we *had* over-scaled it?

Steady. Keep your nerve, I told myself.

Driftwood sculpture

The upper part of the tower was scheduled to house a staircase to be constructed in situ around that central Douglas fir. But the main circular stairway from hallway to the first landing also needed a pivot. While he could have used that

reserve (eighth) Douglas fir, I'd had the impression that Nick intended to revisit an old tactic by using an old ship's mast as the centre post. Instead, he blurted, 'How about that old tree trunk, you know, the one I – *we* – kept back from the pond?'

How could I forget its twisted and blackened interior?

'So *that's* what you had in mind all along. Well, it could work provided you absolutely guarantee it won't attract spiders...'

'I'm sure spiders wouldn't dare... I'll run it by Bob.'

Although Bob raised his eyebrows (it was still fairly early days of the relationship so he was new to Nick's thought processes), he was amenable to the idea so long as the stair treads wouldn't need to rely on the tree for support. In view of its age, this made sense – elm's interlocking grain is resistant to splitting, but we guessed this tree must have been over 100 years old when it finally died, so now must be about 150. Poking and prodding revealed no sign of rot, so Marek manoeuvred the forklift to raise the 20-foot trunk, complete with bark and loose matter, before plonking it onto the concrete foundation, twisting upward in semblance of a driftwood sculpture.

It certainly caused consternation. One delivery driver was convinced that the tree was actually growing in situ.

'You'd better shift that out of there, mate, before it's too late!'

I had to admit that the site did look fairly bizarre, the incipient building consisting of nothing but a fairy circle of 40-foot-high, bark-covered poles, the bole of a mutilated tree and a menacing bulk of bricks that has been likened to a crematorium. With nothing in between.

'Weird place *that's* going to be!' a passing dog-walker was heard to hiss.

Church + Hall

In England, you're never more than 70 miles from the sea; in Suffolk, you're never more than two or three miles from an ancient church. Of Suffolk's 500 medieval churches recorded in the Domesday Book, 417 survive and they say that on a clear day you can see 50 spires from the top of certain church towers. Once upon a time this meant never being more than a couple of miles from a pub either. Often found cheek by jowl, to this day the public house and parish church tend to form the nucleus of any village, but in Westhall, the Grade I listed St Andrew's is shyly withdrawn from The Racehorse by nearly two miles, something that can confuse unwary guests arriving for weddings, baptisms and funerals.

'Church viewing' is a tourism thread in its own right, but St Andrew's is even largely off that radar. Sometimes referred to as 'one of Suffolk's best-kept secrets', its thatched roof and thirteenth-century tower are tucked away in the easternmost part of the parish, approached by a narrow sloping lane flanked by trees, overgrown embankments and fragments of ancient hedgerow. Leaning tombstones surround the church, itself set in a magical glade overhung with spreading trees through which the wind sighs. A dedicated team keeps its restful simplicity filled with flowers and gleaming pews, despite the best efforts of the resident bats.

Like many ancient edifices, it struggles with the fateful combination of damp oak and deathwatch beetle, to the extent that, in 2003, its roof threatened to collapse. The imaginative church warden launched a fund-raising stratagem by tracking down Episcopal churches dedicated to St Andrew across the Atlantic, offering them a piece of the roof in exchange for a donation of hard cash. 'There's a church of St Andrew in Houston, Texas with a congregation of 2,500,' he pointed out. 'What they do not have in Houston is anything approaching the age and – dare I say it – the holiness of St Andrew's Westhall. A piece of carved medieval timber no longer strong enough to hold up the Westhall roof might make a thank-you present to show off in an American church – once the larvae and eggs have been eradicated.'[49]

'I don't think I've ever seen a church which gave such a vivid impression of the high quality of medieval religious art, its imagination and sheer skill,' one enthusiast has written. [50] The first thing to catch the eye on entering is a sixteenth-century stone font; its gesso-work a rare technique occasionally used on wood but almost never on stone. Consequently, it was chosen to grace the cover of Eamon Duffy's seminal book *The Stripping of the Altars*.

Although damaged, traces of original coloured paintwork remain, but it's not at all clear whether harm resulted from the Reformation or the later iconoclastic work of William Dowsing. [51] Interestingly, while Dowsing's journal diligently recorded destructive operations at many nearby churches, including the famous

49 An article by journalist Aidan Semmens on the appeal launched by Adrian Simpson-James. Of 100 appeal letters sent out to St Andrews churches in the USA, there were three replies, one of which came good and received the promised wood in return.

50 For those interested in medieval churches, this blog is definitely worth a look: aclerkofoxford. blogspot.co.uk/2012/04/wonders-of-westhall

51 As 'Commissioner for the destruction of monuments of idolatry and superstition', he carried out a Parliamentary Ordinance which stated that 'all Monuments of Superstition and Idolatry should be removed and abolished', specifying: 'fixed altars, altar rails, chancel steps, crucifixes, crosses, images of the Virgin Mary and pictures of saints or superstitious inscriptions. This was later widened to include representations of angels, rood lofts and images in stone, wood and glass and on plate. In 1643-4 he visited over 250 churches in Suffolk and Cambridgeshire, removing or defacing such items.

Blythburgh Trinity, Westhall isn't specifically mentioned. Born in Laxfield, just eight miles away as the crow flies, Dowsing left a journal detailing much of his activity. Halesworth for example:

> Hallisworth: *2 crucifixes, 3 of the Holy Ghost, and a 3 of the Trinity altogether; and 200 other superstitious pictures and more; 5 popish inscriptions of brass, Orate pro animabus, and Cujus animae propitietur deus; and the steps to be levelled by the parson of the town; and to take off a cross on the chancel. And then the churchwardens had order to take down 2 crosses off the steeple.* April 5 1644

It is worth mentioning that, driven by the same Puritan impulses, there was a parallel upsurge in witch hunts, the notorious Suffolk-born 'Witch-finder General', Matthew Hopkins and his cohorts being responsible for the deaths of 300 'witches' in Suffolk, four of them in Halesworth.

Dowsing's wasn't to be the last wave of iconoclasm. It is almost impossible to imagine the scale and impact of the later wave of despoliation of medieval church windows and artworks under Edward VI's explicit mandate to 'destroy all shrines... pictures, painting and all other monuments of feigned miracles... so that there remain no memory of the same in walls, glass-windows, or elsewhere within their church or houses.'[52] It was after this that churches became so austere by contrast to the vibrant interiors of the Middle Ages. In truth, it was probably the high cost of reglazing a large church that stayed most hands, so that only the most committed Protestants made genuine efforts to strip churches of stained glass. Suffolk pragmatism.

In Westhall, the Norman west door survives. Just step into the bell tower, walk to the opposite wall and turn round. The elaborately carved doorway before you is the main entrance of the original church – which is barely post-1066 – and beyond that is the original nave, now the south aisle.

The painted rood screen, dating back to 1512, depicts various saints including St Michael, who also happened to slay a dragon. Some panels retain bright colours and on the walls, *scraffiti*, marks like graffiti, are scratched into the bright pigments which often adorned stonework of this period. One of the few ways in which the poor could

---

52 Injunctions by the most Excellent Prince Edward the Sixth by the Grace of God, King of England, France and Ireland, Defender of the Faith. 1547

express themselves, this appears to have been tolerated rather than regarded as vandalism. [53]

I can't resist a digression here about 'the Doom', a hugely significant medieval rood screen to be found just four miles away in the village of Wenhaston. Churches commonly displayed paintings of the Day of Judgement, when individuals were upgraded to Heaven or cast down into Hell. Most Dooms were destroyed in the Reformation but, hastily disguised by whitewash, that of St Peter's Church remained hidden from view and forgotten. During restoration work in 1892, a heap of unwanted boards were dumped outside, ready for burning. Overnight it rained, dissolving the whitewash to reveal the original painting, now considered one of the finest Dooms in the country.

The handsome cedar of Lebanon in Westhall's churchyard is said to mark the site of the communal burial of victims of the Black Death, and evidence of nearby settlement has led to speculation that housing was deliberately burned to the ground in an attempt to prevent the spread of the plague. Yet it is likely that the main agent of the Church's increasing isolation was the changing patterns of living, accelerated by enclosures.

The thing that leaps off an early nineteenth-century map [54] is the number of commons and greens that existed in Westhall: Cox's Common, Mill Common or Great Green, Bacon's Green, Nethergate Green, Davy's or Goose Green. [55] Many commons disappeared completely under the Parliamentary Enclosures of 1859, others were built over. Their names live on: Mill Common, the area to the west of the parish where the essential windmill, pub and smithy were located, evolved into the natural focus of the community, but to the east, the church found itself out on a geographical limb, an effect heightened by the slipping gravitational pull of the local manor, Westhall Hall.

The Hall, located on the eastern edge of the parish, had long been the seat of a powerful noble family, the Bohuns. Indeed, a brass plaque in the church above Nicholas Bohun's 1602 tomb-chest traces the family's descent from Thomas Plantagenet. Nicholas's son, Edmund, produced the monumental *A Geographical Dictionary... of the Whole World* [56], a work of immensely valuable reference in a world where maps were scarce and misinformation rife. Edmund went on to become the first governor of South Carolina.

---

53 The face of Christ can be discerned, along with pentangles and 'daisywheels', which were believed to pin demons to the wall.

54 The Barnes Map of 1812.

55 The names probably a legacy from their origins as blocks of woodland. See *Halesworth – an Ecological Society* by Denis Bellamy & Ruth Downing, 2006 2nd ed. Also published on www.cultural-ecology.com

56 *A Geographical Dictionary, Representing the Present and Ancient Names of All the Countries, Provinces, Remarkable Cities...: And Rivers of the Whole World: Their Distances, Longitudes and Latitudes*, 1668

While the existence of a manor is first recorded in the 1300s, the hall as Edmund Bohun knew it was constructed in 1570, although evidence of its actual appearance is fragmentary. A map of 1665 contains the earliest clue in the form of a small sketch indicating a charming arrangement of corner turrets and a formal garden surrounded by trees. Samuel Wilton Rix's 1853 *Diary and Autobiography of Edmund Bohun Esq.* describes the hall as 'a substantial mansion of red brick... flanked by four octagonal towers... numerous thickly mullioned windows...' accompanied by sketches of brick-arched doorways. Landscape historian, Peter Warner, has created an artist's impression based on the 1665 sketch, Rix's evidence and other sources. [57]

After its acquisition in 1829 by the Earl of Stradbroke, who remodelled the hall in the fashionable Queen Anne style, the axis inevitably veered even further east toward his own Henham Estate and away from Westhall village. Unhappily, the hall was victim to the 1960s trend of demolishing stately piles. American visitors may seek their ancestors in the Church but look in vain for Westhall Hall.

With the void created by the loss of the hall and the physical solitude of the church, a tranquillity and a sense of timelessness has settled over that corner of Westhall. Whereas our site, located on the other side of the Parish, was just a couple of fields away from Mill Common and the less than enigmatic Racehorse and village shop (both of which had learned to keep a healthy stock of cheap vodka).

---

57 An Emeritus Fellow of the College and formerly Senior Tutor, Peter Warner has published *The Origins of Suffolk* and *Seven Wonders from Westhall* amongst other titles.

More Technical Stuff

Although admirably industrious, the resident members of *Team Polski* had three unshakeable habits: hard hats (the *not* wearing of), vodka (the excessive consumption of) and feral cats (the injudicious encouraging of).

It's not as if the cats made satisfactory pets, never once stooping to an affectionate roll around or purr. They wouldn't normally venture out to eat during daylight, but the team couldn't resist offering them scraps, so feline grab-and-run tactics developed in plain view. Nick and I weren't keen on this emboldening process, encouraging, as it would, uncontrolled breeding. Nick's not big into drowning kittens.

Hard hats continued to be a battleground. Despite much urging, not one of them would deign to don one, safety not compatible with *Polski* machismo. Concerned that a spanner could at any time accidentally drop onto an unprotected skull, Nick attempted to concentrate their minds.

'You die, I make big hole with digger and bury you with the fellows who fell last week,' he gestures, pointing to the ground. 'Good for me – no funeral money.'

It made no difference.

The *wódka* problem, while admittedly somewhat moderated from the London days, still reared its head from time to time, especially among the bachelors Marek, Piet, Damien and Wieslow who, driven by a compulsion to follow Poland's progress through the European Football Championships, had rigged up a television. (Poland eventually came bottom of its group, which didn't help vodka consumption either.) They were usually satisfied to knock back a mere half a litre at a time (each) but Damien's body could absorb spectacular punishment, so when one Monday morning, Nick tripped over an empty 1½ litre bottle, he only had to raise a quizzical eyebrow.

'Damien?'

Krzysz nodded.

'One night for drinking?'

Another nod.

We just hoped Tony's Stores wouldn't be left with a surfeit of *wódka* stock after the men drifted away, as had happened at the end of the Chediston Street project. The Angel Hotel had seen its profits balloon during the thirty months' worth of heavy drinking by our Antipodean workforce, who made themselves so much at home, the landlord would go to bed leaving them with the key. Profits nosedived the day they quit town.

Despite these habits, we appreciated *Team Polski's* willing exertions through many demanding manoeuvres.

We took delivery of what we hoped would be our third and final consignment of French oak, in readiness for the serious business of constructing the house frame. 'It's all going to China now,' explained Andrew, justifying why each load had been pricier than the last.

Unlike traditional construction in brick or masonry, timber framing is all about forming a skeleton that will hold together independently of gravity and dead weight. Beams and posts are jointed and braced to keep the whole thing rigid in a way that avoids the need for additional load-bearing walls. The conventional prefabricated timber frame, in which joints are cut, fitted and assembled into sections off-site, means that a frame can be raised in just a few days, peg joints stiffening the whole structure.

In our case, the whole exercise promised to be far more convoluted, the frame-assembly process likely to take weeks if not months. Despite the received view that framing should only be carried out by the experienced and skilled – and blithely ignoring the fact that the 'expert' had dismissed it as unworkable – Nick and *Team Polski* found themselves making judgements on the quality of each and every piece of timber and figuring out every complex joint and intersection. They were already accustomed to using a mixture of materials and extemporising, so quickly adapted. When asked if the workers were skilled in working green oak, Nick's standard reply was, 'No, but they will be when they've finished...'

Actually, the construction of the *core* of the house – that is, those parts of the ground floor that excluded kitchen and the single-storey 'east wing' – was essentially conventional even if Bob's request for additional support in the hallway was dealt with, not by traditional strategically placed uprights, but giant iron brackets salvaged 20 years before from the demolished platform canopy at Lowestoft Railway Station. If anything, Nick erred on the side of caution on this level, with chunkier-than-strictly-necessary beams, six-by-six instead of the conventional six-by-two, and placing them in closer proximity than the norm to reinforce load-bearing capacity.

Thus, the construction of the large hall proceeded in a relatively straightforward manner, making use of traditional mortise and tenon, and lap joints, although the interior would come to give the *impression* of complexity on account of the ever-useful *Glasroc*, a flexible glass-fibre reinforced gypsum board that Nick used to create curved dividing walls.

Next to be tackled was one of Nick's favourite architectural devices, the jettied porch, achieved by oversailing the hallway in a structural trick that relies on the cantilever principle. Diagonal 'dragon beams' took the strain – an appropriate term I thought, before finding that the etymology has less to do with dragons and more with a corruption of 'diagonal'. The room above the porch would project by twelve inches on three sides (and the room on the floor above that would project by a further six). Finally, sandstone columns from Rajasthan offered an apparent prop from below, although strictly speaking, the jetty was self-supporting.

The half-moon kitchen was different again. It would be easy enough to spread ceiling rafters out from the main tie beam to the circumference, that is, the semi-circle of windows. However, to Nick's mild aggravation I declared a preference for a plain (non-timbered) ceiling here. The solution? Instead of rafters, he divided the ceiling into three by installing a pair of I beams, fanning out from said main tie beam to the outer rim, with rafters then slotted into the sides of each I beam, all concealed by plasterboard.

The east wing promised to be trickiest of all. At over 38 feet, it was to splay from thirteen feet at its narrowest point to 35 feet at its widest. Traditionally, such a space would have needed two rows of internal posts, acceptable for a barn perhaps, but to apply such a standard formulation would destroy this lovely open space. It required a technical solution. Time for John Rawlings' engineering expertise. In the meantime, there was plenty to be getting on with...

The cascade of curved roofs and irregular shapes ensured that construction would be a tortuous business. Joints had to be cut on several different planes, every one treated as a one-off. Way past 'banana' explanations, Nick's expositions of 'the daily plan' (that day's work) was greatly assisted through the visual aid of the model which, from its more or less permanent place on the back seat of the car, was regularly consulted for the scaling-off of timbers and exploring resolutions to real-space problems. However, while the model indicated the  placement of principal timbers, it didn't go so far as to demonstrate the complex detailing of intersections. Nick's favoured technique was to make dummy versions of tricksy joints, all discussed and worked out through a garbled mix of *polski* and *angielski*. Inevitably, this contributed to slow progress. It helped that joints were secured with extra long stainless steel coach screws rather than traditionally pegged.

Another difficulty arose where roof joined outer wall. In a traditional frame construction, the upper timbers are lifted in by crane. Here we, perforce, relied on extensions to the tines of the ancient *Sambron* telehandler to raise the timbers to the topmost floor. A squad on the ground ensured that the lifting chains and shackles were positioned properly, while another team was stationed on high to manoeuvre the beam carefully into place, up, down and sideways through the maze of already fixed timbers. Admittedly, a crude yet effective working method, *most* of the time...

The tine extender had been fairly mangled in the days of Trans-Africa truck prep, having then been rebuilt with a heavier metal that had left it with counterbalance problems. When loaded and stretched to its maximum upward/forward reach of 25 feet, the inbuilt weight of the extender – which, after all, would need to lift a half-ton of beam – occasionally caused the back wheels of the *Sambron* to lift clean off the ground, threatening to send its load crashing down through the existing framework. A literal tipping point.

'I need Big Power... where Damien?' Nick shouted, the first time he felt the back tyres begin to lift. Quick! *Szybko!* Everyone leapt onto the back of the *Sambron* and leaned out as if to prevent a yacht keeling over. Even weighed down with Damien, it sometimes failed to cope, in which case the timbers had to be manhandled upward using a system of scaffolding poles and levers. This was hard work and, understandably, *Team Polski* favoured the keeling over approach.

Further headaches continued by virtue of the fact that, to all intents and purposes, the house had five roofs: the tower, the east wing and the conventional A-frame porch were manageable, but that still left two complex

ridges to figure out. (The model came in especially useful here.) Both ridge beams were to connect to the tower at one end but, in only one case, would be supported at the other end by a massive post that had been positioned so as to cut vertically through the entire house. A similar post to support the second ridge would carve up the internal space too much, yet the principal roof beam, which formed the very heart of the roof network, needed to be supported by *something*. Nick's answer was a king post truss, which, acting like a keystone in an arch, would link into the tie beam. Tensile forces on the king post would prevent the principal beam from sagging. So far so good, but then it was a question of how to link the truss to the five rafters that were to fan inwards from the front (outside) semi-circular section of roof. In the end, the ridge beam was placed to cantilever three feet *beyond* the king post truss, offering a place to which the five rafters could

link via a series of complex joints, testing Krzysz and Marek's skills to the limit. To their credit, they pulled it off. Bob was happy.

Marek pointed upward. '*Na górże?*'

Eh? Our dictionary suggested it meant 'at the top'. Top of what? Confusion all round until we realised Marek was referring to 'topping out', a ritual akin to ship naming, common to both Poland and the UK. A ceremony to appease the gods, or, in this case, the tree-dwelling spirits that have been displaced from the living wood. It might not have strictly been the apex (that honour would go to the tower), but it felt as if it was the top of the house and, traditionally, the workers signed the last beam before it swung into place, a small fir tree anchored onto the topmost part. Our gang voted for an offcut of oak instead, although I suspected the whole thing was little more than a pretext for a succession of *wódka* toasts.

Not surprisingly, work continued at safer ground level for the rest of the day.

Having come this far, economics dictated that we concentrate on finishing the barns for the first season. The house was put to bed for the winter (getting on for a year as it turned out), its skeleton shrouded with acres of transparent plastic sheeting, endowing it with an unexpectedly ethereal air.

Opening for Business

Arriving at Felixstowe, each of the containers from India, Malaysia and Bali had been efficiently transported to Westhall. Ironically, the most trying aspect of the whole shipping exercise proved to be the decanting of the two Jodhpur containers at this, their final destination. Several tons of granite and furniture had to be unloaded by Nick's capricious forklift within the allotted two free hours, the surly driver tapping his fingers and brightening only after the second hour, when the money clock began to tick. It meant that everything was pushed, thrust and shoved into the maws of the Green Shed in one enormous heap.

Later, fighting the acres of shrink-wrap, we tried but failed to identify exactly what was in each mysterious box, bundle and bale but, armed with the CD photographs, became adept at ripping a corner off the corrugated cardboard beneath the plastic and peering in with one eye.

'That's one of those dining chairs with brass corners, do you remember?'

And nipping something that felt like an ear, 'I think this must be one of those 'tigers'. Where *are* we going to put *them?*'

Every weekend was spent sourcing appliances for the barns: sinks, taps, cookers, fridges, baths, washbasins, showers. However, as well as functionality, a holiday home should surely emphasise the *holiday* element, that is, offer an escape into another world. I'm mindful of the words of designer Johnny Grey who treated rooms 'as a stage for the acting out of a "play"....'. Bedrooms are perfect for this theatrical treatment and the star of a bedroom has to be the bed.

'Nick made the beds,' I later bragged. To all those who (rightly) suspect a certain lack in the domestic department on his part, this was rather startling. What I meant was that he *constructed* them, from scratch, with whatever materials came to hand. By way of example: a line of ostensibly sound council houses had been condemned, having turned out to be built using a discredited method of steel framing. [58] Passing the demolition site, Nick had struck a deal for

---

58 Airey Houses

20 of the rather elegant hexagonal posts that had acted as porch supports. £1 a pair, if I recall. Ah, that old refrain – 'they'll come in useful one day'.

That day arrived when the posts were discovered during the move to the Green Shed. As one, we exclaimed: 'perfect for four-posters'!

A perennial problem for hotels is how to present a glamorous bedhead when the overall bed size is forever switching between twin and king according to need. Our answer was 'to do it with mirrors'. The Jodphur shipment had included two outsize ornate mirrors, of which only one had survived intact so, for the Upper Barn, Nick worked out an ingenious combination of the intact and salvaged elements.

Too high off the ground for short-legged people, that Chinese bed from Malacca, destined for The Granary, was an entirely different proposition. As well as ceilings and floors, many traditional beds even had a door so that, door curtains lowered, the bed effectively became an independent room. Literally, the *bed-room*. Designed to fit into alcoves, making this bed up with fresh linen would be unworkable so, necessity dictating contrivance, Nick fashioned two somewhat lower beds out of the one, with the surplus ornamental segments kept back for use on window reveals and bath panels.

Authentic storage proved a tad more difficult. In old China, it was considered very insulting to lock the door of a room yet, as wealthy households often contained extended family, servants and concubines, lockable cabinets, trunks and boxes became *de rigeur*. There's not even a word for (unlockable) chests of drawers in Mandarin.

In an episode that almost qualifies for 'shopping adventure' status, we visited son Jaimie in Berlin (where he'd repaired to take advantage of the low business rents). As the sorts of things that are imported into one country can be completely different in another, we couldn't resist a bit of shopping, returning with a haul of Chinese ephemera from vintage playing cards, old fans and cigarette posters to fascinating sepia photographs of pre-Mao society. Not to mention a three-foot bronze dragon for the house.

The Granary also came to enjoy the comforts of a state-of-the-art shower, squashy sofas and modern lighting. As the promotional rubric now hints, it's only 'brushed by the Orient'.

Carved pillars, friezes, fretwork and painted orbs meld into Nick's bedsteads elsewhere. With the help of those Balinese doors, batik bed covers and curtains tied back with trochus shells, the Coach House flirts with the concept of 'Indonesian Idyll'. Hoping to add a dash of old-time travel glamour, I also attached those fake hotel labels from Raffles Hotel to battered leather suitcases redolent of the era of steamships and porters... I knew they'd come in useful one day.

Just-for-fun straplines echo the look of each unit, 'A touch of the Raj' being inspired by that painting which Nick had brought home form London and which I'd so disdained. It looks thoroughly at home over the stone fireplace in the Upper Barn. [59] The Stable became a 'Mughal jewel box', conjuring up the glitzier side of the Maharajah lifestyle and the 'Romancing the East' of the Gate House is simply a play on words: East of England meets Middle East, with a side reference to Romancing the Stone. A bit hodgepodge. Sadly, I failed to find

---

59 My instinct was right. With the help of guest Anthony Simpson-James, it has since been identified as cavalrymen of the 10th Hussars in India and based on an illustration in their regimental history, dated India c.1880.

a way to incorporate the word *Levant,* a term embracing that zone between Eastern Turkey and Egypt which evokes such a sense of far-flung places. It also covers a mélange of *objets*; those Syrian ropes of coloured glass balls, vintage hanging lamp, kilims, Ibrik coffee pots and shisha (hookah) pipe, old Ottoman postcards, and paintings detailing intricate *Kasbah* doorways. Not to mention the Aladdin-style, curly-toed slippers found at a local flea market.

It dawned on me that I was effectively furnishing five houses. The haul from Rajasthan wasn't enough in itself, so furniture had to be sourced from local auctions and antique shops. Raids on personal possessions produced a découpaged bookshelf, Baluchi and Berber rugs, Zambian malachite ashtrays to double as soapdishes, while *Masai* bead baskets hold balls of cotton wool, *Tuareg* leather boxes house playing cards and Ethiopian necklaces find a use as tiebacks.

Zimbabwean metal sculptures pop up in the gardens, as do that pair of 'tigers' which are now allocated guard duty to the Upper Barn.

Table lamps were a problem. It would have been so be easy to fall back on the high street, but the lighting needed to fit the mise en scène while being entirely modern in function. My main source was eBay, supplemented with end-of-line finds from here and there. We had also to find 101 more prosaic items: from carving knives to lemon squeezers, toasters to hair dryers, bread bins, toast racks, loo-roll holders, clocks, table mats, umbrellas, torches, log baskets. The list seemed endless.

Through a friend of a friend, I met the gentle and talented Bee, soon to excel on a mature degree course in textiles. She knew just how to set about transforming that array of embroidered silks from Jodhpur into sumptuous drapes. Once these were hung, we were ready for the VisitEngland/Quality in Tourism inspection. Other than unpacking the kitchen paraphernalia.

'Oh, that won't take long,' I said airily. Prematurely, as it turned out...

Each property needed a 4-star or 5-star award to qualify for inclusion within the *Premier Cottages* portfolio. The prerequisite inspection was booked, but I had utterly underestimated the time spent wrestling crockery, glasses and appliances from nail-wrenching and tiresomely obdurate packaging, so we only just managed to welcome the assessor through the front door as Ewa, Krzysz and Marek slipped out of the back. The assessor warned that 5-star guests could be awkward, demanding and incredibly messy, especially if they had 'staff' at home to pick up after them, wealth often nurturing a sense of entitlement.

'Are you sure you're ready for that?' she asked.
'Lord, we hadn't thought of that. We'll have to risk it.'

The Coach House was duly road-tested by friends who provided an invaluable list of desirable tweaks. But the first to go properly public was the Granary, occupied by the owner of the crisp voice who arrived with husband and the three aforementioned terriers. Happily, they have been regular visitors ever since and not in the least 'awkward, demanding and messy'. Our guests rarely are, so maybe we're simply not classy enough.

At that point, we had no glimmer of any impending crisis. Yet, just two months later, the country plunged into economic meltdown coupled with a global recession of proportions unseen since the 1930s.

Shopping Adventure No. 4

The dragon myth seems to be embedded *everywhere*. Even in Egypt. The tombs of Egyptian kings are said to be watched over by Saharan dragons, embodied by Set, the evil god. The serpent-dragon Apep, personifying darkness and weather chaos, to this day battles to prevent Ra, the Sun God, rising each morning. Thunderstorms, wind and rain (a rarity in Egypt) mean he's won the day.
I had had no thoughts of dragons on my first visit.

We're talking the mid-1970s. When the time came to return to England, after five months coping with my inaugural Trans-Africa, Nick and I booked a flight with the second cheapest airline (after the dreaded Aeroflot), Egypt Air. An extra £5 bought a stopover in Cairo from where we'd thought to follow in the steps of early Thomas Cook tourists, not to mention the archaeologists, writers and painters who flocked to Luxor to enjoy Middle Egypt's mild winters.

Six months without a watch had induced alternative time awareness and we managed to arrive at Jomo Kenyatta airport for the 6pm flight rather than 6am. Luckily, there was also an evening flight, which we were allowed to board but not before a pygmy bow and quiver of arrows – secured by Nick in exchange for a pair of socks in Zaire – had been confiscated and stowed in the flight deck. It was way past midnight by the time we emerged in Cairo, having managed to retrieve the bow and arrows from the captain, whom we tracked down to a bar in the bowels of the airport.

Before the days of travel guides like Lonely Planet, it was a matter of finding your own way. The last bus into the city centre was a good start. I can't recall where or why we got out where we did – wherever that was – complete with luggage and bow and arrows, but perhaps the driver mentioned that it was a district known for accommodation. So it was that we wandered the streets trying to get our bearings in the sweltering night air, passing five youths gathered around a street café table engaged in lively debate, as is the Egyptian way.

'You like ice cream?' they called in English as we passed. (How disconcerting when someone knows your nationality just by looking at you.)

Hot and sticky as we were, this was very tempting.

'Yes please!'

The best ice cream ever. The boys proved to be medical students and one of them asked where we were staying. We had to confess – nowhere! They conferred and offered a solution: we were to be taken to Hamadi's home and given a bed for what remained of the night. But first, would we like to see the Pyramids of Giza by moonlight? You bet.

Seven of us squeezed into Hamadi's decrepit saloon, stretching arms to cling to the handles of the back doors that kept pinging open as we hurtled through the deserted streets, arriving just as the moon emerged from cloud to light up the Sphinx, crouching in the shadow of the Great Pyramid that sits at the very doorstep of the city. Dawn wasn't far off by the time we finished scrambling over the eroded limestone blocks and, risking the car again, found ourselves transported to Hamadi's house. Not possessing an outside key, he rang the bell. His mother opened the door in her night attire, hardly expecting to find her son with a couple of white strangers, complete with bow and arrows. She took it very well. Left to wonder what was happening, we were parked in a side room and later led into a magnificent bedroom. What we hadn't realised was that this kindly woman, in accordance with the mores of Egyptian hospitality, had vacated her bed for us. The delay had been in laying fresh sheets.

The next day we were taken to meet Hamadi's uncle who kept an apartment in Heliopolis.

'What do you plan to do in Egypt?'

We explained that we were keen to take the overnight train to Luxor but weren't sure what to do with our luggage. With further manifestation of Egyptian hospitality, he offered a bed on our return and to keep our bags safely in the meantime. What a relief – we had dreaded hauling the wretched bow and arrows around the sizzling south.

With little signage to help unravel its mysteries, the main Cairo railway station proved a manic experience, but eventually we located a set of rickety wooden carriages, ultimate destination Aswan (the reservoir was still filling following completion of the High Dam in 1970) but stopping at Luxor. And, as it turned out, every tiny station en route. Third-class tickets bought entitlement to slatted wooden benches but little else. On these we perched for 12 hours, as the train lumbered from station to station, the windows long-since stuck shut. So it was that we sagged and flopped in heat that increased with every degree south, heatstroke staved off by the cooled orangeade brought by the succession of children who hopped on at the frequent halts to clamber over comatose bodies and hop off at the next stop, presumably to do it in reverse on the next train up the line. At least semi-dehydration obviated visits to the noisome toilets.

Dawn revealed a strip of green cultivated fields in the middle of desert, and on the far side of the *felucca*-dotted Nile, a wall of red rocks: the former Thebes, once one of the greatest cities in the world.

There was the usual tumult of taxi drivers and chancers waiting to pounce.

'You want cheap hotel?'

Our appearance was evidently a giveaway.

Weak-willed from the journey, we followed one chancer into the inner recesses of the old town and checked into a grimy room on the third floor. In retrospect, it couldn't have been that bad as it boasted an erratic electric fan, even if cockroaches did roam the floor. In the streets, pyramids of watermelons balanced on horse-drawn carts and on every corner small boys dispensed freshly squeezed, ice-cold orange juice while pouncing for the kill: 'You buy old scarabs, very ancient,' to be confounded by Nick's teasing reply, 'Ancient? Sorry, I'm looking for new ones'.

On the right bank of the Nile (the town side) two grandiose temples sat two miles apart: Karnak and the Temple of Luxor, between them an assemblage of pylons, obelisks, columns and colonnades. An avenue of 1350 sphinxes had once connected them, but most had long since disappeared, leaving a sadly truncated line as a reminder of past glories. The staggering vastness of the open-to-the-skies Hypostyle Hall contains 134 columns in 16 rows, many 70 feet tall and 10 feet in diameter. Being the hottest time of year, other visitors had had the sense to stay away, so we were able to slalom unhindered through the mammoth moonlit pillars. The drawback of low season was that we stood to be accosted every other minute by under-employed traders and would-be guides who'd offer to escort us, by taxi, bus or bicycle, to the far bank of the Nile where the Valley of the Kings lay behind rock bluffs. One young man, Omar, seemed marginally less pressing than the others and had a more interesting and inexpensive, pitch: donkeys.

'Alright Omar, meet you here at 6am.'

Sure enough, there he was, waiting with two slightly scabby donkeys festooned with plastic water bottles and a bulbous dripping wet sack.

'What's in there?'

'You'll see.'

The sun rose sharply. No hope of shade as we pressed the donkeys past the Colossi of Memnon and over the parched landscape. Hot. Hot. Hot. Not helped by the fact that more time was spent walking alongside the animals than riding them, donkey tracks tending to use short cuts over crags rather than round them. After puffing up a particularly precipitous path, we arrived at a blessedly cool cave that had been hidden from sight below and, astonishingly, marked with graffiti dating back to 1893.

'Here we rest.'

Omar untied the mysterious sack, long since dried out. A rugby-ball of a watermelon emerged, which we eyed with quivering expectation as Omar cut it into slices. Oh, that cold watery red flesh! (The soaked sacking had enabled it to be chilled by evaporation, the same process that Arabs use to cool water in a goatskin.) Revived, we pulled the unwilling donkeys down yet another vertiginous path, arriving at the bottom of the valley in which squats the massive Mortuary Temple of Queen Hatshepsut (in 1997, the unhappy site of the massacre of 57 tourists by Islamists) then onto the *Biban el-Muluk*, Gate of the Kings, leading to the most famous archaeological site in the world.

This unorthodox approach to the Valley of the Kings and absence of people imparted an illusory sense of discovery. Modest entrances to each of the tombs were cut into the rock wall, giving no sign of the splendours within. In exchange for a few piastres, the 'guardian' would instigate an ingenious method of lighting an interior, holding a piece of broken mirror, angled to reflect the sun's rays down the long tunnels to catch other strategically placed mirrors. In this way, light would be bounced many times deep into the earth, even penetrating to the sarcophagus room, often 100 metres in. No need for any camera flash, that light proved bright enough for even my unsophisticated *Instamatic* to record the frescoes, paintings, hieroglyphics and graffiti covering the walls. Yes, from Roman times onward, graffiti had marked the passage of travellers and pilgrims.

On returning to Cairo, we took up Uncle's offer to stay in his elegant sixth-floor apartment in Biouy Mir Nasar and enjoyed the delicious meals of *kushari* and sweet *konafah* that he would serve up on his roof terrace – although I had to steel myself to visit the dark bathroom as, on pulling the light cord, the walls and floor blurred as cockroaches sought sanctuary behind the cracked tiles. The trick was to stand stock still for half a minute until they disappeared. At least the bathroom boasted a Western type toilet; it can be alarming to straddle a squat version, while feeling cockroaches skittering over one's toes, creating an interesting tension between necessarily motionless feet and the other exigencies of travel...

Pushing that last memory aside, I was enthused about returning some 35 years later. Two days before New Year, Nick had blithely uttered the words, 'Let's get away'.

'Bit late isn't it? Still, I'll see what's available.'

This turned out to be a week in Luxor, this time in a 5-star hotel reached by direct flight rather than train. Unlike blistering June, January means pleasant temperatures. This climatic benignity resulted in a full hotel, queues everywhere and side streets that were no longer silent. The food and fresh orange juice were just as delicious though and this time we could afford to eat in actual sit-down restaurants.

We did the 'tourist thing', hitting the west bank of the Nile by bus rather than donkey. Of course, it had all been modernised and, quite rightly, steps taken to protect the tombs from being loved to death. After all, thousands of sweating visitors inevitably create a miasma of humidity that blisters the very paint and plaster. Yet, it was an oddly disassociated experience, what with the long queues treading on raised wooden walkways, glass panels over the walls and electric lighting.

'I'm so thankful for our earlier experience of this place,' I mused, remembering those days of casually mooching around tombs lit solely by sunlight sent deep into the earth by those cunningly placed shards of mirror.

Hot-air balloons over Luxor certainly hadn't existed back then, so our ride over the west bank of the Nile was a first, memorable (to me) as much for my inglorious exit from the basket as for the aerial view of the desert. The excellent Luxor Museum was another fresh feature and this time we attended the rather portentous *son et lumiere* at Karnak Temple. The authorities had committed to rebuilding the complete line of ram-headed and human-headed sphinxes that had originally connected Luxor to Karnak, a controversial project as it meant the compulsory purchase of homes and businesses to clear the way. [60]

The trip climaxed with Abu Simbel, 240 miles to the south. We were the only souls on the bus, its military escort a hangover from that 1997 incident, and the site itself was quiet so there were no queues or razzmatazz to diminish the overwhelming presence and power emanating from the colossal rock-cut statues of Rameses II. The complex engineering involved in re-siting the temples (to avert submerging into Lake Nasser) was just as monumental in its way, but we searched in vain for serious literature on the subject. The artistic heritage was nothing less than fabulous, but Egypt should also highlight the engineering achievement involved.

Purchases reflected our changed circumstances. Instead of cheap little soapstone scarabs and gaudy perfume bottles, we found hanging lanterns straight out of *One Thousand and One Nights,* quality David Roberts prints [61] and dramatic quilted appliqués, their design based on Islamic motifs. Appliqués had originally been associated with tent-making, but as demand for tents fell, the tentmakers (always male) turned to making pieces to be hung in the streets, event spaces for weddings, pilgrimage celebrations and political rallies, as well as items for the home such our bedspreads. It takes many weeks to complete even one piece, during which, we're told, work never stops, even for food and drink.

Augmented by those accretions from elsewhere in the Levant, these finds were destined for the Gate House.

This later story was heartening.

Although relatively small as volcanic flare-ups go, the ash cloud created by the 2010 eruption of Eyjafjallajökull in Iceland closed European airspace for

60 This project has now been completed. However, the Governor of Luxor has been accused of destroying an enormous amount of archaeological data through indiscriminate use of bulldozers.

61 A nineteenth-century Scottish artist especially known for his series of detailed lithographic prints of Egypt, Nubia and the Holy Land.

six days, creating the highest level of air-travel disruption since World War II. Somhow ironic to receive a *cri de coeur* from a couple whose honeymoon flight to Egypt had been cancelled. In the Gate House, they found the sense of 'away' that they'd sought.

Who needs a honeymoon abroad?

Fleshing the Bones

Banking crisis. Credit crunch. CBI warnings. Rising unemployment. Plummeting shares. Falling FTSE. With all this bad news, we feared that our workforce would join the incipient drift back to Poland. For their part, perhaps they worried that we lacked the wherewithal to carry on and Krzysz and Ewa must surely have felt that they'd misjudged their move to UK. All we could do was stumble on and hope that the housing market didn't crash too hard so as to irredeemably devalue Wissett Place, on whose sale we relied to discharge the mortgage that was financing the whole operation. We assumed that market forces would be against us on the holiday front too, but now that the lets were complete, we could, at least, hope for a dribble of revenue.

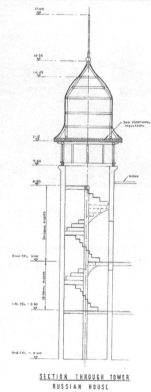

The next step was to put flesh on the bones of the house, or in building parlance, create 'the envelope'.

The tower still had its original encirclement of scaffolding, although the necessary working platforms for materials across the house required nine 'lifts' (that's a lot, I'm told).

By that point, the trees that formed the tower had been left unclad for over a year and the Douglas firs had started to dry out, making it easier to peel off the bark.

The first puzzle was how to set about installing wooden floors on the first, second and top levels of the tower. Nick and John's solution was to brace each of the six posts of the circle against its neighbour and to the centre with oak. Imagine

SECTION THROUGH TOWER
RUSSIAN HOUSE

a wheel rim and spokes running from rim to the central (seventh) pole.

For good measure, each was 'pegged' with a six-inch, stainless steel coach screw and secured with a lump of angle iron. They wouldn't be going anywhere.

'Very ingenious,' acknowledged Bob, in approving John's technical drawing.

A way had to be found to translate the derided 'policeman's helmet' into reality. Creating a shape not unlike a traffic cone, Krzysz bolted wooden struts onto the top of each of the poles. He then cut plywood into varying shapes with which we experimented, Nick holding them against the sky from as high a piece of scaffolding as he could, while I squinted from the bottom of the drive, trying to visualise the overall silhouette at a larger scale. Not exactly fine engineering. Even when we decided on the theoretical shape, it was a matter of devising a method to achieve it. In the end, Krzysz cut forty identical slices of thick plywood and nailed them vertically into place around the required diameter.

After laying short horizontal battens, Krzysz passed the tile-laying to Marek who remembered to install the 'owl hotels' (as he called the owl boxes). He cheated a little, putting a dab of cement on the back of each tile as an extra guard against slippage. After all, it wouldn't be a matter of getting the ladder out every time a tile slipped; more a question of hiring a crane.

'By the time we're done, we'll know how to do it,' was still Nick's annoying mantra.

The last nine feet of the dome finally covered with lead, it was topped with a well-anchored eight-foot spike made from a section of steel scaffold pipe doubling as lightning rod. At least 65 feet from the bottom of the tower to the very tip, when seen from below, the leaded section appeared deceptively foreshortened. A mini landing under the cupola offers a 360° panorama, not to mention a G&T viewing platform, with a distinct air of *Rapunzel Rapunzel, let down your hair!*

At that time, a rumour doing the rounds was that the building was to be a mosque.

Even the routine job of laying roof tile battens was complicated by the curvatures and it took nearly as long to tile the small snaking section that connects the porch to the tower as to tile the entire rectangular porch itself. The south- and east-facing roofs were divided by a valley, and each tapered to a point, meaning the higher from the gutter, the more the tiles had to be cut to fit the shape.

Reclaimed tiles have a character lacking in machined versions, but their kinks and twists added to Marek and Krzysz's battle to achieve consistency – even trickier to judge when they couldn't exactly stand back to see how it looked!

Big Bad Wolf

We had been deferring a decision on the heating front. Unfortunately, enviro-friendly choices tend to involve heavy capital outlay with long pay-back times – sustainability comes at a cost. We needed to find the sweet spot between the outlay and benefit. In the immediate future, we could certainly take one of the most effective steps to sustainability: insulation. But insulating materials would have to earn points on practicality, cost and green credentials, so the contenders were narrowed down to shredded recycled newspaper or sheep's wool, both of which have suitably low U values. A roof space full of moths wasn't too appealing, but when we found that moth-proofed sheep's wool was available, its breathability and fire-resistant properties won the day. A triple layer followed a first skin of factory-reject *Celotex* (as used in the barns), perfect for cutting up to fit the roof's innumerable odd shapes.

Straw converts carbon dioxide into oxygen within its life cycle and, with its super insulating qualities (a U value of 0.13), it is the epitome of sustainability. We planned to use it as infill between the timbers along the whole of the back wall and much of the tower. Moreover, it is non-toxic, robust and cheap (or free when gathered from one's own fields, as here). There's no way the Big Bad Wolf could *really* have blown down a house of straw! Whatever insulating material is used, the trick is in the close butting up to timbers and the sealing of gaps, especially at ground level. As warm air rises, it draws cold air in through cracks at the bottom, the effect getting more powerful the taller the building. (When skyscrapers were first developed, revolving doors had to be invented because cold air rushed in with so much pressure that it was difficult to pull the doors in from the outside or push them open from the inside.)

So, energy efficiency requires a tight build shell, but then again, good air quality requires fresh air, ideally not from random draughts. Heat-recovery systems provide the ideal balance between airtightness and controlled ventilation, but whether directly ducted or integrated into whole house systems (utilising heat from moist air extracted from wet areas), such a system didn't fit our ad hoc approach. They're designed for *organised* people.

Little attention was paid to airtightness in older homes and even now, it can be difficult to achieve where timbers, acting as a cold bridge, are exposed on both sides of a wall. Consequently, it's considered good practice to wrap the envelope around the whole outer skin of the frame, but Piet had been nogging a traditional herringbone pattern of bricks between the kitchen wall timbers, meaning that the entire inside face of the kitchen wall would have to be treated as a whole if it was to be airtight. Leakage invariably occurs around windows, doors, lights, electrical outlets, vents and even holes drilled for pipes and wires, so all must be well and truly sealed if to pass the mandatory air-pressure test that nowadays precedes the issue of the building regulation 'signing off' certificate.

Then there was the question of hot water. While we knew from the experience with the barns that solar panels worked well, we had also learnt that a supplemental source is desirable when the sun isn't in evidence. So, it was back to determining what that supplemental source was to be. Although we had taken the decision to heat the barns with an oil-fired system for entirely pragmatic reasons, it had proved surprisingly cost efficient, to which we attribute the prodigious levels of insulation. Even so, we elected to take another route with the house: a log-burning biomass boiler was the front-runner as it provided the opportunity to utilise wood coppiced on our own land, although wood-pellet fed biomass has become increasingly popular. The disadvantage of both is that the equipment is space-hungry and, looking into the future, a solid wood boiler would require a healthy body to do all that chopping, fetching and carrying.

Ground source heat pumps draw on the relatively stable temperature of the Earth, transferring heat energy from one place to another by way of a closed loop of refrigerant, which repeatedly condenses and evaporates. While initially enthusiastic about a GSHP, we were deterred by the heavy, up-front installation costs as well as running the necessary electric pump – there's no point if the amount of energy consumed by the system exceeds the energy saved. Geothermal is commonplace in other climes, but we remained unconvinced of its ultimate cost-benefit in Britain. A further alternative was electricity-generating photovoltaic panels, but an array sufficient for space heating would be hugely costly. [62]

The only thing we *were* sure about was that heating would be delivered via an underfloor system, especially good for evenly warming high-ceilinged open spaces. Warm water circulates from the boiler (whatever that would end up being) via pipes set under the specially constructed floor. As well as low running costs, it dispenses with wall-hung radiators and all the creaks and groans of traditional piping.

We continued to dither...

---

62 This was before the Renewable Heat Incentive of April 2011 came into being, which provided for feed-in tariffs for domestic systems and consequently made them much more affordable.

Shipwrecks & Stairs

We had a shipwreck to thank for much of the wooden flooring. A freighter coming in from the Far East had foundered off Gibraltar, its cargo of hardwood destined for use as lorry trailer decking (pre-dating the heavy-duty plywood used nowadays) needed to be hurriedly salvaged to allow the ship to be raised. As a result, hundreds of tons of 30-foot long mahogany boards had been clogging up the Gibraltar wharfs. Desperate to be rid of it, the harbour authorities offered it virtually free to anyone who would take it away. Enter a Norfolk dealer. He chartered a ship to haul it all back to King's Lynn and thence in 175 truckloads to his yard, which it clogged up instead.

Consulting his 'contacts book', the dealer noticed that he'd once got rid of a consignment of water-stained marine ply to Nick, for use in preparing trucks for Africa.

'I've got a shipful of wood. I know you'll want it when you see it, it's good stuff. Are you interested?'

Needless to say, Nick was interested.

After utilising it over many years on various projects, the question was now, would there enough left for the house? We concluded that there should be sufficient to stretch to a couple of bedrooms.

These were 'half-lap' planks. Unlike tongue and groove, a gap is left between each board as it butts another, the gap usually filled with oakum, a fibre recycled from old tarry ropes. We left the boards as laid, that is, with the gaps unfilled. Sanded, waxed and buffed, the trailer decking floor looked rather classy, and in the end, stretched to three bedrooms. But not the landing.

Nick looked to see what else was lurking 'round the back' to use for it. Ah yes, those narrow pine boards...

Some years before, he'd been asked to convert a deconsecrated Methodist chapel into a house. This already had beautifully patinated panelling to dado-rail height and, wanting to coordinate a new mezzanine floor, he'd hunted throughout the county for a match. Passing a local village hall in process of demolition (to be rebuilt with a Lottery grant), he'd spotted the very thing.

'How about I take those panels against what you owe me?' he proposed to the demolition contractor, a dodgy scrap merchant who owed him money. From the corner of his eye he'd also noticed some floorboards heaped in the skip, their age and lustre lost under grit and sand.

'You having a laugh...?'

It pained Nick to have to produce hard cash for the panels, but at least he was able to liberate the floorboards, the contractor not seeing any value in those at all.

Painstakingly cleaned by Marek, he proceeded to lay them on the landing.

So far, the flooring consisted of part village hall, part shipwreck. (Overall, as shall be seen, the house floors would end up being an amalgam of these boards, surplus Rajasthani granite and concrete slabs.)

This work highlighted the tedium of constantly shinning up and down temporary ladders. As far as I could see, no spiders had dared emerge from the tree trunk, which was now calling out for stair treads. Helical castle staircases were invariably built to rise in a clockwise direction so that the central post would obstruct an attacker's sword arm, while the defenders swiped downward. The configuration of the tree trunk dictated the same pattern, handy should we ever need to defend our upper floors against marauders. Marek and Piet fitted generously proportioned curved steps of reclaimed pitch pine (supported by wooden 'legs' from below (except where suspended from the ceiling over a slice of the kitchen) and the stairwell was then enclosed to waist height with curved *Glasroc*.

The next step was to plaster it, but before that could be done, there was the dreaded first-fix wiring. I'm always reading that 'lighting should be integral to the design from the beginning' and that one is supposed to create detailed lighting plans, but frankly it's difficult to know where wall lights, switches and sockets should be positioned before the final furniture layout is decided. Jon Lewis had become adept at retrospective wiring, but I felt ahead of the game for once in asking him to install LED lights alongside every stair tread prior to plastering.

Contrary to all contemporary groovy designer wisdom, I remain a fan of traditional centre lights. Old hat they may be, but they're a practical and effective light source when augmented by uplighters and accent lamps. Sadly, apart from the vaulted ceilings of the top room and the east wing, most of our ceilings weren't high enough to accommodate lanterns or chandeliers.

Eventually, the stairwell half-wall was topped with a handrail fashioned from iron tie rods saved from the Chediston Street warehouses. Making these, including rails for a further two sets of stairs, exemplified the exacting effort that attended this stage. The eight-foot long, one-inch diameter rod had to be bent on two planes simultaneously in order to follow the stairs round *and* up. Metal is

usually manipulated through the application of heat, but a trial run with an oxyacetylene gas torch, which can only deal with a couple of inches at a time, merely produced a series of kinks. Luckily, Nick found that the rod could be bent cold when levered between the tines of the digger bucket. The problem was in judging the degree of bend, so there was nothing for it but to keep trying it in situ. In and out, up and down, until it snuggled neatly against the wall. With a final flourish, the newel posts were capped with cast-iron balls that had once adorned the railings at Lowestoft fire station.

At this point, the landing was still open to the stairwell and much to our alarm, given the hard hat (lack of) saga, tools dropped off the edge with worrisome regularity. So, hurrah, finally, it was fitted with metal spindle balusters topped with oak.

Even those spindles had a history. Some years ago, Nick had converted a rather magnificent barn and had later been commissioned to make and erect railings around two enormous ponds in the grounds. Each time the barn changed hands thereafter, he was paid to either take them down or re-erect them. The cycle eventually ended with the much-handled railings tossed in the nettles 'round the back' from where they emerged to be used on the bridge and then here.

Station 365

Google Earth views provide a snapshot in time. Unfortunately, that's not in real time. The 'snap' of Belle Grove Farm had been shot just a few weeks after the excavation of the ponds, revealing sad pools of water surrounded by a jumble of part-demolished buildings, mud, construction materials and the detritus of decades of farming. Hardly reassuring to prospective visitors who must be mindful of press exposés of half-built hotels in dodgy Spanish resorts. Then there was the wartime airfield off to the side. It looked rather close, understandably generating enquiries from potential guests as to the noise effect of low-flying aircraft... This was because the runways and perimeter track of a former military airfield featured on the satellite imagery.

Thinking about it, the construction of RAF Halesworth (Holton) and the many other dromes in the area must have created colossal upheavals. Brand new airfields were rarely sited on handy pieces of wasteland, so farms were vulnerable to requisition. Rubble from bombed cities, used as hardcore along with hoggin from nearby cliffs, was delivered by clattering trains and noisy lorries around the clock, shattering the peace of the hitherto tranquil countryside even before the skies filled with aircraft.

By the time air personnel arrived, the landscape had changed forever – ditches filled in, trees cut down and hedgerows grubbed out. As most young people were in the forces, much of this work was carried out by local women and older people, bulldozers and scrapers only then coming in to level the land. The cement runways were also laid by hand and painted to hide them from the air. [63] From a mosaic of fields, rural Suffolk morphed into a mosaic of military establishments.

Of the early intake of American airmen, one recalled: 'a day or two later we reached Halesworth. The sirens were going off... and then it seemed the whole sky was lit up with searchlights. Guns going off... tracers flying and planes

63 As mentioned in *The War at my Door,* edited by Dick Wickham.

falling...' [64] (To his consternation he discovered that those planes were American, having been shot down by German fighter planes.)

Three million military personnel passed through Suffolk during World War II, 3000 of them at Station 365, as RAF Halesworth was known, where they occupied rows of basic Nissen huts. This 'friendly invasion' had a huge impact. Admittedly, few locals would be invited along to grand occasions when star performers such as the Glenn Miller Band would play in the main hangar, but many civilians luxuriated in the invaders' generosity in the form of nylons, butter, cigarettes and chocolate. Children, including the 30 or so evacuated from Essex and billeted in Westhall, enjoyed the unknown treats of chewing gum, peanut butter and Coca Cola. Thus, the Yanks came, saw and conquered – the local ladies anyway, if tales whispered discreetly in the back row of today's WI meetings are to be believed.

Getting away from the base was high on every serviceman's list but not easy to achieve on account of the heavy training schedule. Bicycles were the standard form of private transport, but even while complaining about the British weather and the 'goddam mud' (and warm beer), the stylish Yanks refused to contemplate wearing the customary cycle clips and simply rolled up their trousers. It's well known that signposts were removed with the aim of inhibiting the movements of invading German forces. Perhaps not so well known is that this contributed to the alarming frequency with which US airmen got lost. (Lack of signposting meant that it was also far from easy for those delivering essentials to find their destinations, especially given the reluctance of locals to give directions to strangers.)

---

64 Tom Baker from *A History of the 489th Bomb Group* pub 1989 by Lt Col 'Charlie' Freudenthal, Group Bombardier.

Close to the coast, Station 365 was ideal for fighter escort missions. As well as the odd bit of strafing and dive-bombing, 56th Fighter Group took on this role to become the highest scoring American group. Aircrew were rarely briefed in advance, but a local lad who worked in the combat mess was able to tip them the wink. 'If the crew got real eggs for breakfast, it were a 'bad' (particularly dangerous) mission but if powdered egg it were 'good'.' [65]

Unsurprisingly, the station and environs became a target for retaliation. Presumably, it had been on one of those reprisal raids that German bombs off-loaded onto Belle Grove Farm.

B-24 Liberators of the 489th Bombardment Group succeeded the Fighter Group and the skies of Suffolk became the arena for the 'assembly' of bombers from different stations across the region. But how to muster multiple groups operating under radio silence? A problem solved by deploying Assembly Ships, older planes painted in a unique and highly visible manner behind which the crews would make the formation for which they'd intensively trained. That serving Station 365, Lil Cookie, was adorned with outsize polka dots.

One of many schoolboys bearing witness, leading aviation historian Roger Freeman, recorded a moment in February 1945. 'It was a freezing morning with excellent visibility. Two columns of bombers were going out, which I could see by the contrails. I counted 28 formations, and knew there'd be about 40 planes in each. So I was looking at more than 1,000 planes – 10,000 men – going to war.' He also noticed the brightly coloured patterns for unit identification. 'They looked like knights in armour,' he wrote [66]

Joe Kennedy, Jnr, the elder brother of John F. Kennedy and the family's prime presidential hope at that time, was one of two aircrew on what was a top-secret operation out of Suffolk using pilotless, explosive-laden Liberators to attack enemy establishments. The crew would fly to 2,000 feet, set course and bail out with the intention that the aircraft continue on its heading and crash into its target. This time something went horribly wrong.

A spectator later described his horror as the plane exploded in a huge fireball over nearby Blythburgh: 'I vividly remember seeing burning wreckage falling earthwards, while engines with propellers still turning and leaving comet-like trails of smoke continued along the direction of flight before plummeting down'.

---

65 An interviewee of Marjorie Shiers as part of an oral history project.

66 *The Mighty Eighth: a History of the U.S. 8th Army Air Force* by Roger Freeman pub. 1970.

After a noise like a double thunderclap, the fireball changed to 'an enormous black pall of smoke resembling an octopus...', shedding burning fragments over Halesworth and Southwold. [67] (The event was filmed from the Perspex nose of a Mosquito aircraft piloted by one Colonel Roosevelt, the son of the then President.) [68]

RAF Metfield is six miles in the other direction and remembered to this day for a devastating self-inflicted blow. In 1944, a colossal explosion, heard up to 40 miles away, rocked the countryside. A contemporary account talks of being blown flat by the blast from a distance of three and a half miles. Windows in Halesworth's main street were blown out and plaster dislodged from ceilings. It seems that a high-explosive bomb had accidentally detonated while being handled, in turn setting off 1,200 tons of high-explosive incendiary bombs, killing five men and wrecking five B-24 bombers.

Suffolk civilians came under renewed attack in the war's latter stages, with the advent of V-1s (or doodlebugs as they were unaffectionately called) launched from out in the North Sea by the enemy. Initially, no one quite knew how to respond on hearing the 'buzz', one individual leaping into the nearest ditch, which happened to be brimming with stinging nettles, while another hoped to derive protection by standing behind a telegraph pole (he was considerably thicker than the pole in question). [69] If an engine cut out overhead, it was a matter of diving under the kitchen table.

In due course, the 489th were redeployed to the Pacific theatre of war. The US Emergency Rescue Squadron moved in with Catalina amphibians for air-sea

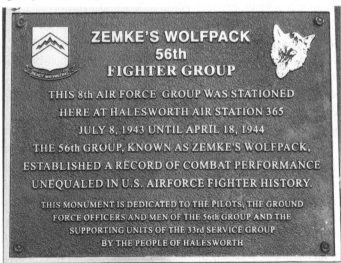

ZEMKE'S WOLFPACK
56th
FIGHTER GROUP

THIS 8th AIR FORCE GROUP WAS STATIONED
HERE AT HALESWORTH AIR STATION 365
JULY 8, 1943 UNTIL APRIL 18, 1944
THE 56th GROUP, KNOWN AS ZEMKE'S WOLFPACK,
ESTABLISHED A RECORD OF COMBAT PERFORMANCE
UNEQUALED IN U.S. AIRFORCE FIGHTER HISTORY.

THIS MONUMENT IS DEDICATED TO THE PILOTS, THE GROUND
FORCE OFFICERS AND MEN OF THE 56th GROUP AND THE
SUPPORTING UNITS OF THE 33rd SERVICE GROUP
BY THE PEOPLE OF HALESWORTH

---

67 Mick Muttitt in his contributions to *The Poaching Priors of Blythburgh,* published by The Blythburgh Society in 2002.

68 All this came to light 16 years later in an article in the *Daily Mail* about the Kennedy family.

69 *Op. cit. The War at my Door,* edited by Dick Wickham.

rescue work, the airfield also used as an operational training base for Mustang P-51 fighters.

Then they were gone. After VE Day in 1945 the 'Yanks' left as quickly as they'd come. It must have been quiet without them. Memorials to these groups and squadrons stand close to the old airfield, dedicated to those American servicemen who served at Halesworth during World War II.

Suffolk remains a magnet for aviation buffs. Although most wartime airbases have been ploughed up, enthusiasts have preserved some runways and control towers. At Halesworth, the Ministry of Food occupied the airfield until the Le Grys brothers turned it into a poultry farm, later acquired by turkey impresario, Bernard Mathews. A memorial museum opens on Sundays, and on bank holidays an aviator throws his P51 Mustang about the sky in thrilling aerial acrobatics.

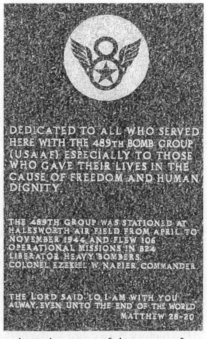

DEDICATED TO ALL WHO SERVED HERE WITH THE 489TH BOMB GROUP (USAAF) ESPECIALLY TO THOSE WHO GAVE THEIR LIVES IN THE CAUSE OF FREEDOM AND HUMAN DIGNITY

THE 489TH GROUP WAS STATIONED AT HALESWORTH AIR FIELD FROM APRIL TO NOVEMBER 1944 AND FLEW 106 OPERATIONAL MISSIONS IN B24 LIBERATOR HEAVY BOMBERS COLONEL EZEKIEL W NAPIER COMMANDER

THE LORD SAID LO, I AM WITH YOU ALWAY, EVEN UNTO THE END OF THE WORLD
MATTHEW 28-20

I couldn't help but observe that this sight elicited a respectful response from *Team Polski*. Tending to be branded as 'ferocious' triggermen, several Polish pilots flew operationally with the fighter squadrons. According to the son of Polish air ace Witold Lanowski, who served at Halesworth for a time, the RAF High Command had to specifically request that they refrain from ramming the enemy when they run out of ammunition and many Polish fighter pilots refused to count the shooting down of an enemy plane as a 'hit' unless the pilot was dead. 'This may seem harsh... but you need to put yourself in their shoes, they were fighting for their freedom, the destruction of the occupier of their homeland and also they were fighting for the freedom of the country that had taken them in, namely England.' [70]

I was moved that this special Polish contribution remained meaningful to the succeeding generations who had again arrived on our shores, this time in search of economic betterment.

---

70 www.witoldlanowski.com

Cross Atlantic

The wartime interchange of cross-Atlantic cultures might be seen as a continuum of the long connection between Suffolk and America. That the names of Suffolk, Norfolk and Essex were given to New England 'counties' is no coincidence. You'll remember that Edmund Bohun of Westhall Hall was made first governor of South Carolina in 1698, but the Suffolk influence over events goes back even further.

Take Bartholomew Gosnold from Grundisburgh. He may not be well known in the history books, but in the early 1600s Spain was storming the New World, and if it hadn't been for Gosnold's like, the eastern seaboard could easily have fallen under permanent Spanish dominion. In 1602, he pioneered a sailing route west from the Azores to what is now Maine and Cape Cod, founding Martha's Vineyard. With insufficient provisions to overwinter, Gosnold was forced back to England. Shakespeare is said to have based the geography of *The Tempest* on accounts of his voyage.

From the family seat at Otley Hall (the same Otley Hall as that of the chimney), he obtained backing for another ambitious voyage and invited along a fellow East Anglian, John Smith who, as later leader of the Virginia Colony based at Jamestown, is considered to have played a crucial part in founding the first permanent English settlement in North America. As the first English explorer to chart that area, his maps played a very significant role in encouraging English colonisation of the New World.

Emigration to the New World was also a means for Puritans to escape persecution. John Winthrop, yet another authoritative Suffolk-born figure, led the first significant wave of migrants a few years after the initial establishment of the Plymouth colony. The authoritarian and conservative nature of the colony where he served as governor, and his vision of the 'city upon a hill'[71] came to dominate political discourse. 'Unconstrained democracy,' he said, was

71 As set out in *A Modell of Christian Charity*.

'the meanest and worst of all forms of government.' His writings continue to influence a long list of politicians today including John Kerry and George Bush Snr. Make of that what you will.

Emigrants from nearby Southwold, Walberswick and other parts of Suffolk tended to be driven by economic impulse rather than ideology, although political heft was added by Suffolk-born Nathaniel Ward who, on emigrating to Massachusetts in 1643 and perceiving that the liberty of the individual was as nothing without law and justice, formulated a code of fundamental principles based on common law, Magna Carta and the Bible. It is said that this code lies at the root of the Constitution of the United States. So you see, this small corner of England has had a disproportionate influence on developments in the New World and therefore globally.

America returned the favour in World War II.

That hadn't been the end of it. The post-war stream of American visitors may have turned into a trickle (most veterans are no longer alive) but later generations are identifying an interest in the military past of their fathers and grandfathers. Just as Westhall had once had a Hall, so Station 365 had had Holton Hall (the USAAF headquarters), and just as those in search of ancestral connections seek in vain for Westhall Hall, those formerly billeted at Holton Hall or on a pilgrimage to their past, are disappointed to discover that it was demolished in the 1950s.

To return to Google Earth and the old airfield – I'm always gratified to be able to assure enquirers that, other than the odd crop-sprayer and helicopter, there have been no flights from those runways since 1946.

Draco Dormiens Nunquam Titillandus

It's one thing to think 'Let's put a dragon on the chimney'; it's quite another to work out what it should actually look like.

Research was needed.

Until opening the imaginary box marked 'dragons', I had never grasped the distinction between those of the East and their Occidental cousins. European versions sport wings and baleful personalities. Chinese dragons are more beneficent and resemble large wingless snakes. Associated with spirituality and wisdom rather than malevolence, their ability to fly is attributed to mysticism.

Claws are hugely significant: the first Ming Emperor decreed that his dragon emblem must have five toes (claws) whereas four-clawed dragons were deemed suitable for nobility – other ranks and the general public were only permitted three. Indeed, improper depiction of claws was considered treason, punishable by execution of the offender's entire clan. (With counterparts across East Asia, a quick identifier is that a Chinese dragon has five toes, a Korean has four and a Japanese, three.)

'Frequency illusion' is where something you just found out about seems to crop up everywhere. Previously unnoticed, suddenly there were dragons at every turn.

On a visit to Barcelona, for example, there they were, 400 or so dragons fashioned in wrought iron, wood and mosaic, lying in wait below eaves, cornices and balconies and camouflaged in lamps, plinths and door handles. Dragons were a recurring motif in Gaudi's work, larger examples being the backbone of the dragon on the roof terrace of Casa Batiló and the famous Dragon Gate.

Our research programme included scrutinising the details of that Dragon Gate. Ignoring the rainwater positively squelching through shoes and dripping down collars (a hazard of winter breaks), we tracked it down to the Güell Summer Pavilion, where its five-metre wingspan magnificently straddles the entrance to the gardens. As the gate opened, it raised its leg and brandished its claws much as *Ladan*, the hundred-headed dragon on which it was based, had protected the golden apples of the Hesperides.

With its jagged teeth and forked tongue filling its gaping mouth, its presence was perhaps a bit too

menacing, not quite the model we were looking for. Even so, I popped some postcards into my file marked 'Dragons Here'.

In the Polish city of Kraków (having taken instructions from Ewa as to Polish manners and good places to eat), we found that a dragon had lived in a cave at the foot of Wawel Hill. The cathedral on the hilltop features a statue of the dragon, together with a plaque commemorating its defeat by the prince who built a palace right over its lair.

More postcards!

We had had no idea, on entering the Banqueting Room of Brighton's Royal Pavilion, that its highlight is the spectacular dragon chandelier. Weighing one ton, this hangs from the claws of a silvered dragon at the apex of the ceiling while below, six smaller dragons breathe light through lotus glass shades. Painted dragons are also found in the chinoiserie-style Music Room, where windows are dressed with opulent blue silk-satin, braced by carved fire-breathers.

I added yet more postcards to the collection.

Eventually it dawned on me that dragons were actually to be found on the carved pew backs and bench ends of medieval churches all over Suffolk, the wealthy wool tycoons of the time just as keen to flaunt their patronage through prestigious sculpturing as the modern moguls who engage fashionably flamboyant architects.

Returning from scrutinising those at All Saints in Wordwell, I even managed to trip over a dragon in the gardens of Ickworth House. Made from gnarled roots and tree stumps, it appeared to be dozing but perhaps was waiting to devour those who flagrantly ignore the Hogwarts [72] dictum *'Draco dormiens nunquam titillandus'*. Never tickle a sleeping dragon... (I didn't.)

---

72 The fictional Hogwarts School of Witchcraft and Wizardry in J. K. Rowling's Harry Potter universe.

My 'Dragons Here' file was beginning to bulge, yet a definitive image eluded me.

I'm ashamed to admit that, up to that point, I had been unaware of Norwich's remarkably strong association with dragons. Two medieval churches are dedicated to St George and the first floor of the medieval Dragon Hall has a splendid crown post roof with a beautifully carved dragon.

Founded in 1385, the Guild of St George introduced an annual procession in which *Snap* the dragon would flap around and taunt the crowds with smoke shooting from its mouth. *Snap* disappeared during the Cromwellian era when the order went out that there must be 'no beating of drums or sounds of trumpets, no Snap-Dragon or fellows dressed up in Fools Coats and Caps...' but returned after the restoration of the monarchy. In the nineteenth century, *Snap* again vanished but, not to be suppressed for long, he is now part of the annual Lord Mayor's celebration, consisting of a horizontal pole (head at one end, tail at the other) with two small wings that conceal the carrier's face. The hands are left free to operate the head and hinged lower jaw which makes a loud click when it shuts, hence *Snap*.

Frankly, these interpretations weren't particularly helpful.

Then fate intervened...

As a gift to mark a 'significant' birthday (one of those ending with a zero), a kind friend presented me with tickets to attend the opening gala of the Hampton Court Flower Show. Sporting a flimsy dress suited for what I had hoped would be a balmy July evening, I found myself mired in the less than romantic sludge created by a day of pouring rain and a thousand tramping feet; the mud squelching through elegant strappy sandals. And that was just the car park! The first item on the agenda had to be the procuring of a pair of wellies. I didn't quite make it as far as the garden accessory exhibitors, however, as greeting me at the gate was a pair of eight-foot metal dragons rampant.

Neil Lossock produces 'individually designed pieces of bespoke garden art in metal and wood' from his workshop in Herefordshire. (It seemed appropriate that he operates on the Welsh borders.) [73] A professional metalworker and a self-styled dragon artist, strongly influenced by 'the Legend of the Dragon', he

---

73 Neil is an Associate of the Worshipful Company of Blacksmiths, www.dragonswoodforge.co.uk

specialises in 'life-size' dragons for ornamental lakes as 'original art for your garden'.

Having never plopped a dragon on a 40-foot chimney before, he took a little persuading that Nick and I weren't mere time-wasters (or tyre-kickers as Nick likes to say) but eventually agreed to journey to Suffolk for a recce.

The scaffolding around the chimney had been removed so his initially tepid reaction wasn't helped by having to measure up while hanging off a ladder propped onto the roof.

'It's feasible I suppose,' he muttered.

Then, warming to the idea, 'Yes, could be interesting.'

Nick pointed out the several fixing points which Piet had integrated into the chimneystack. 'They're certainly strong enough, I'll design it so she can be bolted onto those,' Neil confirmed, taking copious notes and photographs. (*Aha, a female dragon,* I noted inwardly.)

His brief then:

- head with vicious teeth;
- claws (not bothered whether five or three);
- long tail;
- extended wings;
- scales.

We debated whether to introduce fire breathing or at least, sending smoke through nostrils, but the logistics rather defeated us, given that we weren't keen to burn the house down. The idea was abandoned as a step too far, even for us.

Just think, if we'd used a different entrance gate at Hampton Court, we'd probably have missed Neil altogether.

Rustproofing

The house-build having been abandoned in favour of finishing the barns, the roof beams and rafters outfacing the winter under layers of plastic sheeting became whipped and shredded by Arctic blasts. At long last turning our attention to it, we found that penetrating rain had marinated the timbers, which showed grey water marks as well as the dark discolouration caused when the saw blade minerals react with the natural tannins. At least it had hastened the shrinking process, thus mitigating the usual post-build plaster shrinkage. We had avidly watched a *Grand Designs* episode in which one zealous soul spent months hand-scouring water-marked timbers back to an almost virgin state. With our dedication clearly wanting, we felt that a gentle sandblasting would suffice, a process that involves shooting grit at very high pressure through a nozzle to remove the thinnest of layers. In the right hands, it can do much to clean back timbers without gouging the grain and can also clear residual plaster crud, so there was little point in calling in Jim, our sandblasting expert, until Krzysz had finished plastering the walls and ceiling.

But, before that, the window frames had to be fitted.

And before that, they had to be made.

We had followed the softly spoken, unflappable Richard (of Stratton Period Joinery) through his pony-tailed, free-spirited years to a youthful maturity, over which time he's brought his skills to bear on our various projects, whether grand staircases for the Victorian warehouses or hand-built kitchens for converted cow houses. Modestly, he made no reference to rather more prestigious projects, such as that at Highgrove House or those whose establishments have appeared on *Grand Designs*. Now, he was coming to measure our windows.

This was trickier than it sounds. On account of the way some structural oak posts had had to be positioned, many apertures had slightly differing widths. It was safe to say that, of the total of 33 windows in the house, only a handful were truly identical. They just needed to *look* as if they were. If anyone could

pull it off, it was Richard. However, as he'd made such a good fist of the cupola, Krzysz would be left to make the small triangular frames for the non-opening glass corners of the eyelid *lucarnes*.

Lifting the roof off Nigel's model revealed a top floor divided into two rooms, but now the structure was in place, we could see that it would be a pity to interfere with the visual impact of the complex joinery and decided to devote the entire space to the master bedroom. Nevertheless, it needed storage and too many partitions would have interfered with the beam formations of the vaulted ceiling. The problem was solved with stud walls that stopped short of the ceiling to form ceiling-less, walk-in wardrobes (which work fine if you don't mind dusting your clothes from time to time).

Meanwhile, Marek was busy finishing the plumbing in the top bathroom. While he was at it, we got him to tuck taps and a kitchen sink into the one built-in corner cupboard. Short term, it would be useful if we needed to 'camp' out upstairs; and in the long term, mindful that it's two flights up from the kitchen, it would be handy for rinsing glasses and coffee cups on lazy Sundays.

Richard duly delivered the oak window frames (excepting the huge trapeziums for the east wing, which wouldn't be needed yet awhile). He'd cleverly accommodated the variable apertures by juggling the width of the frames, only noticeable on very close study. Marek found that inserting rectangular frames into curved walls involved planing the inside of each window aperture, a challenging and time-consuming process.

As to plastering, we were looking for a finish that was neither polished nor rustic. In our experience, most professional plasterers were quick to protest against compromising their standards by applying the softly brushed finish that we had come to favour, so it was lucky that Krzysz has no aspirations as a drama queen and just got on with it. Once that was done, Jim could be summonsed. His masterly touch lightened the water stains (although they were never going to be perfect) and blasted away the plaster residue. Once the dust and debris from this operation and the sanding of the floorboards subsided, the timbers would be finished with boiled linseed oil.

Opening the way to glazing...

The specification was straightforward: double-glazed, low-emissivity thermal Pilkington K Glass. Ordering was less straightforward and templates were needed for each of the panes under the *lucarnes*, especially where they tailed off into the triangular corners. Nick undertook this precision measuring. If they failed to fit, he'd have no one but himself to blame.

Neil called.

'I've finished the dragon maquette. Any chance of popping over to Hereford to look at it and see if you're happy with the direction it's going?'

'Yes. And yes. How do we find you?'

'You'll see, just turn right at the dragon on the corner.'

The dragon certainly couldn't be missed and we tracked Neil to his lair of a workshop, crammed with hanging dragon heads, tubs of talons and boxes of steel balls that double up as knuckle joints. (Nick swears he saw a box of bloodshot eyeballs, but I'm not so sure.) With its fearsome face and bat-like wings, the maquette was clearly based on the more malevolent European genre, but rather than kidnapping maidens or guarding ill-gotten treasure, it would be protecting our home.

Agreeing that the tail would benefit from some lengthening, we turned our attention to the wings. These were usually fabricated from solid sheets, but to minimise wind resistance, our dragon required wings of openwork metal or mesh. Fabricated in steel, each section would be dipped in a galvanising bath to render it rustproof. So far so good; there just remained the matter of the finish. Initially drawn to verdigris but suspecting that the existence of a dragon on the chimney would draw enough attention as it was, I felt that the finish should blend with the brown-red roof tiles and bricks, rather than act as contrast. That meant a sort of rust colour. Neil suggested a special (and expensive) rust-effect paint that would have to be imported from America.

Rendering it rustproof and then painting it to appear rusty? In this way, madness lies (apologies to Shakespeare).

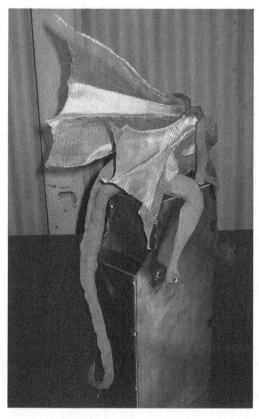

Ad Hoc

With no news of a sale of Wissett Place the mortgage and my four-day week continued to fund progress. *Just.* The financial crisis was blighting many lives but, fortuitously, the barns seemed to be favoured by those still able to splash out for birthdays and other celebrations, so the occupation rate wasn't bad for a fledgling set-up. 'Turn-round Friday' was generally mayhem, given that much of what was needed had to be transported from Halesworth and, my forgetfulness a given, a figurative groove was worn in the road between the two sites.

I was still managing to avoid getting my hands dirty as far as building was concerned, although I was forever slipping out of the office for consultations on this or that, working on the internal layout in our usual ad hoc (that 'daily plan') kind of way. The outer shape of the house inevitably dictated the way the inner space was carved up, awkward kinks and crannies occurring where curved outside wall met straight interior wall.

'Can you pop over here at lunchtime?' Nick would ask. 'I need you to look at something.'

Typically, it would be to adjudicate on a lay-out detail or a design feature. Perhaps it would be Krzysz and Marek manhandling an old bathtub in what was to be an en suite, setting it down this way and that, so I could assess if there was room to manoeuvre around it *and* a washbasin *and* a toilet pan. Only once that was settled would Nick erect the internal stud walls that would form the room.

This approach to building is highly collaborative and in wilder moments, I'd likened it to rock guitarists in full flight of composition.

'Hey, how about using this riff, it starts in G.'

'The key A may work better.'

'Why don't we try D minor?'

Working like this, we were also able to carve out an airing cupboard and a landing cloakroom, the latter going on to rejoice in a copper basin procured from eBay (a devil to keep clean) and a pair of reclaimed brass globe taps. The hard

surfaces of the guest bathrooms were a given, in that we were looking to use up that Indian stone, but I could let rip with the styling, one bathroom taking on an art deco flavour, with a snazzy set of retro-styled taps; another assuming an exotic air, courtesy of a latticed Mughal archway retrieved from my late parents' garage and put over the bath. Quite *why* this was in their garage, I never did determine.

Blowing a further raspberry at orthodoxy was the fact that the main roofs had gone on *before* the straw-bale infill in the north wall and tower. So, while all the activity upstairs augured well, the temporary plastic sheets stretching across the open rear flank of the house provided the only protection from winds that felt fresh out of Siberia.

'This must be the only new-build where the plumbing and electrics have been installed *before* the outer walls,' I tartly observed.

Despite the seemingly relaxed approach, I did have certain *idées fixes*. Objects that just *had* to be accommodated. For instance, the five-foot sideboard that had once graced my parents' 400-year-old Cotswold home (they had become enthusiastic habitués of antique auctions after a lifetime of bland service quarters, so maybe that explains the Mughal arch). I recall

that Dad had once taken it to an *Antiques Roadshow* at Chippenham, where the expert had rather condescendingly explained, on camera, that it was a 'marriage', as they say in the trade: a Victorian piece incorporating Tudor elements of carved ball legs, caryatids and inlaid doors. As far as I am concerned, this mix in no way detracts from its Gothic, in the sense of theatrical, appeal.

'It'll sit in the hallway,' I resolved, calculating that there would be just enough room for it.

Forging a Following

Basic labour for humping beams and bricks or mixing cement no longer needed, come Spring 2009, Piet, Damien and Wieslow retreated to Poland, leaving three stalwarts to comprise the entire workforce. Krzysz and Ewa were now living in town, with Marek sole overlord of the caravans and the cats who, as predicted, had been busy multiplying.

However, the new house had to be put on hold while the trio helped make Wissett Place shipshape for sale. It took three months to work through the to-do list, with constant new additions supplanting the 'done'. Twenty-eight years' worth of clutter had to be cleared, boxes, bundles and bags dumped in the Green Shed in anticipation of the final move. At the very least the paintwork needed

freshening up, so Ewa started by painting one room, but as that merely showed up the next, she painted another, then another, until the surfaces of the entire house were aglow. Adopting journalistic recommendations to deploy neutrals, my approach to styling for sale purposes was very different to that in the barns.

Everything looked uncharacteristically immaculate when finally primped and ready for the professional photographer (*never* rely on estate agent photos). The problem was, keeping it that way for viewings.

My newly negotiated, four-day working week left Fridays free for change-over at the barns. Dirty bedlinen and towels were carted home for sorting and collection by the laundry service, the freshly clean and pressed items delivered back to Wissett Place and then ferried to temporary storage in yet another old caravan. Not ideal.

To launch a business only to be engulfed in an economic crisis hadn't been great timing. Only three months after our launch, the collapse of Lehman Brothers in autumn 2008 threatened to bring down the global financial system. As property prices plummeted, we could only hope that there wouldn't be a repeat of our former brush with financial disaster. Sale proceeds from Wissett Place would be needed soon, *very* soon. And would potential guests now be too concerned about the future of their jobs/pensions to splurge on a holiday? The immediate aim had to be to turn over sufficient income to keep everyone in employment and to do this, we had to concentrate on forging a loyal following.

Amazingly, this started to happen.

I'd been impatient for plant life to grow in order to create the slightly wayward, lush effect I favoured, but even the Crew's Hill shrubs couldn't disguise the newness of the infrastructure. Indeed, the naked corrugated iron fencing probably accounted for this early TripAdvisor review, the first words of which were rather worrying:

> *Anyone arriving at Belle Grove without checking it out, must wonder what they have booked, Steptoe's yard, or the Adams family home.*

Fortunately, it went on:

> *It's only when you step out of the car and take a look round that you see the care that has gone into making this a special place.*

Or the one that read:

> *In movie terms, think 'Mad Max' meets J.R.R. Tolkien, where 'Arabian Nights' take you away from the rigour and stresses of the real world. We all need escapism, and that is exactly what Jo and Nick, in their typical unplanned but inspired way have achieved. It felt quite magical as we turned into the gorgon-flanked gates. We knew we had stumbled on something truly unique.*

And a further review stated:

> To some, Belle Grove may seem a little odd – it is only when you
> get to stay there for a time that you begin to understand what
> extraordinary thoughtfulness has gone into putting it together...
> throughout, there is a great balance between quality and quirk
> – when Nick and Jo put together their ideas for creating and
> dressing the place, they did not hold back on construction or
> design.

Encouraging words, if a tad disconcerting to read that their first reaction had
been to deem the place 'odd'!

Shopping Adventure No. 5

The very word 'dragon' seems, historically, to extend to any creature that is unfamiliar or poses a threat. *African Approaches* recounts our exploration of the Neolithic/Stone Age frescoes on Tassili n'Ajjer, a plateau in the middle of the Sahara Desert where wall paintings act as a window into the Sahara when it was fertile and home to large numbers of giraffe, elephants, gazelle – and 'Saharan dragons' shown attacking humans and wild animals. Over time, elephants and giraffes disappeared from the imagery, but the fearsome dragon remained, presumably representing something that deeply disturbed the community.

'In the sands is gold, treasure inexpressible... and dragons.'[74] The idea of those dragons must have lived on over the centuries as Arabs trading in North Africa tended to attribute any destruction of camels or humans in their caravans to the predations of the so-called Saharan dragons, so the consciousness of dragons seems to have been as present in North Africa as elsewhere.

The strategic position of ancient Carthage/modern Tunisia on the North African coast has encouraged layers of cultures from Berber, Roman, Jewish, Christian to Islamic, Turkish and French. This mixed heritage is reflected in art, music and literature, except in Islam, which prohibits the representation of human or animal life, so depictions in pictorial art, including dragons, had long been stifled. Therefore, in Tunis, we were surprised to find and buy a set of naïvely painted glass panels depicting warriors fighting dragons. It appeared that after the country was declared a republic in 1957, figurative painting enjoyed a revival, along with the traditional technique of glass painting. This explained our purchase.

Over the years, we'd acquired the usual touristy chemically dyed kilims, metal lanterns, olive wood bowls and pottery dishes, but this time, along with the painted glass panels, we fell for a faded kilim of irregular geometric motifs

---

74 As the traveller, Abu Hamid al-Andalusi, recorded.

that, it was claimed, had been used on the floor of a Berber tent. A claim that turned out to be accurate judging from the rather overpowering goaty whiff, which we've since never quite managed to expel, so maybe there is a case for garish chemical versions after all...

Whatever, gentle Tunisian exercises in bargaining stood in stark contrast to the hard sell on carpets and rugs for which Morocco is notorious. Our 'eye' becoming formed over the years, North Africa yielded other objects from mirrors, ceramics and silver to the many Berber rugs from the High Atlas, which we'd pick up in cities such as Rabat where the traders were markedly less rapacious than in tourist-orientated Fes and Marrakech. Sadly, however much we cautioned our overland passengers, invariably they'd be stung by city wasps.

The classic scenario: a friendly, clean-shaven young man, let's call him Sidi, offers to act as their guide through the labyrinthine souks.

'You speak English?' Sidi asks. (Nick's standard reply used to be 'no, we're from Croatia', but all the 'Sidis' became so sophisticated, they'd reply in Croatian or pretty much any language. You had to hand it to them.)

Sidi advises that there's an overpriced, touristy end of the souk and a 'real' end. He'll take the party to that, neglecting to mention his 'uncle's' shop en route.

'Let's call in here,' he'd say after twenty minutes of lulling the party into a sense of security, 'not worry, you don't buy.'

An older, invariably moustachioed personage, waves them in. Sidi vanishes.

Another moustache is on hand.

'Greetings. My name is Abdullah.'

Inside, carpets hang from floor to ceiling. Yet another friendly moustache points out the finest kilims and traditional knotted rugs.

'You like tea?'

The victims sink onto kilim-covered benches and a moustache brings tiny glasses of heavily sweetened mint tea.

'How kind.'

A lean, sweat-stained and (of course) moustachioed underling unrolls carpet after carpet, rug after rug, each with a flourish that implies *this* is the most special of its kind in the whole world.

'You like this?'

'You like that?'

The heat is turned up. 'Choose, choose!'

Our passengers are caught in a rug trap. Each item has a price: one price if you want to have it shipped back, a slightly lower price if you want to carry it away. The mood hardens.

'We take credit cards, not worry.'

'I don't know...'

They don't want a carpet: we don't want them to buy a carpet. After all, they're at the very start of a spartan, five-month trek across Africa. But they're hot and bothered and the 'friendly' moustaches are waiting for them to crack. Some of them do.

In the old days, our stays entailed camping or, at best, sleeping on the roof of the Hotel Foucauld in Marrakech, overlooking the Place Jemaa el Fna. But when another of those birthdays ending with a zero loomed, Nick and I decided to celebrate in proper style in one of the *riads* in the old city, booking a room with a 'matrimonial bed' (as confirmed by fax to my office to the glee of my colleagues). Thinking it would be pleasing to eat in a properly local restaurant, we overlooked the crucial fact that it didn't serve alcohol.

I later reported to incredulous friends that I did indeed mark the Big Day with a drink. Of water. (A twist to this tale was the next decade's Big Birthday, this time in Berlin, where I caught a 24-hour bug. While my husband and son were having a high old time, gadding about the city, I 'celebrated' with, you guessed it – water.)

Many of the Berber rugs and kilims from Tunisia and Morocco seem to have infiltrated the barns, not to mention the house, where they're simply placed one on top of the other, partly for fun and partly as a way of storing them. Apparently layering rugs is a trend that's storming the interior design world. It's good to be on trend for once.

Ochre

Not even the most glamorous structure looks much until the scaffolding is dismantled. I was longing to see our building unveiled, but all the poles and platforms had to remain until every inch of the exterior was painted. Our straw and lime-rendered walls required a suitable product. Ordinary paints can trap moisture, so we needed one which would allow moisture to evaporate rapidly. On the face of it, limewash would work but, given that it needs fairly frequent renewal, the height and inaccessibility of the tower made it impractical. Nick chanced to read about a new product, the permeable (breathable) and allegedly long-lived *Integrasil*. It seemed that the manufacturer, *Sandtex*, had recently been taken over by *Crown*. We called the Helpline for information.

'We'll send you some paint charts,' they said.

These turned out to be several A5 sheets covered with miniscule squares of colour. The small print revealed that most of the colours were not available in *Integrasil* anyway. We tried again.

'You'll have to go to the nearest Crown Decorating Centre.'

'Where's that?'

'Norwich.'

We trekked to Norwich where the staff were singularly uninformed. Under pressure, they came up with the very limited list of colours that *were* available.

'Any chance of samples?'

'We don't do *Integrasil* samples. The minimum order is five litres.'

Further probing revealed that samples of the paint had to be factory-mixed at a cost of £75 each. All we could do now was procure tester pots of the regular matt emulsion which best approximated to the colours available in *Integrasil* whilst knowing that, even if we selected one, there was no telling if or how that version would vary, the textures of the two types of paint being quite dissimilar.

Back at base, Nick painted offcuts of plasterboard with the samples and propped them up against the building. Narrowing our eyes to see the effect close to and from afar, the one and only colour on which we agreed was a dense Suffolk-red, much like the one used on the model. Colour sorted. Or so we thought...

Needless to say, the very colour that we had selected, after so much agonising, proved to be unavailable in the *Integrasil* after all. The red-based tones that *were* available were too dark, too pink or too wishy-washy. Back to the paint charts, ringing the Helpline and braving the decorating centre all over again, this time coming away with a few yellow-ochre-ish paint samples. Again the boards were painted and propped. None were quite right. Off yet again to Norwich to the wretched centre for some darker ochre shades that we'd previously dismissed. We may have seemed to be going to an awful lot of trouble to get this right, but we would have to live with the result for a long time.

While sidetracked by the paint question, the K-glass™ panes arrived. Given his nightmares that the glass wouldn't fit, Nick felt he had to take charge of the glazing, but his care with the templates had paid off. They fitted! Mind you, we couldn't see how we'd ever be able to clean the outside of the glass in the turret once the scaffolding was removed. We had researched self-cleaning glass, but at the time felt that the extra expense wasn't justified, given that the windows would receive little direct rain on account of the deep eaves. However, I did begin to wonder whether the cost would have been justified after all, if only in the turret.

Amid the chaos, Neil called to report that the dragon had metamorphosed into head, torso and toes.

'Do you want to see how it's looking before I go too much further?' he enquired. 'Otherwise, I'll go ahead and start adding its skin and wings.'

It happened that we were due to trundle west to Warwickshire to attend a *Premier Cottages* event anyway, so simply carried on to find, in the depths of his appropriately cave-like workshop, parts of dragon skeleton suspended from the ceiling, and Neil meticulously cutting individual scales out of metal sheets.

'Lord, how many do you need to do?' I asked.

'I expect it'll be at least 1000 by the time I'm done.'

Each four-by-two inch scale would then have to be hand-hammered into a curve before being attached to the body. The experimental ones already fixed to the frame looked pretty convincing. Or should I say *realistic*? It was difficult to get a sense of the creature as a whole though, probably only something that could be fully appreciated when she finally settled on the chimney, wings extended.

The latest set of ochre samples procured at the umpteenth visit to the decorating centre produced an acceptable shade and we placed a cautious 'test' order of two five-litre cans, although we'd be needing thirty litres at the very least. After initial priming, the contents of the first can – a sort of yellow khaki ochre – were applied. It looked great. We prised open the second can. Despite having the identical reference number, it was a completely different colour. On the phone yet again, Nick extracted a promise from *Crown* to send the correct shade by overnight carriage.

In the middle of all the paint hoo-hah, and in complete ignorance of the problems, the new and unassuming *Sandtex* rep called to introduce himself. Poor man, he walked straight into Nick's ire. Maybe it was the strings that he pulled, but when the new batch arrived, the colour, while not quite exact, was acceptable. Three coats were applied, but we did worry that we'd never be able to replicate it. [75] While that's not yet been put to the test, at least its claims to some longevity are being borne out.

---

75 Our fears were justified. Integrasil is no longer made.

12 Weeks and Counting...

November 2009 and an early sprinkling of snow added a certain authenticity to our 'Russian House', especially in the light of its occasional epithet, *dacha*. It's also been seen as Burmese, Mongolian, Chinese, Tibetan, even African for heaven's sake.

Actually, if the house resembled anything at this stage, it was a beehive, the almost resident Jon frantically installing yet more cabling to keep one step ahead of the plasterers and Jim back to sandblast the remaining timbers and scour loose debris and rotten bits from the surface of the tree trunk. This cleansing process transformed it into the smooth sculptural form we'd always envisaged. And no sign of spiders.

The helpful but long-suffering Sandtex rep ventured back once more.

'It's looking good. Is there anything else I can do for you?'

'Well, it would be nice if we could have a complimentary couple of tubs of the *Integrasil* by way of recompense for our travails,' Nick ventured, more in hope than expectation.

'I'm sure we can arrange a couple of tubs of *Crown* paint.'

'We'd rather have the *Integrasil!*'

'Personally, I don't see why not, but I'd better clear it with Head Office.'

He did come back to us on that.

'Well, alright,' had been HQ's grudging reply, 'but in exchange we'd like to use photographs of the house in our marketing'.

Nick's indignant riposte is unprintable. Take it to mean no photographs and no free paint.

The economy had been in crisis mode for at least year by this point, with the financial system seeming to have been built on sand. Despite bloated balance sheets and inadequate capital, banks had continued to play the markets to catastrophic effect. The government had responded to the downturn with bailouts and fiscal stimulus, but the *real* economy was suffering a seizure, with old-established businesses failing, individual wealth declining and personal debt rising. A doom-laden scenario.

So it was a surprise when Wissett Place actually found a buyer. Given the depressed housing market, we were relieved to secure a healthy price that would

enable us to continue with the Belle Grove project. (It helped that the buyers were escapees from London who had managed to secure a decent price for their property in turn.) There was no doubt that taking the trouble to 'present' the property had paid off. Those television gurus were right for once!

I'd always said I'd be happy to pitch a tent in the shell of the new house if a buyer wanted immediate occupation, but I admit to relief that these buyers were keen to defer their actual move until the spring.

That meant in twelve weeks.

We needed to concentrate on preparing the top floor 'campsite'. The windows may have been glazed, but it awaited second-fix plumbing and electrics, as well as general finishing.

By now, Nick was something of a four-poster bed expert and knocked up an elaborate bed in situ, using the jigsaw to cut the triangular pieces of wood that were to top the not-to-the-ceiling partitions. I longed for the woodwork to be finished, so that the power saws and concomitant dust could be banished downstairs, allowing what I regarded as the fun part to commence: the painting and decorating.

With our 'natural house' ambitions, we approve the concept of 'eco' paints. It used to mean fiddling about mixing powders with base paint, but these days they come ready-mixed. However, there doesn't appear to be a cut-and-dried definition of what 'eco' actually means in this context. Some manufacturers use petrochemical-based ingredients, if in low amounts, some use natural solvents which nevertheless contain volatile organic compounds, while others add titanium dioxide (a whitening agent). Given the restrictions on disposing of leftover paint, a definite advantage of eco paints is the useful ability to compost them.

However, confusion over their credentials, the lack of colour choice (this has probably improved since), the relative expense and – crucially – little on-the-shelf availability in the vicinity, meant that, in the end, Ewa painted the bedroom ceiling and walls in bog-standard high street *Moroccan Red* and *Old Gold*. (I gather that such colours aren't generally considered suitable for the requisite calm of a bedroom, but I really can't do taupe.)

The bathroom was to be positioned on the top 'jetty' over the porch, but bathers risked knocking themselves out under the sharp A of the ceiling if we weren't

careful. Following our usual strategy, Krzysz (as the lankiest) clambered in and out of the bathtub as it was shifted from spot to spot in search of the best, and safest, position. It had been so long since I'd seen the Victoria & Albert tub in its showroom glory, that I'd forgotten why we'd chosen it, (apart from the fact that it had been heavily discounted). Happily, finally stripped of its weird shrink-wrap, we still liked it.

On the floor went the last of the £5-a-slab, green-veined granite from India. Although sold in 'unpolished' condition, the surface proved quite acceptable

once brushed with oil-based *Bourneseal.* Another of Nick's ideas was to use a rough-edged granite offcut for the washbasin stand and another on which to perch the bath taps, an oak column hiding ordinary pipes in lieu of a pricey floor-standing set. The concept of the coffin hatch had had to be abandoned to allow room for an egg-shaped shower cubicle, which was sealed with fibreglass ready for the recycled-glass, iridescent mosaic tiles which, incidentally, were the most extravagant element of the whole bathroom, possibly even the entire house. With the last pair of Balinese doors fitted, Ewa set to applying a bluey-green layer of *Chappell Green.* Perfumed candles, fluffy towels and an easy chair would make it less 'campsite', more 'sensuous retreat' (assuming hot water).

All this activity gave an impression of rapid progress, but at ground-floor level, the underfloor heating pipes were only just being laid over the concrete slab.

Come Christmas, a breather and a momentous message from Neil.

'The dragon is ready! I'll get over immediately after the New Year. Weather permitting, that is – we can't go far when it snows round here!'

Smok Lands

As it happened, New Year *was* ushered in by wintry weather. Snowstorms kept the dragon at bay; there was no chance of Neil managing to fight his way out of the Herefordshire hills. On site, outside work was brought to a halt, but it was not exactly warm inside either, given the absence of outer doors or downstairs glazing. Hidden under padded jackets, balaclavas and fingerless mittens, Marek and Krzysz screeded over the underfloor piping, and when that dried, set about laying the slab floor. We'd used these ordinary red-tinted, 20-inch square concrete patio slabs on all sorts of projects over the years, including the barns. Admittedly, they looked pretty unglamorous in their raw state, but a belt sander taken to the reverse side made light work of any unevenness and an application of *Bourneseal* brought out the colour, resulting in an appearance (more or less) of expensive terracotta for a mere £6 per square metre.

By mid-January the weather eased and Neil rose before dawn to set out across the country. I had been amused by the thought of the 25-foot dragon navigating the motorways strapped to a low loader, so was disappointed to see it had been stripped back to five sections for transportation in a white van.

The roof tiles were too delicate to support scaffolding so, mindful of the dangerous antics while constructing the timber frame, Nick managed to borrow a modern telehandler with a high reach to deliver the segments to the top of the chimneystack, where they were to be assembled. (Easy to use it may have been but at a hefty £30,000 to buy, we decided to hang on to our poor old *Sambron*). On his first visit, Neil had had to balance on a dubious ladder; this time, Neil had the scarcely safer mission of manoeuvring the components into place from a precarious platform cantilevered off the chimneystack. He fitted the body and wings together fairly easily, but the neck projected further from the chimney than anticipated, so fixing its head meant, quite literally, walking the plank. Up to this point, Neil had been assisted by Krzysz, but their combined weight plus that of the head tipped the plank upward (think of a see-saw), and there was a horrible moment when they all wobbled, trying to decide whether to save themselves, the head or the roof tiles beneath. Remembering the sweat that had gone into tiling that section of roof, Krzysz made a hasty retreat, stabilising the plank but leaving Neil clutching the head, regaining his balance with the poise of a seasoned surf-boarder.

In a way, it's a shame that Neil's' work can't be seen up close, as only then can its intricacy – claws (five let it be noted), scales, fangs and all – be appreciated. The nearest one can get is to stare at its tendrilled face from a particular point in the tower or crane out of the top bedroom window to glimpse the end of the arrow-head tail. However, the silhouette had been the priority and Neil really pulled this off, especially those meshed wings that rise above the body as if it's just landed.

We're not sure if we had ever got across the dragon idea over to Krzysz, Ewa and Marek so its arrival was probably a shock although, as ever, they were inscrutable.

I point. '*Polski* for dragon?'

'*Smok.*'

Wow. That is uncannily like Tolkien's *Smaug*. Feeling that personalising inanimate objects can be a tad naff, I had resisted naming it *Snap* but somehow *Smok* stuck...

'I prefer Sidney,' mocked Nick.

In China, it is disrespectful – and therefore very bad luck – to position a dragon in such a way that prevents it ascending into the sky. That is, with its head facing downwards. We hedged our bets, ensuring that while the dragon's neck had a definite downward swoop, its head tilted upward. Furthermore, it appears that dragons are associated with Earth energies and we discovered that the house is very close to an energy current or ley line. [76] It happens that ley lines are also known as dragon lines and that the St Michael dragon line [77] cuts across England from the furthest point west in Cornwall to the easternmost point of Suffolk and thence out to the North Sea. *Smok* had chosen an auspicious roost.

Smok's advent provoked bewildered excitement, a stream of concerned posties, van drivers, delivery workers and meter readers all enquiring, 'Are you *sure* it's safe?'

'Don't worry, he's soundly attached,' we reassured them. 'We're not exactly keen on the idea of it crashing through our bedroom ceiling one windy night either.'

---

76 The phrase 'ley line' was coined in 1921, referring to supposed alignments of places of historical and geographical interest, such as ancient monuments and natural ridge-tops. Ley lines have since taken on a more mystical connotation but remain phenomena that no one seems to understand. It has been suggested that the lines carry an altered form of the Earth's magnetic field and an article in *New Scientist* magazine of 1987, claimed that species as diverse as pigeons, whales and bees navigated using the Earth's magnetic field. Dragons not mentioned.

77 A line that commences on St Michael's Mount in Cornwall, and travels across southern England linking sites like Glastonbury Tor, the Avebury Henge and the abbey site of Bury St Edmunds. This alignment has become known as the St Michael Ley.

Patience

So it was that *Smok* presided over the continuing void that was the single-storey east wing, the space that was to be topped with that sedum roof. The main roofs had been tiled long-since, but this space remained open to the skies, those huge roof beams from France, eight inches square and 33 feet in length, awaiting placement.

Conventional timber framing follows the cross-beam method which divides a building into bays. The trouble with this system, tried and tested though it is, is that the size of the main beams has to increase in ratio to span if sagging timbers are to be avoided. In our case, supporting the roof with posts, in conformity to this formula, would destroy the point of what is intended to be an open, light and airy space. Our configuration, with its flared shape, large apertures, ultra-long timbers and shallow roof, posed genuine technical problems.

All the way through, Building Control had been helpful and supportive, if occasionally flummoxed by Nick's 'alternative' suggestions but Bob was (rightly) concerned that the weight of the roof would cause the timber to deflect, like a shelf sinking under too many books. You may recall that our structural engineer friend, John, had been working on this. His strategy was to increase the load capacity by installing a steel ring beam to clench the exterior walls together. A steel crossbar would also be inset in the ceiling to bond the side walls to each other.

In practice, this meant that the room's width would be connected by a shallow A frame to which the timbers running the length of the room could be bolted, in effect, hanging from the A frame.

Part of this engineering device had been implemented, Nick having already installed the top ring beam as well as burying one end of the steel frame into the chimney, but the other end, comprising a steel column and wind braces (diagonal stays), was yet to be entombed in the, as yet, non-existent straw bales. So what was the problem?

Well, it was our responsibility to 'prove' that this solution would work, which meant submitting technical details to Building Control. Lack of manpower had led the department to contract out complex and time-consuming issues to a private firm of structural engineers, a firm whose website, I noted, claimed to offer a 'prompt and decisive' response. John had already submitted detailed drawings, accompanied by eleven foolscap pages of – horror of horrors – handwritten calculations. The response had been resounding silence.

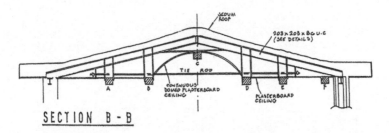

SECTION B - B

We cast around for other things to be getting on with, but there could be little movement with the kitchen either, as only the sale proceeds of Wissett Place could finance that expenditure. All we could do was concentrate on finessing the 'campsite' in anticipation of the approaching move.

So Jon continued to grapple with the second-fix electrics, frequently putting me on the spot with questions.

'What light fitting goes here then?'

'Err. I'll go and rummage round.'

Unless I'd already sourced a second-hand, specific-for-purpose item from eBay, my usual answer involved rootling around in the Green Shed. Bathrooms usually require 'new', however, and at the same time, there was a surprising dearth of functional yet chic bathroom lights in an acceptable price bracket. Magazine photographs of glamorous chandeliers suspended over baths often failed to mention whether they were IP (building regulation) rated.

Lucky that the supplanted coffin hatch wasn't needed for furniture. We managed to haul up and round the stairs a table, some chairs, a red leather retro suite, mirrors and a television. For the four-poster he'd built in situ, Nick fashioned a headboard from a Rajasthani wall hanging studded with tiny mirrors, which sparkle and glitter as they reflect daylight from windows and the miscellany of table lamps at night.

The 'campsite' was pretty much ready.

I could, *almost,* begin to feel that it was somewhere we were going to live, something I had not allowed myself to think up to then.

Part 3

A Magical Pile

April 2010, the month and year I retired from legal life; April 16th 2010, the day to say goodbye to Wissett Place and take possession of Dragon House, the local tag that had taken over from the unlamented *dacha*. We'd been lucky to be able to move in stages, the pain of the final day minimised thanks to the open-jawed Green Shed, into which many belongings had already been dumped, the theory being that we wouldn't need much while camping/squatting on the top floor.

Kind friends brought house-warming offerings that included a sensational four-foot, green and gold (yet somewhat fierce), handmade papier mâché dragon, an ingenious pixelated picture of the house and a light-hearted verse, penned by the friend who wrote of Sutton Hoo with such insight.

Thoughts on a Grand Design

Is it a house, a castle or a mosque?
Is it lying in wait or totally lost?
Floating free from a fairly Grimm tale
Or conjured up after pints of real ale.
It harbours its very own Hansel and Gretel
Who ply you with wine or put on the kettle
The walls are not gingerbread, sweets or a lolly
So to lick them or bite them would be purest folly
If you venture towards this wonder at night
The moon full out, the wind soft and slight
A shape on the chimney will loom into view
Smok the dragon is spying on you
He's made his wild mark on the country around
Seen high above trees, glimpsed clear from the ground

A Grand Designed house, with travellers' spells,
Treasures with stories, its own Book of Kells
Fun, art, invention; a magical pile
To enliven our landscape and raise a warm smile

But celebrations were muted. Unhappily, the very day of moving coincided with Ikki's funeral. He had been ill for some time and we were woebegone over the loss of this kind man and exemplary neighbour. It would have been such fun living next door. Karen carries his torch on the G&T front, even if she is wont to say things like, 'did you see the Muntjac deer this morning?' and when we say, 'no, when was that?' replies 'Oh, five-ish'. Now Karen, do you *seriously* think we're conscious at five a.m., let alone looking out of the window?

'Is it wise to have so many stairs?' Jaimie had questioned, when panting his way to the second floor, with the killer appendage, 'At your age?'

I suppose from the vantage point of his age, being in one's 60s seemed positively antediluvian. Looking at the years ahead, maybe he had a point, but we wouldn't have undertaken this project at all if we'd been sensibly cautious types and, in any case, we're mindful of the medical wisdom that asserts, the longer you can keep managing stairs, the more mobile you are likely to remain. The same principle applies to hanging onto my old MG roadster, in and out of which I'll swing my hips as long as they'll let me, although it *does* seem to get more low-slung every year...

It was comfy enough up in the campsite, certainly compared to the tents in which we had spent a considerable portion of our lives. Electricity. Running water. Bed. Flush loo. TV. What more could one want? (Well, a phone line and broadband would have been nice but that's another story.) Icy draughts were the main problem due to the continuing absence of outer doors or downstairs glazing. A blanket across the stairwell offered makeshift defence, but the wind had a way of funnelling from the back field, taking a sharp turn left through the porch and upward, whipping aside the blanket and bringing with it the fine powder issuing from constantly whirring saws and drills, depositing it into the corners of our eyrie, just as on the beach, sand infiltrates every crevice. It was a huge relief when the whine of electric screwdrivers and thump of nail guns came to a halt at 6pm. Pity the draughts didn't do the same.

The top of a feathery silver birch seemed to tickle the windows as it whipped in the breeze. Only recently planted, it had thrown up extraordinary growth – perhaps its roots had found an old cesspit or a dead cat. Surrounded by the swaying greenery of more mature trees, it felt much as if I were surveying the sea from the captain's bridge of an ocean liner.

At dawn, vociferous birdsong would invade my consciousness and black shadows skim across my line of vision, the barn owls (with perfectly good nests in the ash trees lining the railway) having been beaten to their 'hotels' by forceful jackdaws. Come the evenings, despite the empty echoings of the ever-so slightly spooky site, we felt snug and safe behind the Balinese bedroom door. An unwanted effect of the deep eaves and double-glazing is the banishing of the sound of rain beating on the glass but, from the warmth of the bed, we relished the rhythm of raindrops drumming on the two rooflights and the twit-twoos of tawny owls from nearby thickets of trees.

Even I, 'Queen of Mess', longed to create order out of the chaos. The ceiling-less 'walk-in' wardrobe awaited garments and slatted shelves awaited shoes. At least the bathroom was functioning perfectly and although the minuscule 'kitchen' consisted only of an ineffectual caravan fridge, a superannuated microwave, toaster and kettle (the only thing that worked properly), delicacies could still be conjured up. I embraced this way of entertaining. After all, we were merely carrying on the Elizabethan tradition of entertaining in the bedroom, if not *in* the bed.

'Come round for an indoor picnic,' was my default mode – so much easier to top up at the deli than slave over the microwave. (One can get away with an awful lot as long as the wine keeps flowing).

Certain friends had been urging adherence to *feng shui* and I was astonished to discover the degree to which its principles do influence architecture. Apparently, Donald Trump changed Trump Towers in New York to gain a more 'auspicious' view of Central Park and, more predictably, all major buildings in Chinese cities are built to *feng shui* principles. Such projects require deep pockets but, in a way, Khan's concept of 'natural building' can be seen as *feng shui* by another name. It seems we'd already encouraged 'bad energy' by locating the bed opposite the windows, a no-no. The placement of mirrors and other objects was hardly propitious either and even though it's considered far too stimulating for a sleeping zone, we were desperate to bring Wi-Fi into this, our only functioning room.

This was proving a problem.

Unfortunately, the site was (and is) in a mobile signal black spot, so a new landline was crucial, especially for the business. Moreover, no line equalled no internet. We endured several months of exasperated calls to BT (via India) as well as the intermittent digging up of highways. Unexpectedly, an older, that is, thoroughly seasoned not to say battle-hardened, OpenReach engineer dropped by.

'We've been thinking about the problem back at the exchange,' he said. (Not having realised anyone cared, I was impressed.) 'Let me just tweak something in that post up the road.'

Whatever he did, it worked! Experience tells. However, in all the angst, BT overlooked our request to keep our old telephone number (it was on the same exchange). We'd only had it 28 years after all. In the trauma of solving that, the original broadband order was overlooked. It meant starting from scratch. All this meant that I was forever plaguing former colleagues by diving into my old office in town to ride on the back of their broadband. [78] So much for retirement.

Apart from this major irritant, one effect of no longer shunting between Wissett Place and the barns, was that life became less complicated. The linen caravan became redundant and the old coal shed was converted into a large store, now Ewa's domain.

---

78 Pleased to report that nowadays, we have radio-transmitted broadband. Bliss.

Anyone for Dinner?

My tombstone will probably read, 'She acted first and thought later (usually better of it)'.

The sale of the house released funds to propel the kitchen forward, and so, carried on a wave of excitement, I blithely invited 18+ relatives to a grand family dinner on the eve of my brother Keith's second marriage [79]. The numbers were manageable as I'm congenitally incapable of making a small meal after so many years of feeding housefuls, and after years of camp cooking over wood fires, 'making do' is in my blood. However, even I recognised that I would need more than a dodgy microwave and a toaster for this affair.

Quite apart from the question of having somewhere to prepare meals, would the east wing even have a roof by then? Would there be enough seating? Would we end up with a wedding-size Chinese takeaway?

Then again, there's nothing like a deadline...

Nowadays, the kitchen tends to be the principal room of the house, a multi-purpose space encompassing everything to do with food and eating, plus television, laptops and e-devices. Indeed, if one believes glossy magazines, it's reached the point where the well-heeled need *two* separate kitchens – a 'family' kitchen as showpiece and a practical space for caterers. For most of us, the kitchen has to function as somewhere to prepare food *and* for people to gather. This had certainly been the function of the 'farmhouse' kitchen in Wissett Place, housing a circa 1948 solid-fuel Aga, a *lino* floor that tolerated muddy boots and a scrubbed pine table which had hosted scores of convivial gatherings. There, cooking was practised casually, partly on account of the much-loved (and forgiving) Aga whose temperature responded more to the direction of the wind than the thermostat. In a procedure that appealed to my inner slattern, I'd simply open the door and cast food inside, knowing it wouldn't spoil too quickly

---

79 Sadly, my sister-in-law, Rosey, had died many years before.

if I forgot about it (something for which I was... *ahem*... infamous). The Aga kept the chill off the draughty room too and its friendly presence was much missed whenever closed down for the summer.

So, although an Aga had been on the wishlist, why now did we decide against one? If our theories were correct, the south-facing orientation of the kitchen windows, combined with the building's insulation properties, would result in permanently warm space. We recognised that there would be summer months when the last thing needed would be a device upping the temperature. It seemed perverse to expend serious money on something that we'd only use for half the year. [80] So we went from an appliance with no controls at all to a Britannia multi-fuel range cooker with a dozen knobs. And a griddle. And a wok burner. We'd had no intention of buying anything when idly looking around the John Lewis showroom, but it had been on sale at an extremely knock-down price, a customer having ordered it in a non-standard, blue enamel finish but rejecting it on account of a teeny knock on the bottom corner.

'Might as well take advantage and worry about the colour later,' I'd calculated.

There had been no kitchen to receive it at the time, so the cooker had been deposited in the Green Shed while we worked out what we really wanted from the kitchen. Not surprisingly this was space, light, storage, warmth and comfort. Although I had loved our old kitchen, even with the Aga one couldn't have called it toasty and there had been no margin for the comfort element in the shape of a longed-for settee. A 'lazing' area was now a prerequisite. I'm not enamoured of that modern favourite, the 'island unit', but a rounded peninsula would separate the food preparation zone and the slumping zone, an outside door providing a natural division.

I had hoped to squeeze in a kitchen table as well but had overlooked one crucial thing: headroom. The circular staircase was partly suspended over one end of the kitchen, and while a work surface could easily slot beneath, it reduced the usable floor space, only leaving room for a table *or* a sofa.

'Definitely a sofa,' I said. 'What I'd really like is a curved one.'

'Hah! You'll be lucky!'

As with the bathrooms, the best way to see how the kitchen would function in practice was to do a mock-up. For this, Nick cut two four-foot diameter circles from large sheets of plywood and balanced each on an oil drum, which in turn were balanced on cable reels to achieve the requisite height.

---

80 If only we'd known about the Aga Total Control, which wasn't launched until 2011.

An evening in the company of *Gordon's Export Proof*, shuffling around these props, testing heights and body space, facilitated arriving at the optimal layout: no filler panels, no wasted recesses, no hard-to-reach corners. We made sure to translate it to paper before we forgot anything that made perfect sense at the time...

The next morning revealed a sketched layout that, even on sceptical examination, still worked: a convenient spatial relationship between sink, cooker and dishwasher and differing worktop heights for differing tasks. No wall-mounted cabinets though as I have an aversion to them; just as well because there was precious little room, what with the upper half of one wall consisting of nothing but a row of windows and the only small section of flat wall opposite reserved for appliances. Give me a kitchen that honestly displays the paraphernalia of eating and drinking – hiding it behind doors is almost a metaphor for an attitude to life. Why open two cupboards and a drawer each time you make a cup of coffee when you can reach to an open shelf holding all you need? Why put plates away every time they're washed when you can make a wall-mounted drainer do double duty as storage? Applied ergonomics or laziness?

Of course, *some* cupboards are desirable. The outer wall of the half-moon shaped room would be fitted with floor units to follow the curve, but we were stumped as to deep storage. As with electric sockets, one can never have enough, especially as the Christmas just past reminded me that all those things which emerge only once or twice a year still need a home.

We had the layout. All would be in the detail.

'Richard is coming tomorrow to look at the kitchen,' I reminded Nick. 'He needs to be properly briefed.'

The floor units would have concave fronts echoing the curvature of the outer wall, but the run would need visual breaks. Our brain cogs whirled. Having successfully incorporated old corrugated iron in the fences around the barn gardens, I wasn't at all surprised by Nick's suggestion.

'We could use 'wriggly tin' for door panels.'

'Ye-e-s-s-s-s, I suppose we could. I need to remind myself what it looks like though.'

So we trudged up to the back field, where, sitting in heaps, were the remains of the corrugated iron that had once formed the lean-to workshop. Each and every one of the 50 or so sheets had to be lifted, inspected and evaluated on artistic merit. Splodges of rust made fetching piebald patterns but the majority merely had rusty edges. Where was the rust when you needed it? But Nick was right. I could see how its shades and texture would provide a counterpoint to the smooth oak, the curves of the corrugations echoing the overall shape of the room. And after all, rust is but oxidised steel. Sounds quite chic put like that.

The deep storage problem was to be resolved by taking advantage of an awkward pointed corner formed where a curved wall converged with a straight. Double doors, panelled with the wriggly tin, would open into every cook's fantasy – a walk-in larder/pantry.

Just as well Richard possesses an excellent technical brain. He didn't so much as blink when presented with our scrappy page of notes, even when we mentioned curvilinear and concave cabinetry, corrugated iron and a bowed-leg peninsula, as well as the three-tier, wall-mounted draining rack that I craved. He took measurements, scribbled notes on his own equally scrappy paper and departed.

Miraculously, it was a mere three weeks before he returned, having conjured up doors ready for the tin panels, a set of drawers and the circular peninsula. A tour de force, its four-foot diameter was supported by outer 'banana-style' legs that tapered inward onto open shelves. The whole structure curved on several planes at once, and even incorporated two drawers, which, in order to function, have also had to be cut on different planes. Not only that but, by employing vertical stainless steel rods set in oak, Richard has painstakingly constructed an elegant plate rack in sympathy with the kitchen's other curving elements. The reflected light from the mirror mounted behind it brings that section of wall alive.

All this workmanship at less cost than a bog-standard, high-street kitchen.

That Green Roof

If only the rest was going as swimmingly. We hadn't heard anything from the structural engineers retained by the council to check John's calculations.

Nick called. 'We're stuck with what to do next. We must crack on you know.'

'We need to come out and look,' they said.

'There's nothing to see really. The calculations and John's drawings should make it clear, but fine, if you wish.'

The pair of young men, who have been unfortunate enough to inherit the job, found nothing to assist their cogitations – little to look at save the five oak beams languishing on the ground and the sky above. Of course, the steel to receive the ends of the proposed A frame had long since been buried in the chimney breast, as had the wind braces in the straw wall so, to be fair, in that respect they had to rely on John's theoretical calculations.

'Alright, we'll think about it.'

'Bloody hippies!' one of them grumbled in a loud whisper as he left.

Weeks passed. Nick chased.

'We need to come again.'

'Nothing has changed you know!'

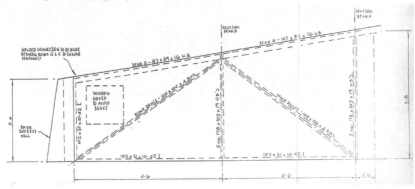

Actually, the one thing that *had* changed was that the long beams were now balanced on a rig of scaffolding and, unsurprisingly, had a bit of spring in them when walked on. The visitors looked worried. The real problem was that their training didn't seem to have prepared them for the unorthodox and they were acutely suspicious of John's handwritten computations, as if only something generated digitally could be trusted. Did they ever wonder how the world managed before the advent of computers?

The stand-off continued, certainly the longest delay on the job so far. His frustrations doubtless heightened by what must be a drain on the department's budget, Bob decided to short-circuit matters by verifying John's calculations himself.

'After all,' he said testily, 'I've never known John to be wrong in 20 years. I'm sure it's spot on, but I'd better run through it myself.'

This was beyond the bounds of duty and possibly a reflection of his exasperation with the new order.

'If I'm satisfied, you can go ahead with the steelwork.'

He was.

I suspect that the engineering duo were only too delighted to be absolved of the responsibility.

At last, Nick could move on to finishing the roof, firstly completing the recommended A frame and suspending from it those massive eight-inch square beams, half of their size hidden behind plasterboard. Following that original sketch, the model showed a peculiar if distinctive 'hump' at the ridge, so yet another question: how to create it from scratch? As our default expert, Krzysz applied lessons learned from constructing the cupola, forming the hump shape by cutting diminishing twins of

plywood reinforced with sections of timber. In a way, a budget version of a glulam beam.

The final layer was the 'living' element, chosen in lieu of the zinc or aluminium possibilities. We had considered buying the plants and installing the roof ourselves, which would have been significantly cheaper, but ultimately decided that this was one area where experience would tell. So in this case, the plants, grown on a 'blanket', were harvested like turf and rolled out on top of a substrate of waterproof membrane. The installation, undertaken with great thoroughness by professionals familiar with its demands, took a week with only one hiccup.

'If I were you mate, I'd put in extra leaky pipes.'

We had been led to believe that sedum, a succulent, thrives without water, but from his experience the contractor (as opposed to the supplier) strongly recommended a comprehensive irrigation system. Excess water, whether from rain or irrigation, would drain into gutter-like gullies around the edge of the roof and escape down a pair of muscular chains that function in lieu of conventional downpipes.

Rainwater goods can easily disfigure a façade, so at the back, water from the tiled roofs would be caught by a stock ogee gutter, discharging into a continuous length of plastic downpipe concealed in the wall, the rainwater gushing out into a drain at the bottom. At the front, a bog-standard, half-round plastic gutter was hidden behind an oak fascia, itself lined with lead.

Fire regulations are stringent when it comes to habitable, second-floor accommodation. To avoid fire doors on the staircases, Bob agreed that the green roof (which sits below the top east-facing windows) could act as a fire escape route, accessible through special fire windows. These seemed quite small but, as he remarked, 'If you had flames licking your backside, you'd be out of there quick enough, you can be sure.'

It was only then, with the east wing floor laid (those cement patio tiles) and with a roof, that we could contemplate installing those straw bales.

9

BELLE GROVE
FARM

11

12

13

14

15

Belle Grove

Start Field Walk 40mins

Walk Finish

Walk Finish

Noller's lane

Lower Common

Local line to Beccles

KEY

1 Griffin Gateway
2 Prototype 'Rocket'?
3 Vintage Scammell Scarab
4 The Temple
5 'Dragon House'
6 The Barns & Gardens
7 Bridge
8 Pond Walks
9 Courtyard & log store
10 Covered Arch
11 Summerhouses
12 Pre-war sugarbeet harvester
13 Camera obscura & Kadai beacon
14 Totem
15 Crytic car/old hayrake
16 Floating Duck Pavillion
17 Rajasthani swing
18 Signal Hill
19 Farm workshop
20 Paraphernalia
21 Shepherds Hut
22 Bathtub heaven
23 Vintage crawler
24 Grassy play area

16

A Good Hat and a Pair of Boots

Flashback to August, two years before. The combine harvester had scoured the wheat off the 'back field' leaving short, hard stems of straw, which Nick then baled 'ready for next year', as he had optimistically put it. Mindful of their proposed use as building blocks, the bales had been compacted extra firmly before being loaded onto trailers and left standing on the old Holton airfield to await the right moment, being that elusive conjunction of phase of build and prolonged dry spell.

That happy combination finally arrived. The rest of the country may have been suffering an endlessly wet summer, but East Anglia was living up to its reputation as the UK's driest corner. The ponds had been reduced to slimy puddles and the grass to yellow stubble. Perfect!

One thing worried me though and I asked Nick the (to me) obvious question.

'I know you draped tarpaulins over those bales, but it's rained so much over the last two years, is the straw still good enough?'

'It's so dense that rain sloughs off the surface and the air dries it out very quickly,' he explained. 'The main thing is to make sure it's not standing in a puddle otherwise water will wick inside.'

This is indeed the main issue with straw-bale building. Water penetration from below is the main enemy, so large roof overhangs and high plinth walls are recommended, accounting for the prescription 'a good hat and a good pair of boots'.

It wasn't so much the damp but the fire risk that was of concern to those who had never heard of straw-bale building (in this, I don't include Bob and Building Control, who were very open-minded about it).

We used the analogy of a telephone directory. 'Try and burn one. Loose pages of paper burn easily, but flames need air, so you'll find that the tightly packed pages mean it won't catch fire at all easily.'

Besides, once bales are plastered on both sides, there is even less chance of burning. Straw-bale construction is even used in bush-fire risk areas in Australia.

Despite this and its excellent insulation qualities, straw-bale construction remains unorthodox. Late nineteenth-century America first came up with straw-bale houses when farmers in the state of Nebraska, lacking the conventional building materials of stone and timber, saw the possibilities offered by the newfangled baling machines. That which had been 'waste' was transformed into fully load-bearing building blocks, and even though the resultant structures were viewed as temporary expedients, they were found to keep so warm through winter and cool in summer that they became permanent. About a dozen of these 100-year-old houses are still inhabited today.

The twentieth-century love affair with cement sidelined the technique, but the 1970s saw a US revival. Straw structures became known here too,[81] but the British climate encouraged a different methodology, the weight of the roof carried by a wooden framework with the straw used as infill. To acquire a more hands-on technique, Nick had already attended a residential workshop under the instruction of straw-bale guru Barbara Jones, which included a 'work experience' project to build an arts centre for the local community utilising the infill method.

The bales were transported from the airfield, unloaded and lined up on blocks just in case of rain (this was England after all). Preventing rain splash-back from the ground onto the base of the walls was a particular concern, so Nick had already made sure that the 'feet', the block plinths, were high enough to lift the first row of bales out of harm's way. It helped that the site was on a gentle slope with clay subsoil, as this meant that French drains should keep it clear of rushing water, should that ever occur.

81 Following the publication of Steve MacDonald's 1991 *Straw Bale Primer.*

The bales had one smooth(ish) flank and one distinctly prickly one. Although given a haircut by snipping off particularly long, hairy bits, they were still horribly scratchy, as Nick had discovered when manhandling them during his workshop.

'Make sure you wear thick, long sleeves and trousers,' Nick warned what remained of *Team Polski* who, in their usual summer uniform of skimpy vests and shorts, took as much notice of that as of the hard-hat warning. So he was amused by Marek's complaint on lifting and embracing his first bale. *'Au, ałe to bolało. To cholernie bolalo. Placczzego nas nie ostrazeglés?'* which we gathered meant something along the lines of, 'Ouch, that hurt. That's bloody prickly, why didn't you warn us?'

'I *did* say wear a shirt!'

Bricklaying is mathematical and precise, whereas straw-bale building is intuitive and forgiving, certainly a new experience for the depleted *Team Polski*. Under Nick's direction, they pinioned the first layer onto the block plinth by way of a reinforcing rod and, above that, butted the bales together in a 'running bond', secured with long pointed oak sticks hammered through the bales. Not quite the giant Lego brick build they had been expecting.

'What about mice – or worse, rats?' A visitor squeaked at the very thought.

'They're not that interested,' Nick assured them. 'The straw's no more likely to attract furry creatures than anything else.'

Desirable residences for rodents tend to be cavities and underfloor in old houses, (as well we knew in Wissett Place which required regular de-micing), so as far as they're concerned, straw bales compare unfavourably, there being no gaps. Nick tried but failed to poke a finger into the straw. 'See how tight it is – no chinks at all.'

This compaction also made the walls acoustically and thermally efficient. The one drawback I could see was that hanging heavy pictures could perhaps be problematical.

Working with the bales afforded opportunities to create all sorts of bendy shapes, something not possible with any other material except, ironically, its polar opposite, cement. Pronounced arcs and bends can be carved in situ by chainsaw and subtler curves achieved by bending bales over strong knees or the traditional 'persuader', a large rubber-headed hammer. Although not needing to be bent, our bales did need to be fitted around the standing timbers, a process that resulted in frayed edges. This is where the traditional 'needle' came in: a 20" length of steel rod, ¼" in diameter, pointed at one end and flattened at the other to the size of a 20p coin. A hole in this forms the 'eye' for the twine used to sew up the severed section, to keep it from falling apart, rather like stitching a hem to prevent it unravelling.

With cooperation and common sense, Krzysz and Marek continued until the vertical posts of the entire northern wall and tower had been infilled, ready for rendering.

On the inside, Krzysz covered the (relatively) smooth wall with mesh, to which the first coat of lime plaster was to adhere. Its 'hairy' face meant the outer surface had no need of the mesh, but the render had to be applied to a bone-dry surface. The weather threatening to change, Marek quickly used a high-pressure compressor to blow the render into the rough. At the straw workshop, they'd recommended a mix of clay, dung and horsehair (which helps prevent cracking), but not being quite so zealous, Nick took a shortcut with lime and sand, mixed, for the third and final layer, with miniscule nylon fibres in lieu of the horse hair.

Finished, the flaring wall took on a solid beauty, its curvaceousness brought to life. The softly irregular lime surface conveyed an almost monumental feel, like that of stone but warmer.

Transformation

Sills having been added to the double-opening door from Rajasthan earmarked for the front door, it could at last be fitted. A champagne moment, somehow even more significant than the 'topping out', although visitors were disappointed that they could no longer walk in at will and holler up the stairs.

Pointing to a large and ostensibly deep split in an upright timber, one asked, 'Should it be like this?'

'Oh, that's only shakes.'

'What the hell is that?'

'Don't worry, it's not from overdosing on vodka, just the name for those long splits in the wood'.

Nick explained that all wood contracts to some degree and although some wood shrinks less, oak is inherently stronger, any split stopping at its heart.

'On top of that,' he said, 'the wood becomes harder the more it dries out, which makes up for any weakening on account of shakes. In fact, it gets so dense, you can hardly put a nail in it.'

I was still disconcerted to see the splits down the length of some of the beams but assured myself it added character.

'What are you going to do when that dragon rusts away?'

This *was* a good question, showing the effectiveness of the rust paint.

'Don't worry.' I went on to explain, but then pointed to the fascia boards of the east wing.

'Now that is *real* rust.'

Fascia boards and soffits would normally be wood, but there was no way that an oak beam could be flexed to follow the tapering roof so, looking around for an alternative, Nick's eyes had lit on some rusted steel sheets, whose former life had been the floor decking of an old Leyland truck long since cut up for spare parts for an Africa trip. Despite flaking and frayed edges, at only an eighth of an inch thick, this lent itself to nailing onto a flexible plywood backing plate.

One day the steel really will rust away, but Nick shrugged this aside, merely commenting dryly that it was his duty 'to keep the builders of the future employed'.

The rainwater goods were in situ, the glass installed and the exterior painted. Hurrah! The scaffolding could come down! Every dismantled section of metal poles and wooden planking unveiled another slice of the building. For the first time, the complex roof contours could be seen in synthesis, the chimneystack and tower offering crisp silhouettes, while the window glass shimmered as it reflected the sky. The whole structure seemed more honed, more harmonised.

Alive.

Shopping Adventure No. 6

That neither letterbox nor knocker seem to have been a requisite in Rajasthan was a drawback to that front door. We installed a rather splendid hanging bell, but it tended to get overlooked, visitors looking everywhere but upward. What we needed was a good old-fashioned knocker.

It was on a visit to Turkey that we spotted the very thing.

The earliest known depiction of St George and the Dragon is from eleventh-century Cappadocia and his imagery is still strong within the Eastern Orthodox Church. So, it was no surprise to find dragon iconography all around us – including on a metal door knocker that was not anything other than twentieth century (if not twenty-first), albeit verdigris imbued it with a vintage look. Haggling in the customary way, we procured the knocker much too cheaply for there to be any genuine age. It was obviously new; for one thing, there were three the same. Unfortunately, the security officers at Antalya airport disagreed. While aware that Turkey bans the export of antiquities, we had no idea that a modern door knocker could fall into that category.

The existence of the door knocker in our cabin bag had been identified by a scanner and officials positively radiated gratification in having caught 'smugglers' red-handed. In vain, we tried persuasion, not easy when neither side speaks the other's language. After much flustering and blustering, a decision was passed down from the top. Send the offending door knocker under police escort to the local museum for authentication. That should settle matters. Shouldn't it? We kicked our heels on the wrong side of the check-in counter as the queue of departing visitors shrunk and then disappeared altogether, the arrivals hall becoming alarmingly empty. Two hours dragged by while Nick provokingly tapped out the theme from *Midnight Express*.

We suspected that the museum curator would be highly amused (or not) by the appeal to his expertise. Sure enough, the fake knocker eventually reappeared in the arms of its crestfallen custodian and handed back without further ado or explanation, in exchange for a signature to a document that could have been an admission of trafficking illegal goods for all we knew.

The civilian airport manager rushed us through check-in, immigration and a second tier of security, who also threatened to get excited about the wretched door knocker! It took quite a lot of convincing before they believed we'd already been vetted. With visions of the knocker going to the museum for a second time, we were rescued by the airport manager who clearly sparred with security on a daily basis and who hurried us onto the apron, where a taxi awaited to deliver us to the waiting aircraft, only to be greeted by a bank of resentful stares.

The knocker sits well on the front door though.

Concrete or Corian?

Worktops triggered something of an impassioned debate. Modern laminates are a perfectly reasonable choice but unfashionable – I was just not feeling the love. Having conceded concrete foundations, I quite liked the idea of a concrete countertop, [82] partly to be ahead of the fashion curve, but also because of its useful property of taking on any shape. (It is pretty much the only other material from which we could have built such a curvaceous house.) A precedent exists in the form of terrazzo, popular in the 1930s, a polished white cement incorporating chips of marble and aggregates which looks surprisingly chic. It would require homemade moulds though and I failed to convince Nick who, sensibly (how annoying), pointed out the drawbacks, from getting the moulds absolutely right, efflorescence and honeycombing in manufacture, to susceptibility to stains, not to mention the sheer weight.

Alternatives were composites like *Corian*, suited to odd shapes but extremely expensive, or stone such as granite (our supplies from India having been exhausted). Then there was the question of colour. The kitchen windows look out over a swathe of meadow grass fringed with tall trees, to which I was aiming for a strong visual connection by encouraging the eye to roll across and out. That suggested green, but the right shade proved elusive. Until, that is, I idly threw a green and black spotted scarf across a workbench. Eureka! But a lesson in how to make life difficult for oneself. A 40-minute drive took us to a good stone merchant where we scrutinised slab after slab. I'd suspected that it was going to be tricky to find a material even approximating the desired colour and I was right. The only greens were in depressing leaden granites and murky marbles.

'What's this?'

---

82 See *Concrete Countertops* by Fu-Teng Cheng, Taunton Press, Inc. 2002, for some stunning examples.

From the back of a shelf, Nick unearthed a sample book full of brightly coloured squares, the unloved cousin to all the polished stone samples on display. It was *Silestone*, a composite in which binders and pigments are mixed with quartz particles to produce a material said to be more durable than granite. The sampler included a sort-of lime green, probably rather blatant for most tastes. The test was my scarf. Allowed to borrow the swatch for 48 hours to check the colour in situ, I held it up to the light, scanning it this way and that, concluding, 'I don't think we'll do better'.

The high cost of stone or composite worktops is, in part, due to the precision required in measuring and fitting. With all the curvatures, our worktops promised to be more complex than most, so to minimise costs, Nick undertook the preparation of templates and installation. In the meantime, I learned not to excitedly flash my scarf in illustration of the worktop colour as this invariably led to raised eyebrows...

Having rather enjoyed our enforced picnics upstairs, I'd come to favour dining with minimal ritual. A 'soft' area of chairs and cushions would be perfect for lounging about with newspapers and low-key entertaining.

'Wouldn't it be fun if we *could* find a curved settee.'

Returning from the stone merchants, I'd resisted popping into the furniture store in Diss with tawdry SALE signs plastered over its windows, but Nick had insisted.

'You never know.'

Damn it, he was right (again)! The very first thing we clapped eyes on – and indeed the only thing worth looking at in the whole place – was a curved-back sofa of precisely the right size and colourway. Even better, it was marked half price.

Having already decided to dispense with a conventional kitchen table, we made do with a group of small, round, low tables set between a couple of low-slung armchairs and the new settee. But we hadn't eschewed a proper table altogether. A formal dining space is useful for 'occasions' and I embrace the image of a generous table groaning under the sort of fine china and elaborate glassware that isn't often allowed to emerge these days. So the hunt was on to find a suitable table for that grand family dinner, one that would have to be more than a few lengths of plywood balanced on trestles.

Herding Cats

Substantive work on the house was drying up and, rather than look for work elsewhere, Marek decided to withdraw to Poland. Quitting the caravans meant abandoning the ferals and his best mate, a brawny, three-legged tomcat who rejoiced in the name Mr Kot (Polish for cat) and who was leader of the gang. Despite acquiring a bicycle, Marek rarely ventured off-site, other than sorties to the village shop for ready-meals, vodka and cigarettes. Unfortunately, the cats had become reliant on him to supplement their diet of shrews and without his scraps, they reverted to roaming, and more or less bullying Belle Grove guests into feeding them.

Worse, they'd been producing litters in unreachable lairs beneath old sugar beet harvesters and farm machinery. Their numbers grew to well in excess of 20 (as far as we could tell, they were difficult to count).

Something had to be done.

At the Country Cat Shelter in nearby Beccles I asked, 'We have too many cats – what can we do?'

Cat assistant: 'What do you mean?'

'Well, how do we, er, *deal* with the problem?'

Accusingly, 'Surely you don't mean you want to get *rid* of them?' (I did actually.)

I retreated under her moral indignation and found the Cat Protection League around the corner. Rather more realistically, the staff recommended a neutering programme, agreeing to loan special traps to catch and transport the cats to the nearest vet, warning, 'They can be a bit vicious you know'.

Handling a frightened cat, let alone an aggressive feral, can indeed be perilous. Ewa was the only one who could get anywhere near them, so was nominated trapper-in-chief. The knack was to position a trap near bushes where a cat could feel safe and bait it with stinky food while leaving the fold-down door open. Poor Ewa spent long periods crouched in the bushes holding one end of a very long cord attached to the open door, which ran over the top of the cage toward her. The idea was that the, by now, distinctly skittish cat would sniff the food, let hunger get the better of it and venture inside whereon Ewa would yank the cord to shut the door and fling a dark blanket over the cage.

The kittens, not having quite learnt mistrust of humans, were the first to be captured. Some of the cannier cats escaped, snarling, spitting and doubly wary on the second attempt, rewarding Ewa with nasty scratches. I was on permanent standby to transfer each 'catch' to a carrying box and rush to the veterinary practice seven miles away. Usually the cats calmed down once under the blanket, but Mr Kot was so outraged by the indignity that he continued the fight, furiously hurtling around the inside of the cage all the way, nearly propelling me into a ditch.

It took a couple of weeks to entrap them all. After neutering, a corner of their right ear was snipped off so it was obvious which cats had been 'done'. We could only hope that their numbers would decline by natural wear and tear.

It wasn't exactly in her job description, but at least Ewa could add herding cats to her CV.

The Club Room

Just as architects are jealous of their status, professional interior designers rather condescendingly assume that the untutored have little instinct for creating a comfortable and visually satisfying environment, as opposed to one that is a mere assemblage of chattels based on need and exigency. Yet, plenty of non-professionals have the aptitude to create a pleasing environment without the help of yet another mood board.

A journalist writing for a glossy magazine later posed the question, 'When you first started, did you have a strong idea about how the living room was going to look and did it end up that way?'

I answered, 'From a structural point of view, yes. Having proceeded by way of an architectural model rather than conventional plans, we could visualise the shape of the room, windows, placing of the timbers and so on. We always saw it as a big dramatic space.

'Stylistically, no. Usually, we wait to see a space from differing vantage points, opening and shutting doors, standing in corners, walking around, flicking lights on and off. In this case, and most uncharacteristically, we had succumbed to an expensive if funky metal floor-standing light in anticipation of a vintage vibe. We got it completely wrong!'

That is to say, *I'd* got it wrong.

This was because the Tudor sideboard (as I inaccurately call it) failed to fit in the hallway by a matter of eight inches. The only other space for it was the east wing and as soon as it was placed, the mood shifted, its presence dictating a different dynamic.

That sideboard went on to house some special items. My early years had been spent in post-war Germany, the little information from that period gleaned from older brothers who describe fields littered with crashed aircraft and children playing barefoot amid piles of broken masonry. Later in life, I quizzed my parents about those days and the provenance of a dozen beautifully enamelled

Bavarian coupe glasses displayed in their china cabinet. These, it appears, had been acquired from a local family in exchange for scarce commodities like sugar and coffee. That's how it was. Their history somehow adds another layer of meaning to the ownership that has since passed to me. I can't look at them without fleetingly wondering about that family who had had to part with their prized possessions, in order to sustain life in the economic fallout of war. It doesn't hurt to be reminded that not to have been at that end of events is a mere accident of fate.

Fittingly, the Latin word *focus* means fireplace and certainly our room was to be traditional in the sense that a fire would be its focus. A living room without a welcoming hearth is unthinkable, so an enormous opening, lined with those sooty bricks, had been left in the chimney. The open grate in our old house had been fed with great chunks of steam coal and wood off-cuts. However, knowing just how difficult it is to build a new chimneystack that doesn't belch smoke into the room (chimney building is a dying art), we felt it safer to install the *Franklin* stove that had been knocking about the Green Shed for years, especially as it could burn with the doors either open or closed. The fireplace still needed some sort of surround though.

'Remember that wooden fire surround I picked up at Beccles Auction?' Nick quizzed. 'It must be buried *somewhere* in the Shed.'

I did recall something being brought home with the confessional words, 'I know, I know – it's big (it was six foot by five foot six), but that's why it's cheap. No one has room for these any more. The feet have rotted off, mind. It's a bit of a mess'.

I also remembered my retort. 'You can say that again. *And* there's scorch marks all over it. *And* I'm not keen on those decorative twiddles.'

Twenty years later, Richard pruned the despised twiddles and restored the feet. Propped into place, I had to admit that its scale suited that of the room. Yet, despite its handsome proportions, somehow it looked lost.

'What it needs is an over-mirror to reflect light back into the room,' I announced. 'Try one of those old mirrored wardrobe doors laid on its side. It'll give some idea.'

'Yup, that's it!' I decide.

With a wooden mirror frame devised by Richard to match detailing in the fire surround and a pair of salvaged carved columns, it ended up an unholy patchwork of badly stripped old pine, elm, new pine and mahogany. But applying paint is like waving a magic wand: a coat of primer, then *Daylight*, a light cream eggshell, and the mess merged into one. With the addition of bevelled mirror glass, the edifice transformed into an elegant chimneypiece.

Echoing 'topping out', any malign spirits that may have crept in during building work are said to be driven away by the ceremony of 'warming the hearth'. It has to be said that most of the warmth generated in the *Franklin* disappeared up the chimney. (Later we splashed out on a more up-to-date and expensive model. Hence, nowadays, you'll see a contemporary *Stovax Riva Studio*.)

The end wall and the south wall consisted primarily of windows, but having ditched the window shown on the model to preclude cold northerly draughts, the north wall had no windows at all. I felt that this somehow unbalanced the room, so I asked Marek and Nick to find some of the mirrors which I was sure were lurking in the Green Shed. They retrieved a hotchpotch, including a couple of dressing table mirror-glasses, all ranked along the wall alongside that old mirrored wardrobe door. They looked horrible.

Nick raised an eyebrow. 'Are you *sure?*'

It was another of those 'have faith' moments. As with the fireplace, all the frames were brought together with applications of *Daylight*. The mirrors bounced light from the windows back into the room, providing the visual counterbalance I sought.

It had always been our intention to line the high end of the room with bookshelves (one end is nearly thirteen feet high, sweeping down to eight). Books represent a lifetime of reading choices as well as chronicling one's inner life, so the cull on moving hadn't been as ruthless as perhaps it ought and four thousand volumes remained. Krzysz was called upon to make a floor-to-ceiling bank of shelves (to house Travel, Art and Gardens) but, this only accounting for a fraction of the overall shelf space needed, he carried on all over the house: in my study (Africana), in Nick's study (Architecture and Transport), on the landing (History, Modern Literature and Crap Fiction) and in the bedroom (Miscellaneous). Although I tried to arrange them coherently, I mourned the fact that I'd never again be able to lay my hands directly on a particular volume, as I had been used to doing.

What with the bank of windows, the many mirrors, the bookshelves and the fireplace, there was little wall space left, but we managed to squeeze in a few *Tinga Tinga* and, an old favourite, an appliquéd cloth depicting a monkey bought in the Republic of Benin back in the 1970s. They represent rather different shopping adventures (as recounted in *African Approaches*).

The sun streaming through the large windows, the leafy houseplants and the bamboo 'bar' (handy, if démodé) together create something of a colonial air, reinforced by the fireplace, squashy armchairs and fraying rugs. 'No sooner do two or three Englishmen meet than they form a club,' the saying goes. After sourcing an outsized metal chandelier from eBay and adorning it with a brace of antlers, I sensed that the room was indeed taking on something of a clubby ambience. All that was missing was a *punkah-wallah* and a choleric colonel sitting in the corner reading *The Times*. Even in the winter, the lowering sun deliciously cosies the space, the mood transformed by the changing of cotton summer 'throws' for furry winter ones. In this way, the east wing morphed into the 'Club Room'.

In which I did manage that big family dinner. By then, the Britannia was in situ, surrounded by makeshift worktops (the *Silestone* to be fitted later) and the kitchen floor temporarily surfaced with plywood, on which young nephews and nieces were encouraged to scribble. The best gadget so far was the boiling water tap, justified by 'if I can't have an Aga, I'll have that'. I learned to embrace

the cooker's sky-blue enamel, a counterpoint to the green walls chosen to complement the *Silestone*. I would never have set out to choose that shade of blue but, as it happens, it was perfect. I do believe one can make anything work in the right colour context – yes, even the dreaded 1970s avocado bathroom suite.

Instead of a bodge-up of trestles, the score of guests clustered around a newly acquired but second-hand, extendable walnut table. Would you believe it, the feet around the pedestal consisted of carved dragons (which, by the way, only sported three claws).

Those dragons were getting everywhere.

Shopping Adventure No. 7

The Donatists of Mauretania – a fourth-century breakaway church based in North Africa – preached that man must actively fight evil. By 'evil', they meant dragons, seen as demons incarnate. As Mauretania is pretty well the only place we *haven't* seen manifestations of dragon culture, they must have been successful...

In the latter days of our safari business, we had seen the potential for a different kind of travel in parts of Francophone Africa that weren't on the British radar: Mauretania, Algeria, Mali, Burkina Faso, Niger. All places we'd driven through but never targeted as destinations *per se*. British operators never seemed to be interested in opening up this market for short-haul travel, preferring to concentrate on the former colonial zones of East and South Africa. With a view to working together to promote the area, *Point Afrique*, a French company that specialised in desert trips, invited us along on one of their trips.

'How about one of our Saharan treks?' they'd suggested. A bit arduous methought. An unusual train trip looked more promising:

> *'Sans conteste, le moyen le plus original pour découvrir le désert, ses oases, ses villes, ses campements nomades et la vie qui s'articule le long de la colonne vertébrale que représente la voie ferrée pour le Nord de la Mauritanie'.* (Undoubtedly, the most original way to discover the desert, its oases, towns and nomad encampments that revolve around the railway in the north of Mauritania.)

Nick and I had always been intrigued by this *train du désert* that takes iron ore from inland mines to the coast, a train so long and heavy, it has to be pulled by three massive American locomotives and, at five kilometres, supposedly the longest in the world. On one occasion, one of our 'Trans' trucks had even been transported on an empty train from the coast inland, the passengers riding for free in the empty bucket wagons (more about that in *African Approaches*). Thus, we opted for the train, although hoping for a bit more style than a bucket wagon...

So it was that Nick and I found ourselves competing for a seat with scores of babbling tourists on a charter flight out of Paris bound for 'Atar International' in Mauretania, an airport consisting of a sandy football pitch and a tin hut, albeit on the outskirts of a beautiful oasis famed for its dates.

Happily, on decanting a few hours later, the hordes dissolved and we and a few others were scooped up by a *cheche* [83]-wrapped Mauritanian and conveyed, by way of Land Cruiser, to our first night's bivouac. Tiny flickers of light beckoned through the darkness as we churned over the sandy *piste*, the moon emerging to shine, as if to order, on an exquisite open-sided Bedouin tent supported by long ropes. Closer inspection revealed that those lights came from myriad oil lamps with the rope-ends buried beneath the surface of the sand, bracing the tent as firmly as a ship's anchor. The floor was the desert itself, covered by rugs and tapestries, and eating arrangements were a matter of sitting cross-legged around an oilcloth, while sleeping consisted of a mat and sleeping bag wherever we dropped. The best spot was right under the edge of the canopy, so we could fall asleep while looking up at the overwhelming celestial brilliancy.

Before the train part of the journey from Choum to Nouadhibou, a series of 4WD vehicles, trucks and camels carried us over endless dunes, sand seas, dramatic rock escarpments, canyons, gorges and *gueltas*, as well as the Pass that leads to thirteenth-century Chinguetti, one of the holy cities of Islam (nowadays more of a village). Surrounded by dunes up to 200 feet high, it is threatened by remorseless sand, but for now is known for its *bibliothèque* or repository of ancient manuscripts and religious texts. After that, it was *le train,* but it turned out not to be the main iron ore train after all. We had hoped for a tad more style than a bucket wagon and we got it, in the form of redundant Italian rolling stock pulled by a single engine. Someone else's reject it may have been, but a lot of trouble had been taken with the décor, the single carriage having been lined floor to ceiling – *and* ceiling – with overlapping lengths of indigo patterned printed cotton, the banquettes wrapped with kilims, and the floor with matting scattered with elaborately figured leather *pouffes*.

'I've simply *got* to find some of this.'

I fingered the indigo cotton with a view to adding to my capacious chest, already crammed with African textiles and which every so often I'd open and drool over the contents before reluctantly folding them away. (And to think, I used to mock my mother for doing the same with her fabric finds. Mother, I recant.)

---

83 Six-foot long turban-like veils worn only by men.

The carriage had two levels: one for eating and lazing, one for viewing. Better still, it had an old-fashioned open platform at one end, like a classic London Routemaster. Health and Safety officials would have had a collective breakdown had they seen us happily swinging off the pole with the train in motion.

Actually, the pace was slow, the breeze perfect for cooling off. As a stopping train, it offloaded water at tiny 'stations' that had come to be the modern equivalent of watering holes, with herds of fractious camels and goats. From time to time, it pulled into a siding in deference to the main iron-ore beast heading toward us on the single track. Although there was a timetable, the only sure way we could assess whether a train was oncoming was to listen, ear down, to the vibrations of the track.

The first shopping opportunity arose during a two-night stop-off in a *campement* located by the monolithic rock at Ben Amira, where a bevy of shy but determined Bedouin women set up in their black tent of heavy goat's hair

cloth, its open side facing away from the sweeping wind. Nomads are particularly known for cushions, boxes, bags and rugs and we succumbed to the jewel-coloured patterned leather cushion covers, etched wooden bowls and – the *pièce de résistance* – an old Moorish style box, the wood strapped with decorative brass with its key still attached by a dirty strip of rag. No fabrics to be seen though.

Nomadic tradition has spilt into urban settings and different Mauritanian cities are known for producing specific items: one city produces carpets and bags; another is famous for weaving and tie-dyeing and so on. Unfortunately, the port of Nouadhibou, the only city on our itinerary, was known for none of these things. However, its Grand Marché presented a second shopping opportunity by virtue of being stuffed with bale after bale of traditional West African fabrics: *pagne tissé* (a thick woven cloth) *bogolanfini* (cloth dyed with fermented mud) and *bazin riche* (dyed and beaten cotton). Much of this would only be worn for special occasions, but cheaper stamp-printed cottons of natural indigo and wax prints imitating handmade Indonesian batiks were also piled high together with the local lightweight *mulafa,* the everyday wear for women comprising a six-yard length of vivid muslin wrapped around the body and again around the head.

Ignoring Nick's exasperated sighs, I amassed lengths of *mulafa* and indigo prints to add to my war chest. A stamped-metal, hand-washing kettle and bowl found in the Marché went on to find a home in the Gate House (sitting well with the Arabic coffee pots) and the oval, jewel-coloured leather cushion covers have taken a starring role pinned to our landing ceiling. There really wasn't anywhere else to put them.

The arrangement with *Point Afrique* fizzled out. Just as well. Since then, active al-Qaeda and other militants have been increasing their operations in the region, kidnapping and killing foreigners.

Indoors...

In the early days of my legal career, a client, an uptight civil servant, complained to my superior about the state of my desk. If only I'd had the nous to quote Albert Einstein: 'If a cluttered desk is a sign of a cluttered mind, of what, then, is an empty desk a sign?' There is a respectable school of thought which holds that it makes perfect sense to maintain a messy desk when weighed against the time cost in keeping a surface free of papers by filing them in cabinets.[84] Not to mention the serendipity of digging through papers in search of something, only to stumble on an even more important task which would never have been done if hidden away in a filing cabinet.

As much as anyone, I admire those magazine spreads showing the Zen-like spaces of those for whom 'less is more'. Yet, I just can't join the vogue for 'let's not get bogged down with possessions'. I *like* possessions. Luckily, so does Nick. There's solace to be found in cherished belongings, a timeline of life – where we have been, how we spend our days, what and who we have loved, what has inspired us. Whether sentimental or utilitarian, they reflect who we are. They are friends. And there's always room for another friend...

We wouldn't call ourselves collectors; we're just attracted to certain things and then, well... they sort of... accumulate. Perhaps we're more akin than we know to the Australian bowerbird, which spends hours decorating its nest with shells, flowers, feathers, berries, coins, nails, pieces of glass and shiny discarded items.

So, yes, while the timber frame expresses the form of the building, the contents could be said to reflect its soul. The lack of straight lines and hard corners within the house are, in many ways, a delight but do impose restrictions. Or should I say discipline, as curating is kept in check by the curved walls which repel most things angular. Nonetheless, we have managed to squeeze in a miscellany of paintings including the first possessions I'd save in a fire: the

---

84 *A Perfect Mess. The Hidden Benefits of Disorder*. E Abramson & D H Freedman, Orion, 2006.

closely-observed drawings, land and seascapes by our stupendously talented friend, Vanessa Clegg. [85] On the rich backgrounds of blue *Ball Gown* and red *English Fire*, these jostle for room with other favourites including a series of old African maps, some of which depict spectacularly inaccurate lakes and mountain ranges. Ptolemy's version of Africa's landmass had held sway right up to the fifteenth century, when Portuguese explorers and traders started to unroll the coastal fringe. They had little incentive to explore inland so cartographers simply filled the void with fictitious features. It feels appropriate that some have the words *hic sunt dracones* – here be dragons – drawn on their edges. [86]

Even when geographical information became available in the nineteenth century, 'the dead hand of the past, reluctance to embark on the costly enterprise of re-engraving, inertia and resistance to change' [87] delayed updating. At least the Flemish 1920s linen map of 'Afrika', wrapped around a convex wall, is accurate. (A gift from Jaimie. It's quite often the case that when asked the provenance of something unusual, we chorus 'our son gave it to us'. 'He's a chip off the old block then,' is the usual reply.)

The somewhat Gothic works of Rosalie de Meric have found their way onto the curving stair walls. Her visions hint at the supernatural and, to quote an obituary in *The Independent*, 'her drawing and use of colour had a dynamic energy... the simplification of forms to express their essential quality, transmitted to the viewer with a directness and power...' De Meric and her husband, the barbiturate-addicted poet Thomas Blackburn, formed a triumvirate with the

85 www.vanessaclegg.co.uk

86 Meaning the territory is unexplored and potentially perilous.

87 *Maps of the African Continent and Southern Africa*, R V Tooley, 1968.

artist Francis Bacon and many of her works have sold for hundreds, if not thousands of dollars. However, the miscellany of frayed canvases and painted boards found in a leaky garden shed weren't exactly in mint condition when put up for auction in a local saleroom. (In her final years, the artist lived near Halesworth with her daughter, respected local author Julia Blackburn, whose memoir gives a raw insight into her troubled family. [88]) The first catalogued sale had had high reserves and little was sold, so we could only assume that the reserves were withdrawn as, at the following sale, Nick managed to secure a dozen de Meric works at breathtakingly low prices. It wasn't about money though; we embraced the imperfect condition of the canvases, which somehow befitted her disturbing images.

At the opposite end of the spectrum, I respond to the romanticism of the aviation prints to be found in odd corners. Maybe it's on account of my family RAF background, but even in paint, the sight of Spitfires and Hurricanes soaring above broken cloud makes my spine tingle.

And as generations of gentry have found, a stairwell makes an excellent place for a portrait gallery. In the absence of suitably august portraits, tribal masks and carvings are amassed on the steps that link the third floor to the turret.

Modest displays of fossils, artefacts and oddities were popular in Victorian times, but long before that, one of the wonders of seventeenth-century London had been 'Tradescant's Ark,' the first and definitive cabinet of curiosities, more of a room really. An extraordinarily eclectic collection, it included a dodo from Mauritius, a supposed mermaid's hand, a dragon's egg and feathers from a phoenix's tail. [89] We're drawn to seeing into an object, not only for its aesthetic quality, but for memories. Hence our own Cabinets of Curiosities. While containing no mermaid hands or phoenix feathers (shame), they *are* crammed full of African *objets trouvés*: quirky stones, tools, weapons, trade beads and

88 *The Three of Us* by Julia Blackburn, Vintage, 2009.

89 The collection ended up in the Ashmolean Museum, Oxford.

jewellery, pygmy calabash pipes, fish teeth, camel hoof boxes, porcupine quills, monkey skulls, weird-looking seeds and nuts, even tarantulas and scorpions encased in resin sold by priests at a Catholic Mission in Central Africa. Reluctant to dump these potent reminders of a life, they live in four oak cabinets that Nick commissioned from Richard for a long-ago birthday and now sit in the room designated as my study/office. The problem is that these, plus the ranks of travel books and my messy desk have inched me out, so these days my 'office' is my accurately named 'laptop', hauled from room to room.

The downstairs cloakroom is another useful repository, housing oddments from the bullet belt Nick acquired in Afghanistan in the 1970s to African carvings to the basket of cones from those Douglas firs.

'How do you keep all this dusted?'

I confess to astonishment at this surprisingly frequent question. How can one prioritise dusting over daily reminders of beauty and memories? I empathise with the Quentin Crisp approach: 'After the first four years, the dust doesn't get any worse'. Fortunately, my *wyluzowany* (laid-back) approach to housekeeping has not been tested by spiders, which appear not to be as drawn to the old tree trunk as I'd feared.

We'd intended to arrange for the ends of the dragon beams (the diagonal timbers that support the jettied porch) to be sculpted into a pair of 'grotesques' but have somehow never got round to it. Instead, they form perches for a pair of metal dragons (found at a car boot sale, naturally). The dragon motif is continued on the landing by that three-foot bronze Chinese dragon, acquired in Berlin. As iron filings to a magnet, it's *Smok*'s presence that seems to attract them in the form of candlesticks, lamps, and all sorts of dragony knick-knacks. They come our way just as a collector of say, china pigs will be deluged with presents of nothing but china pigs.

I have to keep insisting, 'We don't have a dragon fetish, you know. It's all come about quite accidentally.'

Really.

...and Outdoors

The short carriage train that trundles between Ipswich and Lowestoft on the single-track line has started to run hourly instead of every two hours. Much as that is convenient, I had rather dreaded a negative reaction from guests, but they seem to like its old-fashioned chuggy presence. In any case, I realise that the odd rumble is infinitely outweighed by the sense of enclosure brought by the densely wooded rail embankment. Without that, we would be looking at the adjoining field, nothing *like* as interesting.

The swallows that had abandoned their annual pilgrimage to the farm, presumably in disgust at the disruption, have returned to the eaves of the Green Shed, swooping, gliding and skimming in great curves over the ponds. Rather than introduce fish, we'd simply waited to see which creatures would naturally colonise the waters and, sure enough, the hollows soon became alive

with swarms of silvery damselflies, iridescent dragonflies (very appropriate) and an array of water creatures: striders, scooters, skaters, skippers and spiders. Moorhens fight at one end and mallards occupy the other, while the shiny salamander-like bodies of newts often migrate onto the car standing. Meanwhile, the bulrushes have erupted into the waters, as have the willows, metamorphosed into 30-foot trees. Nowadays, we spend more time hacking back than encouraging things to grow.

Just as the ponds have been allowed to mature naturally, we've left the grounds 'unmanicured' so butterflies have been quick to find the nettles and buddleia that insistently appear. There are ongoing nationwide fears for the declining bumblebee population, but here they thrive, rotund bodies propelling over the tussocky ground.

We've abandoned lighting the *kadai* every Friday, but it is kept ready with firewood for special moments. Despite the mass neutering of the cats and consequent decrease in numbers, the few that linger are as pestilential as ever when it comes to hunting the progeny of the mallards and moorhens. Hence, the advent of the 'floating duck pavilion'. Unlike versions sold to questionable MPs (duck houses will forever be associated with venality), Nick constructed this at  zero cost using the top circle of a cable drum, a halved plastic oil drum and roof vent, all daubed with red oxide and buoyed up by superannuated life belts from a Lowestoft trawler.

Other unlikely additions to the landscape include 'Signal Hill', a circle of six telegraph poles perched on top of a mound to announce, 'here is a mobile signal spot'. There's also the 'shepherd's hut' that Nick cobbled together by mounting an old twin axle trailer with a corrugated iron body, lined with oddments of panelling left over from the 'sun rooms' and now housing cricket bat and balls, a croquet set and a telescope. Not forgetting the walk-in camera obscura, another construct utilising materials whose fate would otherwise have been the skip, the apex of its roof crowned with a long piece of pipe topped with an old copper ballcock.

In what I *hope* is seen as a tongue-in-cheek tribute to the hot-tub culture, we retrieved an ancient and algae-encrusted roll-top bath from one set of nettles and installed it in another, complete with shower head fashioned out of a bent colander, duckboards, Victorian soap dish and brass towel rail. We can but hope that people 'get it'!

As former meadow, with a distinct lack of manicured flowerbeds and immaculate lawns, the billowing uneven grass in front of the house can't really be honoured with the word 'garden'. The terrace is the key element, laid by Krzysz with mellowed York flagstones sourced from a Lancashire brewer's cellar. Its expanse is anchored by the weathered presence of a five-foot stone carving of a figure fending off a dragon with a spear. Acquired at the same auction house as those de Meric's, now beloved of *Flog It* and *Bargain Hunt*, we had believed this to be St George, but it transpires that it represents St Michael, who also had

dealings with a dragon. In its glory days before the salt-laden breeze started its corrosive process, it had adorned the façade of a Convent in Clacton-on-Sea. Flat-backed St Michael is set against a dark green yew, which, apart from the apple protected by Krzysz, is the only 'ornamental' tree that has survived from the old Belle Grove.

Silver birch saplings have been planted in the last of the Balinese terracotta-lookalike pots and the remaining Balinese granite troughs manoeuvred into place with the forklift and sown with herbs, their weight meaning they'll never be shifted again. For tables, I hankered after those wooden cable drums that look like outsize cotton reels. Old ones proved hard to find until, fortuitously, Nick spotted a herd of possibly abandoned cable drums on an industrial estate near the infamous paint centre in Norwich and tentatively asked if he could buy one or two.

'Have the lot mate,' he was told, 'we don't know what to do with them.'

Handily, assorted cable drums slot together to make a staggered surface surrounded by a set of vintage metal chairs. It's a relief to have some sort of organised space outside the back/front door (that is, the kitchen door which is at the front – very confusing) instead of a sea of mud. Somewhere we can sit with a glass of wine or three and contemplate the copse of newly planted Alder, Hawthorn and Hornbeam, amongst which is tucked a seven-foot, stone Celtic cross. (If the building can be eclectic, why not the garden?)

The terrace captures the sun beautifully during the day but later becomes shaded by trees, so Nick and Krzysz constructed an extravagantly romantic

summerhouse to capture the evening rays. The width of the exotic assemblage dubbed 'The Temple', had been governed by a set of Mughal pillars comprising four elliptic columns and a cross beam, its depth dictated by a quantity of salvaged encaustic floor tiles long hoarded for a suitable destiny. The walls boast offcuts of decorative plaster cornice and assorted panelling leftover from the shepherd's hut (in turn left over from those sun rooms, which were leftovers from the Chediston Street project...you get the picture...). Such 'leftovers' are beginning to offer thin pickings, but there's always something for more crazy constructions.

Ducks, moorhens, pheasants and green woodpeckers wander nonchalantly over the grass; muntjac deer chew my new plants and appear to have a taste for tulips. They all think the place belongs to them, as do the remaining pesky farm cats, making trouble in paradise.

We have been perfectly comfortable for some time, but it wasn't until I started messing around outside that I allowed myself to feel that this really *was* where we'd live until we can no longer manage those stairs.

Loose Ends

The house passed the mandatory air-pressure test and, after making one or two minor adjustments to satisfy fire regulations, we were duly 'signed off' by Building Control. In case you're wondering about the boiler, we opted for an Air Source Heat Pump. Its flaw, compared to a Ground Source version (which relies on the stable temperature of the earth), is that the more extreme the outside temperature, the harder it has to work to extract usable heat energy. However, it being much cheaper to install than a GSHP, we proceeded on the premise that such extremes are rare in East Anglia.

A balance has to be struck between capital outlay and life's ongoing expenditure, but feed-in tariffs have made feasible an array of photovoltaic panels, now mounted on the roof of the Green Shed. Having said that, insulation remains the key – all that *Celotex* and sheep's wool makes the place seem warmer without heating than Wissett Place ever was with central heating full bore. Well, perhaps I exaggerate, but the warmth is beautifully spread, so no one need hog the fire. Nick was right; the kitchen would have been much too hot with an Aga. (I still miss one though.)

Sentimentally, we'd been rather loath to get rid of those happy scrawls on plywood underfoot in the kitchen, but in the end, we plumped for the pleasing finish offered by engineered oak, stipulating a so-called 'rustic' effect, that is, one with plenty of random knots. When it came to fitting it, half the boards had to be sent back to the suppliers. I wonder how many complaints they get because the product is 'too perfect'?

It would be so easy to put one's feet up on 'retirement' and retreat into a cosy, self-contained little world. No chance of that. Despite the potentially disastrous timing, we're weathering the effects of the financial downturn (so far) by creating a niche destination for those looking for somewhere 'extra special'.

Along the way, we've met some extraordinarily nice people, making new friends and drinking partners.

My best friend at school had been Polish, her parents having escaped to England from behind the Iron Curtain in the 1950s. I had been fascinated by her family's gravelly speech and unfamiliar food, so I embrace the ongoing Polish connection. Nowadays, many foods, from *kiełbasa wędzona* (smoked sausage) to roasted buckwheat groats can be found on the shelves of our small local supermarket. Hard-working Ewa is official housekeeper, Krzysz is Nick's right-hand man and their two children are thoroughly integrated into local life. With their English much improved, Krzysz and Ewa can be relied upon to keep the 'balls in the air' in our absence.

Our 'tiger/leopards' haven't adjusted to England quite so well, limbs wobbling, bodies cracking and yellow fungi sprouting over their hindquarters. Eventually, one simply rotted away (its wooden head saved and mounted on a wooden shield in ironic tribute).

The other has been rebuilt and wrapped in the same sort of fibreglass used to waterproof the base of the showers. As the in-house decorator, Ewa had volunteered to paint it with leopard-like spots. Herding cats, painting tiger/leopards – that's what I call a multi-faceted CV!

Still bearing traces of their agricultural genesis, the Barns at Belle Grove received recognition in the prestigious VisitEngland Awards as 'Self-Catering Holiday of the Year'. That was in 2012, the year London hosted the Olympic

Games, especially memorable for the email that had plopped into our inbox purporting to be from the Department of Sports, Culture & Tourism. It attached an invitation to an Olympic venue as guests of Her Majesty's Government. As we are notoriously unsporty, this seemed so unlikely as to be a scam; the email promptly deleted. A reminder arrived. That was binned too. Only after a slightly testily-worded third email arrived did I scrutinise it rather more carefully, forwarding it to a friend who had already bought tickets.

'Does this look real to you?'

'Yes!'

So it was that, as a 'thank you for services to tourism', we spent a day of red-carpet treatment at the Olympic Hospitality suite and in the Velodrome saw Laura Trott win gold. And there was I thinking I'd never be interested in cycling.

As for the house itself, the internal layout has had to live up to the dominance of the exterior but, for me, it was never all about the challenging architecture but how it would work in practice. It turns out that it is fun to be in *and* admirably meets our needs. In the face of Jaimie's doubts, we continue to mount the stairs, even if I do sometimes have to pull hard on the 'tie rod' handrails.

Living in one's own creation highlights unplanned benefits, mistakes and oversights. I'd always fancied a conservatory and as I sit in the Club Room, with sun streaming through the glass amid luxuriant greenery, it's just that. During a heatwave the tower, a variant of stack ventilation, acts as a wind catcher, a traditional device found in Middle Eastern architecture to send cool air into the heart of the house. On the other hand, with its wooden floors, it's what the Dutch call a 'noisy house' and I quite see why apartment leases require tenants to lay carpet.

Anticipating issues with the ups and downs of living over three floors, we'd integrated a three-storey shaft intended to take a mini 'dumb waiter', minimising the need to stagger upstairs laden with books and drinks or down with armfuls of dirty bedlinen. However, small off-the-shelf elevators proved both expensive and not too adaptable to the shaft size so, dismissing the idea of a hand pulley as too much like hard work, we settled on a small electric motor from Screwfix. As we had failed to consider noise minimisation in the original duct design, its grinding echoes through the house rather intrusively. Thus, we continue to stagger upstairs laden with those drinks and books and down with that bedlinen.

The final result can only really be assessed once the oak has had a chance to shrink. It is already doing so, hence those 'shakes', but the prolonged build process worked in our favour as the oak had already started the process before the outer and inner skins were added. The timber exposed to the elements is silvering nicely and people are often surprised to discover its newness. The sedum has been successful on the whole, providing an ever-changing carpet of colour through the year although alarming bare patches do appear on the southern side. So far solved with plant food dressing and extra 'leaky pipes', this demonstrates that even succulents need moisture and nutrients. All the same, we still can't work out why sedum grows quite happily on nothing more nutritious than a sliver of junk metal over by the Green Shed but is so fussy on our roof.

Our vision that the house should feel part of its environment has, I think, been realised. Maybe it doesn't conform to architectural doctrine, but what's wrong with an impish, even subversive, bending of the rules?

Nikolaus Pevsner's *The Buildings of England* series, usually referred to simply as 'Pevsner', was part of his 50-year quest to document English architecture. In his 1955 Reith Lectures, 'The Englishness of English Art', Pevsner explored the qualities of art and architecture which he (as a German-born) regarded as peculiarly English and what they said about the national character. In this he identified continuity and reticence. We can claim continuity in the sense of reusing local materials but, with our 'visual noise', I suspect we fall down on the reticence front. So for Belle Grove Farmhouse to be featured in an updated edition was an honour and a true validation.

The description, accompanied by a photograph, makes an unusually subjective reference to it as a 'fantastical house...' before proceeding to a scrupulous summary of the building [90].

> *Three storeys, the plan composed mainly of overlapping circles with a slender round tower on one side and tall brick chimney on the other...The materials mostly traditional and local...but even the three-storey jettied porch has been subverted and looks exotic.*

And an entry in *Suffolk's Hundred Best Buildings* [91] reads:

> *The main house has been rebuilt with more than a hint of architectural fantasy...*

and continues

> *... many of the details look familiar but are exaggerated or expressionistic: others are more quixotic, like the open-work metal dragon crouched on top of the chimney...Yet the design is practical and well thought out. The tower and the cascade of curved roofs with ribbon windows offer good views from a snugly finished interior in which further chapters of the story unfold*

90 The full entry may be found in *Pevsner Architectural Guides: Buildings of England, Suffolk: East* (pub. 2015, the first since 1974) amplified by architectural historian, Dr James Bettley.

91 Authored and edited by architect Tim Bauxman, pub. 2014. www.imemlifts.co.uk

through features like the wonderful tree trunk spiral staircase. This is a personal vision, unexpected and eccentric, yet warm and welcoming.

A gratifying culmination to the project was the announcement that the house had been named Overall Winner of the prestigious *Daily Telegraph*-sponsored, *Homebuilding & Renovating Magazine Awards* which resulted in a ten-page spread in the magazine's January 2012 edition. One of the judges commented:

> *The winning schemes were those that displayed individuality and pure ambition... It's the sort of thing you can only really put your finger on when you walk through the front door. I've never seen a house that says more about its owners than Belle Grove.* [92]

There was even a prize. Much to the mirth of friends, this turned out to be a bracing spa break rather than, as theretofore, a hedonistic hotel weekend. Still, I was delighted that Nick's vision had attracted the accolade; I think of it as his magnum opus, a monument to the fusing of practicality with creativity. Yet I confess to discomfort with the *Daily Telegraph's* febrile description which, while recognising the 'extraordinary architecture', suggested that the house was designed 'by a combination of hobbits, wizards and gingerbread men'. I suppose it made good copy.

Of course, not all of the people can be pleased all of the time, as this email from a resident of a neighbouring (five miles away) village demonstrates.

> *I'm sorry, but I am writing to complain about that hideous edifice next to your barns, which looks as though it has bounced across from Disney Land [sic]: how on EARTH was planning permission ever given??! It is an insult to a trained eye and to the beauty of the surrounding countryside, and should NEVER have been allowed to happen. It is an ignorant design, demonstrating the most appalling taste and vulgarity that one could ever conceive in a building: I am absolutely and utterly outraged! My mothers ancestors lived at Heveningham Hall in the early 19th century – so perhaps I am ultra-sensitive to this kind of thing...But really: to impose that kind of grotesque lump of a building upon people locally is an act of the grossest insensitivity and ruthlessness. I feel truly sorry for those who have to suffer the sight of it on a daily basis: fortunately, I live some miles away!*

Gosh, this could have come straight out of *Blott on the Landscape*, [93] in which distaste for Victorian architecture screams off the page, Handyman Hall being 'an amalgam in stone and brick, timber and tile and turret, a monument to all that was most eclectic and least attractive in English architecture...'

---

92 Jason Orme, editor of *Homebuilding & Renovating Magazine,* as quoted in *The Daily Telegraph.*

93 By the inimitable Tom Sharpe.

Nor was I sure whether to be more affronted by the reference to Disney or amused by the thought that 'taste' was a gene inherited through an ancestor who had lived (in the attic for all we knew) at Heveningham Hall. Our neighbour's steadfastness is appreciated all the more.

Our eyes had also been opened to the exigencies of filming when a three-man crew took two and a half days to shoot footage for a short slot on HGTV's *Extreme Homes*. A more comfortable experience was for Channel 4's *George Clarke's Amazing Spaces*, but it makes me all the more relieved that *Grand Designs* hadn't shadowed us.

It seems naive now, but the degree to which we would become objects of curiosity hadn't for one moment occurred to me in the hatching stages. Rubberneckers in cars and on bicycles have been known to screech to a halt and train passengers hop off at a nearby rail station to follow the railway line back to see if their eyes really could be believed. Deliverymen politely ask if they can 'snap' the dragon to show disbelieving children.

Privacy, especially needed when the trees are stripped of their sheltering leaves, has been achieved by blocking the 70-yard eyeline from the highway into the kitchen with an old steam locomotive (dubbed The Rocket), or at least what appears to be one at cursory glance. In reality, it's Nick's amalgam of an old boiler with vertical pipe welded on top, a curved section of Anderson Shelter at the back and two pairs of mismatching iron wheels.

As seen, the forging of settlements in America and wartime bonds of respect, even the direct impact on the Kennedy family dynasty – one of the 'what ifs' of history – add up to a meaningful connection between this part of the Old World and the New. But here's a personal twist: our son Jaimie has married Tatiana. While both living/working in Berlin, they had met online, as is the modern way, and discovered that they had both been born in the town of Ipswich – one in

Massachusetts, the other in Suffolk. Thus, the thread persists. A further, less romantic connection between Suffolk and the USA has been the advent at Belle Grove of a wild American mink, which has made short work of the mallards, despite Duck Island.

As to the dragons. Well, when coming up with the notion of a dragon for the chimney, we had had no notion how very pervasive the idea of the creature is in our heritage, let alone within global culture. The Dragon Boat Festival at nearby Oulton Broad, 'borrowed' from an ancient Chinese tradition, has been absorbed into Suffolk life, attracting over 40 teams to battle it out along the waterways. Now there's Norwich's Dragon Festival, with its exhibitions, storytelling and performances. This fits in nicely with Nick's stock explanation for children:

'It was a cold winter that year so a lady dragon decided to follow the dragon ley line across the North Sea in the hope of finding warmer lands. As she was rather hefty, most people in the towns below didn't like her resting on their houses in case she broke their roofs, so she had become very tired what with all the flapping of her wings.

'Eventually, she found herself cruising over Westhall and, as the chimney looked nice and solid and there wasn't anyone about, she decided to take a break. It was so comfortable she slept for a whole night and a whole day and then said to herself "I wasn't looking forward to that chilly old sea-crossing and now that my underbelly is nice and warm and I've got a great view all around, I think I'll just stay put. I hope the people who live here won't mind".'

They don't.

Frequent Q & As

Q   *What advice would you give to anyone looking to take on an unconventional build project?*

A   If the design is at all unorthodox, seriously consider commissioning a scale model. It's a tremendously useful tool in the planning process and not only does it assist in visualising the outcome, it helps resolve potential structural and design issues in the course of the modelling. And should you want a dragon on your house, find a professional dragon maker!

Q   *How long did it take to build?*

A   That's a bit difficult to say as the barn conversions and house build were, to some extent, concurrent and other projects popped up, including preparing our old house for sale. The overall work on everything, including rehousing Nick's Mum and landscaping, took about five years, and the house was actively worked on for about half that time. As Nick is wont to say, if the house had been built in straight lines it would have been ready a year earlier. Moreover, as anyone who has built a house knows, the work is never *quite* finished...

Q   *How large is the house?*

A   3,220 square feet

Q   *What about a building warranty?*

A   The structure may be unusual but it has integrity. There is no NHBC warranty, but a Structural Surveyor friend bravely committed to providing it with a Certificate.

Q   *How much did it cost?*

A   We've got to be vague about this too. Major outlays included ready-to-pour cement, the green oak from France, services, the bespoke oak windows, doors and kitchen, bathroom fittings, glass and, of course, labour. Otherwise, most materials were recycled so all in all, we guesstimate £275,000.

Q   *Do you feel that you compromised any 'green' ambitions?*

A   In part, particularly in the barns, where we had to watch start-up costs; sustainability comes at a price. But forget location, location, location – the most significant thing one can do is insulate, insulate, insulate!

Q   *Anything specific that you wished you'd done?*

A   In retrospect, triple glazing everywhere plus self-cleaning glass in the tower – but there again, many decisions were driven by a tight budget. Originally, there was to have been a window in the upper north face of the tower, but we omitted it thinking that guests could feel overlooked. In reality, it wouldn't make much difference so maybe we'll get round to inserting a window there one day, as it would lighten a darkish spot.

Q   *Or anything that didn't work, either in the house or barns?*

A   While I love them in the house, the lighting circuits are a mixed blessing in the barns – it takes time for guests to become accustomed to the concept, so there's a tendency to switch each lamp off individually, causing confusion all round when later they won't illuminate at the flick of the main switch. As for that dumb waiter...

Q   *And you'd change?*

A   The richly coloured hallway makes a welcoming intimate space in the winter, but if I'd thought about it, I would have made a lobby behind that double Rajasthani front door and installed internal floor to ceiling glazing, so that in the spring and autumn, we could fling open the solid doors to allow extra light to penetrate whilst keeping warm. In summer, we leave the doors open anyway. It's still doable. In the meantime a talented friend has painted the hall ceiling in faux medieval manner to lighten the space and the senses. [94]

---

94 Marcus Cotton of www.talliston.com

Q   *Anything you'd have liked if available?*

A   A device charging worktop or at least sockets with USB ports. And we'd definitely have looked into thermodynamic panels if they'd been around (and those new Agas).

Q   *Have there been any problems with the dragon sculpture?*

A   *Smok* has managed to stay aloft in the face of a force 8 gale and long may that be the case.

Q   *Can we come and look round?*

A   Only by arrangement with Invitation to View, a neat scheme in which small historic houses open to the public on certain days of the year. We were privileged to be the very first new-build on board. Owners take small pre-booked groups on personally conducted tours ending with tea. See www.invitationtoview.co.uk.

Images

Black and whites

Colour plates (separate page numbering – all clockwise)

Page 1
the sketch that sparked it all off, Nigel Purdy working on the scale model and the model at various stages

Page 2
digging the tower footings, the builder's bag of vodka bottles, the old Sambron struggling with 40' Douglas Firs, seven poles upright at last, the recovered elm trunk, working on the chimney, Krzysz and Marek, porch skeleton.

Page 3
The sandstone columns from Rajasthan, roof timbers, infilling with straw bales, the pair of old railway brackets, oak spoke design for tower floors, stair treads constructed around tree trunk, one of three 'wheel' trusses in tower

Page 4
Tower taking shape, progress, installing lightning conductor, more progress, rooflines, laying tiles in curves

Page 5
Nick selecting corrugated iron for kitchen, result, views of finished kitchen

Page 6
Hall, doorways into study and cloakroom, hall ceiling, my 'office'

Photo credits

Brian Benson (www.bbphoto.me)
Chris Wright (www.chriswright.net)
Vanessa Clegg (www.vanessaclegg.co.uk)
Darren Chung (www.darrenchung.com)
Tony Hall (www.tonyhalleyepix.com)
Pixabay.com
Waveney Valley Dwile Flonking Association.
Jane Davis
Ewa Sobel
Peter Warner
Judy Boyt
Jo Jordan

Also by Jo Jordan:

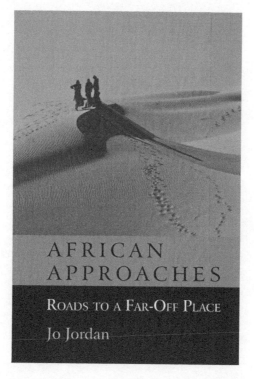

African Approaches: Roads to a Far-Off Place (published 2012)
ISBN: 9781780032627